15,00

JAMES, SEUMAS & JACQUES

Unpublished Writings of

James Stephens

JAMES,
SEUMAS & JACQUES

Unpublished Writings of

JAMES STEPHENS

Chosen and Edited with an Introduction by

Lloyd Frankenberg

NEW YORK

THE MACMILLAN COMPANY

Library of Congress catalog card number: 63–15680

Printed in the United States of America

Acknowledgments

The editor wishes to thank The British Broadcasting Corporation
for permission to reprint the James Stephens broadcasts. Some of the
broadcasts appeared, in full or in part, in *The Listener.*

Permission has been granted to quote from the following publications: *Finnegans Wake,* copyright 1939, by James Joyce, reprinted by permission of The Viking Press, Inc.; *Letters of James Joyce,* edited by Stuart Gilbert, copyright 1957 by The Viking Press, Inc., and reprinted by their permission. "On Poetry" from *Quite Early One Morning* by Dylan Thomas, copyright 1954 by New Directions, reprinted by permission of New Directions, Publishers. "The Leaden Echo and the Golden Echo" from *Poems of Gerard Manley Hopkins, Third Edition,* edited by W. H. Gardner, copyright 1948 by Oxford University Press, Inc., reprinted by permission. *A.E. Collected Poems* by George W. Russell, Macmillan & Company Ltd., St Martin's Press, Inc., and Diarmuid Russell. *Collected Poems* by William Butler Yeats, reprinted with permission of the publisher, copyright 1903, 1906, 1907, 1912, 1916, 1918, 1919, 1924, 1928, 1931, 1933, 1934, 1935, 1940, 1944, 1945, 1946, 1950, 1956 by The Macmillan Company, copyright 1940 by Georgie Yeats.

Gerald Bullett's contribution to the broadcast "Poets on Poetry" is reprinted by permission of Mrs. Bullett.

A Word of Thanks

I had hoped to thank Cynthia Stephens (Mrs. James Stephens) in person. We met only by letter, and twice, long ago, over the telephone. But I am privileged to feel that we were friends. It was a shock to realize that all the considerate pains she took were at a time when taxing problems were to prove too much for her health.

Iris Wise, Mrs. Stephens' daughter, and her husband, Norman Wise, have been so kind and warm and generous in so many ways I can find no words adequate to thank them.

Alan Denson transferred to me the enormous helpfulness he was already showing Mrs. Stephens. Much of the groundwork for this book is his. *Letters from A.E.,* which he has edited for Abelard-Schuman, Ltd. (1961), contains relevant correspondence concerning James Stephens, and some of the letters Stephens mentions in his talk on A.E.

P. H. Newby, Timothy Eckersley, and Jean Kempton of the B.B.C. were instrumental and indefatigable in searching out transcripts of James Stephens' talks. Without them, the book would scarcely have been possible.

And Lovat Dickson, of Macmillan & Company, Ltd., besides giving his blessing, was more than gracious in having photocopies sent me of a mass of material to select from.

There are many others who know, I hope, that I thank them. To include every name might make all seem perfunctory.

For constant help, advice, and encouragement, not just in the present instance, I am most happily in debt to Padraic Colum.

L. F.

Contents

JAMES, SEUMAS & JACQUES

For Seumas

In his talk on "Talk" James Stephens regales us with an indiscreet confession of La Bruyère: "We write as well as we can, but we can never write as well as we talk."

But Stephens can. Even from the deepest, darkest silence of type, his words go straight to the ear.

"One day, away in a place, I saw a spider," he confides at the outset of "An Irishman's Days." Only a voice could have written a sentence like that. We're ready for anything else at all he may choose to tell us.

What's more, he can go in reverse. He can talk like a man writing.

"Everything you write," he complains—this again in "Talk"—"has to be halted down to the pace of the letters of the alphabet."

Try saying that aloud. You will hear what it sounds like to write for the eye. No writer who writes for the eye could have said it. A few seconds later, adjusting his cuff, Stephens has the impudence to add, "Speech isn't prose, in spite of Molière."

But for James Stephens prose has always been speech. His writing sounds like talk, and so does his talk. It sounds that easy.

It is this that gives his books their deceptive simplicity. We don't feel we're reading *The Charwoman's Daughter* or *The Crock of Gold* or the stories in *Here Are Ladies;* we're overhearing them. They seem to go on in us; we make them up as we go.

Who but ourselves could have dreamed up the lovely credulity of Mary Makebelieve? have abducted and reabducted the daughter of Meehawl MacMurrachu? We are the donkey in *The Demi-Gods* suddenly braying his views. It is we who live the nightmares of *Etched in Moonlight* and find them all the more real for having been dreams; who are about to die of starvation in "Hunger"; who fall with a tightly clutched "Threepenny-Piece" through limitless space.

Even the poems—the poems especially—have occurred in us. We share the feeling that first prompted them. Reading Blake one night, Stephens says, he put the book down. "I can do that!" he cried, and wrote twenty-five.

It's true that our memory sometimes slips a cog. But carried away by talk, whose doesn't? Sometimes we remember the books were Blake *and* Browning. The very first poem was not "The Rivals" but "The Fifteen Acres." "It is the honourable characteristic of Talk," as Wordsworth might have put it, "never to say quite the same thing twice."

It is evident, in retrospect, that Stephens was born to go on the air. Talk was the soul of the man; speech-rhythms, the open secret of his crackling style. He talked to himself in bed and on the Dublin streets; to friends outdoors and in; to audiences at home and all over the United States.

On one of these tours he wrote from Chicago to his friend Stephen MacKenna:

Populations have shaken me by the hand, and more and mightier populations are waiting to do it again. I will be bawling out of me twice a day here for six days, then I go to Cincinnati and bawl there, and will bawl myself thence to P and Q and Z. I give to unaccountable multitudes, in unheard-of and incredible places, an imitation of myself howling like a wolf, and they pay me for it!

It is said he was often heard on the Irish radio, though no scripts or recordings have come to light. He kept none of the former, and the latter, most likely in the early twenties, were seldom if ever made.

By the late thirties, whether from his own ill health, the premature death of a favorite and only son, or other discouragements, Stephens had practically ceased writing. His last full-length book of prose, the collection of stories somber and incandescent, *Etched in Moonlight,* appeared in 1928. He published two more books of poems, *Strict Joy* in 1931 and *Kings and the Moon* in 1938.

Ironically, all Stephens' other books had been overshadowed by the success, in 1912, of *The Crock of Gold.* It was as if the readers of that book were so charmed by it they could not imagine him writing another line. Or they wanted him to go on writing the same book.

This he would never do if he could. It was against his nature to repeat. While the features are unmistakable, each new departure strikes out on its own.

He had planned a series of five books to be based on *The Cattle Raid of Cooley,* the collection of Irish legends with the Gaelic title *Táin Bó Cúailgne*. It stopped short at two. Probably he could not abide the thought of the same style, the same *tone,* at such length. Already *Deirdre* (1923), the most dramatic of his narratives, and *In the Land of Youth* (1924), with its playfully shifting sequences of time and place, were very different books, alike only in being drawn from the common source. How could he go on multiplying variety?

Stephens is at his best with a subject that lets him cavort about it. Most of them do. With a donkey, a friend, or an idea to chase all around the mulberry bush, he runs as we read. We are happy and panting and full of achievement when, like the boy in "A Rhinoceros, Some Ladies, and a Horse," he races to the post office and around it and back with a letter he was to have mailed. The letter was only a pretext.

The rather few manuscripts Stephens left reveal his continuing search for a major pretext. There are scattered notes for an autobiography, for which the "Rhinoceros" story seems to have been intended. There are trailing-off memoirs of George Russell and Stephen MacKenna, which keep turning autobiographical. And there is the beginning of a biography of Byron, which accomplishes the feat, in some twenty chapters, of never getting its hero born.

Stephens seems to have been trying to "Byron" himself into Byron; to apply his own counsel to a biographer to "refuse to avail himself of letters from or anecdotes about the person he is celebrating." Instead "his aim should be to release from the stories the character which is entangled in every page of them."

This, from an early "Essay in Cubes," is the very purest of conceptions. But Stephens' own genius is always for talk and anecdote. His forays into "writing" writing betray his impatience. And he was perhaps wise in another way in dropping these themes. Their development would have entailed him to facts; and facts, to him, are a millstone.

As he says himself in the memoir of MacKenna that turns into A.E. but is mainly himself:

This writer . . . has two strange advantages over many another writer—that is, he has a double memory. With one of these memories he forgets everything that comes to his attention: with the other he remembers everything whatever that has happened to him. He does not recollect the dates, or the names or the looks of those who were connected with such happenings, but the happenings themselves are with him as though they were cast in bronze.

What we miss most is the autobiography. That might have been stranger than any of the tales he told. Where *was* he born? and when? and to whom? It is possible he did not know himself.

He answered, as he says, to "James, Seumas and Jacques," with apparently no documentary evidence for any one of these names. Sometimes he gives himself a father who died when he was very young, and a stepfather from whom he ran away. Then again, he claims to be descended from gypsies.

As the "Seumas Beg" of his childhood poems in *Insurrections, Songs from the Clay, The Rocky Road to Dublin,* we find him encountering goats, larks, coneys, satyrs, centaurs, old women, pirates, elves, and the devil. Was that populous childhood passed, as he more than once suggests, in a village? At other times he is alone in the Dublin streets.

Most likely he migrated, vagrant or truant, between them. In her book *James Stephens: A Literary and Bibliographical Study,* Birgit Bramsbäck has gathered some of the legends surrounding these early years: that he slept in parks; that he fought with a swan for a piece of bread (in one of his stories he shares it with a dog); that he might have starved on the road to Belfast, but was taken in by a woman who fed and bedded him; that he left when it dawned on him his presence in her room was cramping her trade. (According to George Moore, she was "a charitable applewoman.")

Is it truth or a myth that he was for a time a circus clown? that his dearest ambition was to become an acrobat? that he did teach himself shorthand?

More verifiably, it is as "James Stephens," typist in T. T. Mecredy's Solicitors' Office in Dublin, that he was discovered by A.E. and fostered to friendship and fame. And as "Jacques" he was the ofttime resident of Paris and habitué of the café La Closerie des Lilas. At its tables, his daughter tells me, occurred one of the more spectacular disappearances.

Losing and finding is a leitmotiv of Stephens' career. *The Crock of Gold* is one long hide-and-seek between the little, the bigger, and the biggest people. Its imaginary wealth goes back to its imaginary owners; beings so small it would take a gigantic eye to see they weren't there. Reality, always a laggard, has now caught up: we believe most in what we can't see.

The book itself seems to have joined in the spirit of the plot. Part of it is said to have been written at La Closerie, which proved very convenient, too, for celebrating its completion. When Stephens got home, the manuscript had vanished.

It was a small—one suspects a *very* small—waiter who retrieved it.

To these three names, "James, Seumas and Jacques," should be added a fourth, "James Esse." Stephens sometimes used it—as if to assert his "being"—as a nom de plume for his own, perhaps, sobriquet.

With all these changes of name, he remained small. The fact, like most facts, rankled and amused. Cyril Connolly has said that in every fat man there is a thin man struggling to get out. Something of a contrary nature seems to have gone on with Stephens.

His wife once asked him why it was, in group photographs, he always managed to be placed next to the tallest man present. I think he felt that by nature he belonged there. In proportion to his body, especially his legs below the knees, he had a very large head. Could this have been due to the *thought* he took, as a boy, to grow big?

Exercising a great deal, he hoped, would add cubits to his stature. But he could only get tall horizontally, by running faster and faster.

Later, he tells us, he became a gymnast. "I was short and light and strong and seventeen years of age," he says in what is now Part III of "On His Poems," "and there's nothing better than that except to be tall and heavy and stronger and twenty years of age."

In the end, apart from these tantalizing glimpses, he left his early life a mystery. That is perhaps the way he preferred it himself: a mystery enlivened by brilliant sparks. We can only wish he had chosen to throw out more.

Into the breach of his major pretexts sauntered the B.B.C. In 1925 Stephens had moved from Ireland to England. He took a little house in Kingsbury, an outlying section of London. In "Eversleigh," as it is called, on Queen's Walk, he settled down more or less permanently, though he still kept his Paris flat in the rue Campagne-Première and made trips to the United States.

It was in 1928 that the B.B.C. asked him to give his first talk. At least it would appear, from the incomplete records, that "I Remember: Reminiscences of J. M. Synge," which went over the air on March 15th of that year, launched his association with the B.B.C.

He seems to have given his next on New Year's Eve, 1930. Then there is a break, or lapse of statistical memory, to May of 1937. From that date on, until his death in 1950, Stephens was quite regularly featured on the B.B.C. A good number of the scripts have now been found; true *objets trouvés*.

A selection from these scripts, plus two sure and two possible exceptions, forms the present book. The certain exceptions are "A Rhinoceros, Some Ladies, and a Horse," first printed in *Irish Writing,* 1946; and the memoir "Arthur Griffith" from an essay appearing serially in *The Review of Reviews,* 1921-1922, which was later incorporated in the pamphlet *Arthur Griffith, Journalist and Statesman* (Wilson, Hartnell & Co., Dublin; undated, probably 1924).

The two uncertainties are "Stephen MacKenna (II)" and "On His Poems (III)." Both of these were found typed in a form similar to transcripts made by the B.B.C., but there is no indication whether they were ever delivered.

Even the known scripts preserve a characteristic air of mystery. Not all of them are to be found in Stephens' own files; and of these, many are in rough draft or preliminary version. He must have gone on perfecting them—as he said, "Now I must irradiate it"—up to the moment of broadcast.

Once his words were in the air, it would seem, Stephens felt rather like William Blake, that they were published. The spirits could read and the manuscripts were of no further use. Quite a few of them did, in fact, find their way into *The Listener*.

For the others, taken down out of the wild blue ether, buried in crocks and finally dug up again, the B.B.C. transcripts are often the only, or the most reliable, sources. Again, losing and finding plays its dominant role.

This is as it should be. The evanescent, the ephemeral, are Stephens' grist. In his hands—on his tongue—that fugitive form, talking on air, takes shapes of dazzling versatility. Whether he is telling a story, mulling over a poem or a friend, or remembering a cow, the form and his temperament coincide. If the form holds him to thirteen or twenty-six minutes, he simply packs more into it. And it always sounds casual, just-this-minute thought up.

This is especially plain on the recordings, the dozen or so that survive. Having the gift of the tongue, Stephens has no need for the occupational therapy of radio. He never sounds like a man trying to sound like a man talking.

As with his books, this apparent effortlessness is deceptive. He is quite right to complain about prose. For a talk that is planned is a piece of highly articulate prose. And for prose to sound like talk, every syllable has to be plotted.

The number of variant scripts among his papers shows how hard he must have had to work to achieve this effect of spontaneous ease. In turn, they have made some of my choices difficult. For he has had to leave out—no doubt for the sake of that exigent, staring, and stopless needle—things almost as good as what he left in.

How else are we to account for this lovely, but discarded, beginning to "Mogue, or Cows and Kids"?

When I was a boy there were all kinds of creatures about, and one with no trouble made friends with every one of them. There were goats and donkeys, and in a place that I remember there was a tame deer that loved to walk between two people with its head bobbing up and down. It would never walk with one person, but two people entranced it. Then, suddenly, from between them, it would go bounding away, all stiff-legged, jumping for height and from delight in the fact that she knew you were watching her. All animals love to be looked at—so do some people.

This is almost a conversation. At least, the heads are wagging together. Stephens converses with everyone and everything, especially *tall* things. He quarrels with a mountain. He interviews an enormous fish. He reduces a bull to bewildered docility.

How often, in his descriptions, height is a focal point. MacKenna is "a man about six-feet-one, slender as a rake." Shaw is "a very lofty, slender gentleman . . . he peering away down at me and I staring away up at him."

Sometimes Stephens lays them low. When Shaw, irritated at having been "stood up," voices a distaste for frenchified Irishmen, Stephens—now at the *top* of the steps—rejoins, "I don't like Cockney Irishmen."

In "The James Joyce *I* Knew," Stephens says: "We were very different-looking people. Joyce was tall, which I wasn't; he was thin, which I wasn't; he looked down at me, which I couldn't; he rubbed his chin at me, which I wouldn't."

In another account of their meeting: "Joyce, as I remember him then, was a very good-looking young man. He was tall and slender, with a finely-cut face, beautiful hands and a lovely tenor voice. I was the exact opposite to all that and had obviously been assembled rather hastily out of old boots held together by chewing gum."

The offhand but unconcealed chagrin of this is more often a magnanimously admiring envy, as in "The Great Man" he introduces Gentleman Jim Corbett: "He was about six-feet-three all up and down."

Would we go so far as to say that size was the grit in James Stephens' oyster? That still doesn't tell us much about how he came to surround it. After all, as we know, it was a little man who first imagined himself Napoleon; but he was the only little man to get away with it.

There *is* a decided competitive streak in Stephens. A sparring quality is his native style. It feints and shifts; leads with a mocking left; follows up with a solid right of affection; or vice versa. "First Meetings and Last Words" would describe much of his writing; and the last word is not always his own.

"Jamesy," says MacKenna to him, at the end of that talk on "Talk," "your poetry is the worst in the world, and your prose is getting to be nearly as good as that."

This is banter; but Stephens' delight in it is symptomatic of his fiercely affectionate involvement with all. Everywhere he is on terms of loving rivalry. Not only with his friends, of whom the two greatest—he is fond of telling us—were Stephen MacKenna (the philosopher, not the novelist) and that mythical Irish mystic George Russell who, owing to a faulty pen, came to be known under the pen name of A.E.

There is more than one account of a famous conversation with A.E. Each of the not-quite-contradictions makes a true point.

" 'When you come to my age,' " says A.E. in the broadcast Stephens gave in 1948, " 'if you can claim that you have had six friends in your life you will be a luckier man than any man has a right to be.'

" 'I am one of your six,' I boasted.

" 'You are one of my four,' he replied severely; and something like desolation fell on him for half a minute."

In another version Stephens counters, just as quickly, "You are one of my two."

And in the unfinished memoir, Stephens puts it in still a third way:

"Two friends to a lifetime is not failure," said A.E. . . . "for that is one more than one deserves."

"A.E.," said I, "who are your two friends?"

"You are one," he said—and then, with much mournfulness, "I am the other. . . ."

"You do love Yeats," said I.

"I do not," said he.

Even the pastime, which seems to have been rampant in the Dublin of those days, of pinning the donkey's tail on Yeats, is never without affection. With Stephens, affection and donkeys' tails go hand in hand; and of course he loves donkeys. It is not just friends he is friends with. In his contentious way, he identifies with everything under the sun.

His very first poem, as he sometimes says, was "The Rivals," in which he outdoes and, in the same breath, is outdone by a bird. The enumeration of his love affairs, nearly always reciprocated, is legion. In their several ways "A Rhinoceros, Some Ladies, and a Horse" all fall in love with him, not without various hazards to his person.

And there is that matter in "Living—Whatever That Is" of his "bushing" himself into a bush; a bush, furthermore, that bears a curious resemblance to himself—the self he presented to James Joyce—"It had got itself up regardless." With all this and each that and everything else he has the more than metaphorical proximity that is poetry.

Stephens has too nimble and darting a mind to be that solid citizen, the critic: to take a ponderous stance; to command a withering view. He dances and prances about his subject; harries it this way and that; ropes it in with whirling opinions.

What matter if the opinions are ours? Once in the ring, we share them. We find ourselves, like Stephens himself, going in every direction. "Were I an Englishman," he says in "W. B. Yeats," "which I am for the duration . . ."

We accept that Yeats is good because Yeats gets so much of himself into his poems. We easily agree, too, that for that Yeats is to be scolded. Doesn't the great poet keep his personality out of his poems? Isn't it just that—of course it is— that makes great poets so frequently dull? As it is, Yeats is almost as bad as "the Shakespeare who poked his own personal nose out-of-joint into half-a-dozen of the sonnets." Poetry is to be "simple, sensuous and passionate"; there's too much passion in Yeats' poems to call them love poems. Had he lived long enough, he might have refined the sensuality out of them. No wonder it will take criticism at least thirty years to catch up with him; has it caught up with any other poet in three hundred?

We're left with a series of nips and tucks: at Yeats; at poetry; at life. The last word has not been spoken. It never wanted to be said in the first place. The great thing is lively and ceaseless and gadfly attention.

When Stephens in one place says, "Truth is not a thing" and in another berates Blake for being "untrue," he may not be logical but he is right both times. His remarks on Blake are perhaps the most extraordinary of all, considering how much Stephens loves him. Blake has put critics in the position of having to take him or leave him. On the whole, the Irish are all for taking all of him, the English for leaving him. Stephens leaves him; then takes him right back; which is as it should be.

For all the speed of his insights and verve of his style, Stephens can be very obstinate. He appears like a bantam among good-natured Goliaths, in a series of group broadcasts he took part in in 1941. The panel included writers and actors, on the general theme of poetry. "Is Verse-Speaking a Lost Art?" was one of the titles.

Like many discussions on the air, they stayed right up there. The points Stephens was making, with some temerity in such company, are put more tellingly elsewhere, especially in his 1937 broadcast "On Speaking Verse." But over and again, when the others think they have him safely outnumbered, up he pops like an incorrigible jack-in-the-box to re-iterate his contention that a poem is *not* communication, or that actors *cannot* read lyric poetry.

They are as exasperated as later, in the one group discussion included, "Poets on Poetry," Dylan Thomas pretends to be. That broadcast—Thomas' side of it—appeared in the posthumously published *Quite Early One Morning,* and was the first inkling I had that Stephens' broadcasts were other than readings and comments on his own work. It was tantalizing to speculate on what had aroused a reaction like:

I'm not going to argue with all that. Sometimes I just sits and thinks. I agree that music-hall songs can be good poetry—so can limericks, drawing- or tap-room—but I don't think cracker-mottoes

etc. ever have been. I think, Stephens, you must be pulling my (comparatively) young leg.

Now we are able to see what provoked that, and that
Stephens is up to his usual serious mischief. He has his private
definitions, and he is not to be shaken from them even if they
shock the unshockable Dylan Thomas. They goad Thomas,
too, into some witty and wonderful eloquence.

Stephens' sparring match with James Joyce was of longer
duration. His estimate of Joyce, both as writer and as man,
went through interesting changes. In 1917, in a letter to
W. T. H. Howe of the American Book Company, he referred
to *Dubliners* as "a rather disconnected, unpleasant prose work"
and to Joyce himself as "a disappointed, envious man . . . a
succès de scandale is all he can hope for." Twelve years later,
visiting Howe in Cincinnati, Stephens formally revoked these
sentiments in a postscript to the original letter.

Perhaps the first opinion helps pinpoint the date of that
first meeting, which Stephens has variously described. The
last thing to expect of him is consistency, that vice of *big*
men.

His memory, or his tongue, is beautifully wayward. In
"The James Joyce *I* Knew" he has Joyce confide "that he had
read my two books; that, grammatically, I did not know the
difference between a semi-colon and a colon. . . ."

In the almost identical, and therefore omitted, remarks
that preface his discussion of *Ulysses,* Stephens says: "We
told each other that we had never read each other, and we
managed to convey in a kind of song without words that
we never would read each other anyway."

One fact Stephens never falters on, and that is dates. None
ever obtrudes itself upon the narrative. So he may say, "Two

years later we met in Paris," but the fact remains safely and beautifully shrouded in mystery.

This can prove irritating to the historian, but it contributes an aura of fable to everything Stephens touches. By ignoring the inessentials on which so many writers hang, how often he brings us swiftly and surely to the matter at hand. In that sentence, "One day, away in a place, I saw a spider," instead of the actual, we are confronted with the real. Its almost active suppression of any dull whereabouts brings us face to face with the spider. As he says about Synge, "He learned the craft of packing a phrase until it is explosive with adventure."

And as he says in "Yeats the Poet," "Truth is not a thing; truth comes hurrying after with a bucket and a broom." In "An Irishman's Days" the truth—or the matter of fact—comes seeping in. Gradually we learn that the spider is in a pond; that the pond is in Kentucky. The facts arrive with the precision of a dream.

So with books and writers; they are for Stephens just such an adventure. Watch him deploy about *Ulysses* and *Finnegans Wake.* He is not summing them up; he is savoring them.

His talks on *"Finnegans Wake"*—and possibly *"Ulysses"* too, as the brevity of the text would suggest—ended with a generous selection from the book. As with lengthy quotations from Coleridge's "Ancient Mariner" and "Kubla Khan" and John Donne's "The Anniversarie," which depended on sound for their effect, these have been omitted from the text. It's a real loss that apparently the recordings do not survive. After Joyce himself, Stephens would have been one of the best of his vocal interpreters.

But Stephens' choices are interesting and revealing. He introduces them effervescently:

Dear Listener! Dearest Listener! Finnegan would say Darling —but then Finnegan was asleep at his wake. . . . Is this the tale of a poor little girl who couldn't take it? Who is switched at one shake from the Bride to the Widow, and in French at that—Madame Isa Veuve? Surely these are the three most desolating words that were ever uttered since the Serpent hissed his whispers to the Mother of us all. . . . Thank heaven I am not whatever it is, and I don't have to whatever it may be, and if you listen with only one ear you may be glad you didn't listen with the other. . . .

At the start, he says, "there's a fog and a sleepiness, and there is a question obscured by sleep and fog and the mist that does be on the bog":

What was thaas? Fog was whaas? Too mult sleepth. Let sleepth. But really now whenabouts? Expatiate then how much times we live in. Yes?

We are led from this, the beginning sentence on page 555 (Viking, Compass edition) to the following page, where Isobel is sleeping "in her april cot"—"a memory dreamed by her or about her—and every dream is a memory":

night by silentsailing night while infantina Isobel . . . [on to] win me, woo me, wed me, ah weary me! deeply, now, evencalm lay sleeping; . . .

Then Stephens goes back to an episode on page 194: "Wherein the days of youyouth are ever mixed mimine . . ." Here Isobel's mother, "giddygaddy, grannyma, gossipaceous

Anna Livia," holds forth—or is held forth about—till the anonymous chronicler (Earwicker or Joyce) "lifts the life-wand and the dumb speak."

They speak in the French language of ducks: "Quoiquoi-quoiquoiquoiquoiquoiquoiq!"

Stephens concludes with page 157: "Nuvoletta in her light-dress, spunn of sisteen shimmers . . ." following this on, with breaks, to the conclusion of the passage: "I'se so silly to be flowing but I no canna stay."

Such are the episodes Stephens chooses: all women, all tender, all—as he says—"otherwhere." Of course, Joyce is everywhere "otherwhere."

James Stephens recognizes this with affection, with exasperation. The exasperation turns up more prominently in three pages not included in the text. They are headed simply, "Joyce."

From other notes it would appear that Stephens delivered, or at least prepared, a broadcast on Joyce in January of 1941. These pages may have been part of it. It is not clear whether they represent a considered or discarded opinion.

A comparison suggested in the 1946 broadcast, "The James Joyce *I* Knew," is more fully developed: "French litera-ture has never known anything like Marcel Proust, and English literature has never suffered anything at all that resembles James Joyce."

Both had "somewhat the air of being foreigners. Proust only seemed to live in Paris. His real life was passed in one room most carefully arranged so as to exclude what was to him the devil's own self; that is, a draught. Joyce had seemed to live in Germany and Italy and France, but his soul flitted to revisit another town entirely."

They were alike too in health, "Proust with a set of lungs

that weren't worth having, Joyce with a pair of eyes that he
could do nothing with except to shut them when he wanted
to go to sleep."

Each had a prodigious memory, practically "nothing else
but that. . . . They died at twenty-three and buried themselves into their memories." Both were "completely uninhib-
ited" writers flinching at no detail. "Indeed they both loved
the details of a matter almost more than they loved the matter
or its completion."

What they remembered was a France and an Ireland that
had already "gone indeed with the wind." Stephens questions
"whether either of these very singular men can be called
creative artists in the sense in which we normally use that
term. . . . In a sense they are epical artists, and their message
is, that all this we write about is dead."

Stephens concludes: "They were both spoiled poets, and
like the 'spoiled priests' of our legends, that's something not
quite worth being."

Yet in the surely later estimate, *"Finnegans Wake,"* his
pulse quite naturally responds to the "speech" in which it is all
written. He recognizes that speech, through all its Hydra-
tongued puns, for "Dublin talk." And unerringly, through all
that talk, he finds and seizes and re-creates its perennially recurring rhythm: "honey here and honey there and heather-honey
on the mountain."

Perhaps the oddest part of it all is that Stephens is talking
about a book he might well have had a hand in writing. It may
have been before their second, Paris, meeting and subsequent
friendship—described so gayly and datelessly by Stephens—
that Joyce wrote from the rue de Grenelle, 20 May 1927, to Har-
riet Shaw Weaver (in *Letters of James Joyce,* edited by Stuart
Gilbert: Faber & Faber, 1957):

. . . As regards that book itself [then called *Work in Progress*] and its future completion I have asked Miss Beach to get into closer relations with James Stephens. I started reading one of his last books yesterday *Deirdre*. I thought he wrote *The Return of the Hero* which I liked. His *Charwoman's Daughter* is now out in French. He is a poet and Dublin born. Of course he would never take a fraction of the time or pains I take but so much the better for him and me and possibly for the book itself. If he consented to maintain three or four points which I consider essential and I showed him the threads he could finish the design. J J and S (the colloquial Irish for John Jameson and Son's Dublin whisky) would be a nice lettering under the title. It would be a great load off my mind. I shall think this over first and wait until the opposition becomes more general and pointed. . . .

On May 31st he writes from La Haye, again to Miss Weaver:

. . . It is rather singular that for the last three years I have been carrying three photographs of Tuohy's portraits in my pocket— those of my father, myself and James Stephens. The combination of his name from that of mine and my hero in A.P.O.T.A.A.Y.M. is strange enough. I discovered yesterday, through enquiries made in Paris, that he was born in Dublin on the 2 February 1882. . . .

Over two years later, Joyce writes to her from Torquay, 16 July 1929:

. . . J. S. coming down here on Saturday for a weekend to talk about giving lectures. He seemed to be much impressed and moved by my proposal to hand over the work to him if I found my sight or the opposition demanded it and said I could rely on him to help me in anything. But he says I will do it and added that A.L.P. is the 'greatest prose ever written by a man'! . . . I thought it better my proposal to J. S. should come now so that if I am forced to it in the end it may appear less abrupt and more spontaneous. . . .

Finally, on November 22nd of the same year, Joyce announces with evident satisfaction and relief:

. . . James Stephens was over here for a week. I saw him nearly every day and explained to him all about the book, at least a great deal, and he promised that if I found it was madness to continue, in my condition, and saw no other way out, that he would devote himself heart and soul to the completion of it, that is the second part and the epilogue or fourth. I was very glad to speak with him and we will leave it at that for the moment. . . .

Truth with her bucket and broom has come straggling after and we have now, perhaps, the approximate year, if not the exact date, on which the "tall, beautiful, blind gentleman" left his calling card with Stephens' concierge.

If Stephens, as it turns out, never wrote any of *Finnegans Wake*—and what a major pretext that would have been— Joyce did write some of Stephens. He translated the poem "Stephen's Green" (later called "The Wind") into German, Latin, Norwegian, Italian, and French. The versions are to be found in his letter to Stephens dated 7 May 1932.

I wonder if Stephens ever knew about the sweetest gift of all which, on page 211 of *Finnegans Wake,* Joyce playing Santa Claus (or rather, playing Anna Livia Plurabelle playing Santa Claus) hands out from his mixed "mealibag" of tricks. Is he recalling the occasion of their first meeting when he had looked down and Stephens had, as always, to look up?

Besides being a gift, it seems to be a wager concerning Stephens' inner impression of his height and to refer as well to his head, that large crown with its roving wreath of hair.

And Joyce, whose allusions include nothing if not everything, may have had in mind too Stephens' assertion that his later books should have gotten medals as big as cartwheels and oversized barn doors. (*Deirdre* did receive the Tailltean Gold Medal, listed in one reference book as Tallman.)

Whatever the full implications, in the midst of some rather bizarre largesse distributed to all and sundry, appears the affectionate tribute:

... for Seumas, thought little, a crown he feels big; ...

LLOYD FRANKENBERG

Paris, 21 février 1962

Around and About the Style

Taken down as many of these were, off the air, the scripts did not present a uniform stylistic behavior. I have tried to bring them into line without imposing too great consistency on Stephens' own usage.

Punctuation, for him, was often a thing of the moment. Commas, dashes, semicolons, colons served much the same function: a breath between phrases. To dashes in particular he gave a certain idiosyncratic verve—a hurry-up call between words, phrases, sentences, even paragraphs. And wherever they seem to convey this sense of urgency—

"And wherever do they not?" says James—

I have retained them.

He had a way, too, particularly for broadcasting, of writing straight along without paragraph breaks, relying on his inflections to supply them. Once anything was to be printed, however, he took care to provide pauses for the eye. I have done the same for some of the scripts, with no assurance that my sense of the drama and his coincide.

As to poems, including his own, he had that marvellous Irish gift of quoting by heart. That doesn't mean at all that he was ever letter-perfect. On the air, this can add to the excitement. For print, as I'm sure he would have done, I've tried to square quotation with original text.

Choice and arrangement posed the trickiest problems. Between alternate, sometimes several, versions, which is the best? It's not always clear in what form a talk went on the air. As a rule I've given the fullest as being the most likely. I have, too, in a few cases, omitted what seemed like interpolations of timely but not lasting interest.

Another problem was fitting together the several talks given, sometimes several years apart, on Yeats, A.E., and Joyce, and on his own poems. Occasionally these repeat a point or quotation, or tell the same anecdote in other words. I have tried to include the point at its sharpest, the quotation at its aptest, and the anecdote where it seems most pungent.

Not all such repetition has been eliminated. Even slight shifts in emphasis may throw revealing lights on changes in Stephens' attitudes. With Yeats and Joyce especially, who were both "friends and others"—often for the same reasons and at the same time—it would seem important to preserve all the shades of feeling.

There are indications in Stephens' papers that he thought from time to time of weaving some of these talks together into more extended essays. The beginnings he made with A.E. and Stephen MacKenna are too obviously tentative to include. But the groupings of his talks—without taking his own liberty of rewriting them—may be in part a carrying out of his own intentions.

The three main groupings of talks are (1) mainly stories, (2) mainly about people—first people Stephens met, then people he met in books—and (3) mainly about himself. Within these, after bringing Yeats next to Yeats, A.E. to A.E., and so on, the course is mainly chronological.

I have to say "mainly." The divisions are nowhere cut-and-dried. One pair of hands, sifting and pondering these papers before mine, labelled a miscellaneous bundle "Broadcasts not especially autobiographical."

L. F.

FABLES

A Rhinoceros, Some Ladies,

and a Horse

(1946)

O<small>NE</small> day, in my first job, a lady fell in love with me. It was
quite unreasonable, of course, for I wasn't wonderful: I
was small and thin, and I weighed much the same as a largish
duck-egg. I didn't fall in love with her, or anything like that. I
got under the table, and stayed there until she had to go wherever she had to go to.

I had seen an advertisement—"Smart boy wanted," it said.
My legs were the smartest things about me, so I went there on
the run. I got the job.

At that time there was nothing on God's earth that I could
do, except run. I had no brains, and I had no memory. When I
was told to do anything I got into such an enthusiasm about it
that I couldn't remember anything else about it. I just ran as
hard as I could, and then I ran back, proud and panting. And
when they asked me for the whatever-it-was that I had run for,
I started, right on the instant, and ran some more.

The place I was working at was, amongst other things, a

theatrical agency. I used to be sitting in a corner of the office, waiting to be told to run somewhere and back. A lady would come in—a music-hall lady that is—and, in about five minutes, howls of joy would start coming from the inner office. Then, peacefully enough, the lady and my two bosses would come out, and the lady always said, "Splits! I can do splits like no one. Look!" And thereupon she did a split right there on the office floor. And one of my bosses would say, "I'm keeping your splits in mind." And the other would add, gallantly,— "No one who ever saw your splits could ever forget 'em."

One of my bosses was thin, and the other one was fat. My fat boss was composed entirely of stomachs. He had three baby-stomachs under his chin: then he had three more descending in ever larger englobings nearly to the ground; but, just reaching the ground, the final stomach bifurcated into a pair of boots. He was very light on these and could bounce about in the neatest way.

He was the fattest thing I have ever seen, except a rhinoceros that I had met in the Zoo the Sunday before I got my job. That rhino was *very* fat, and it had a smell like twenty-five pigs. I was standing outside its palisade, wondering what it could possibly feel like to be a rhinoceros, when two larger boys passed by. Suddenly they caught hold of me, and pushed me through the bars of the palisade. I was very skinny, and in about two seconds I was right inside, and in three seconds the two boys were running away, and the rhinoceros was looking at me.

It was very fat, but it wasn't fat like stomachs, it was fat like barrels of cement, and when it moved it creaked a lot, like a woman I used to know who creaked like an old bedstead. The rhinoceros swaggled over to me with a bunch of cabbage sticking out of its mouth. It wasn't angry, or anything like that, it just wanted to see who I was. Rhinos are blindish: they mainly see by smelling, and they smell in snorts. This one started at my left shoe, and snorted right up that side of me to my ear. He smelt that very carefully: then he switched over to my right ear, and snorted right down that side of me to my right shoe: then he fell in love with my shoes and began to lick them. I, naturally, wriggled my feet at that, and the big chap was so astonished that he did the strangest step-dance backwards to his pile of cabbages, and began to eat them.

I squeezed myself out of his cage and walked away. In a couple of minutes I saw the two boys. They were very frightened, and they asked me what I had done to the rhinoceros. I answered, a bit grandly, perhaps, that I had seized it in both hands, ripped it limb from limb, and tossed its carcase to the crows. But when they began shouting to people that I had just murdered a rhinoceros I took to my heels, for I didn't want to be arrested and hanged for a murder that I hadn't committed.

Still, a man can't be as fat as a rhinoceros, but my boss was as fat as a man can be. One day a great lady of the halls came in, and was received on the knee. She was very great. Her name was Maudie Darling, or thereabouts. My bosses called her nothing but "Darling" and she called them the same. When the time came for her to arrive the whole building got palpitations of the heart. After waiting a while my thin boss got angry, and said—"Who does the woman think she is? If she isn't here in two twos I'll go down to the entry, and when she does come I'll boot her out." The fat boss said—"She's only two hours late, she'll be here before the week's out."

Within a few minutes there came great clamours from the court-yard. Patriotic cheers, such as Parnell himself never got, were thundering. My bosses ran instantly to the inner office. Then the door opened, and the lady appeared.

She was very wide, and deep, and magnificent. She was dressed in camels and zebras and goats: she had two peacocks in her hat and a rabbit muff in her hand, and she strode among these with prancings.

But when she got right into the room and saw herself being looked at by three men and a boy she became adorably shy: one could see that she had never been looked at before.

"O," said she, with a smile that made three and a half hearts beat like one, "O," said she, very modestly, "is Mr. Which-of-'em-is-it really in? Please tell him that Little-Miss-Me would be so glad to see and to be—"

Then the inner door opened, and the large lady was surrounded by my fat boss and my thin boss. She crooned to them —"O, you dear boys, you'll never know how much I've thought of you and longed to see you."

That remark left me stupefied. The first day I got to the office I heard that it was the fat boss's birthday, and that he was thirty years of age: and the thin boss didn't look a day younger than the fat one. How the lady could mistake these old men for boys seemed to me the strangest fact that had ever come my way. My own bet was that they'd both die of old age in about a month.

After a while they all came out again. The lady was helpless with laughter: she had to be supported by my two bosses —"O," she cried, "you boys will kill me." And the bosses laughed, and the fat one said—"Darling, you're a scream," and the thin one said—"Darling, you're a riot."

And then . . . she saw me! I saw her seeing me the very way I had seen the rhinoceros seeing me: I wondered for an instant would she smell me down one leg and up the other. She swept my two bosses right away from her, and she became a kind of queen, very glorious to behold: but sad, startled. She stretched a long, slow arm out and out and out, and then she unfolded a long, slow finger, and pointed it at me—"Who is THAT??" she whispered in a strange whisper that could be heard two miles off.

My fat boss was an awful liar—"The cat brought that in," said he.

But the thin boss rebuked him: "No," he said, "it was not the cat. Let me introduce you; darling, this is James. James, this is the darling of the gods."

"And of the pit," said she, sternly.

She looked at me again. Then she sank to her knees and spread out both arms to me—

"Come to my Boozalum, angel," said she in a tender kind of way.

I knew what she meant, and I knew that she didn't know how to pronounce that word. I took a rapid glance at the area indicated. The lady had a Boozalum you could graze a cow on. I didn't wait one second, but slid, in one swift, silent slide, under the table. Then she came forward and said a whole lot of poems to me under the table, imploring me, among a lot of odd things, to "come forth, and gild the morning with my eyes," but at last she was reduced to whistling at me with two fingers in her mouth, the way you whistle for a cab.

I learned after she had gone that most of the things she said to me were written by a poet fellow named Spokeshave. They were very complimentary, but I couldn't love a woman who mistook my old bosses for boys, and had a boozalum that it would take an Arab chieftain a week to trot across on a camel.

The thin boss pulled me from under the table by my leg, and said that my way was the proper way to treat a rip, but my fat boss said, very gravely—"James, when a lady invites a gentleman to her boozalum a real gentleman hops there as pronto as possible, and I'll have none but real gentlemen in this office."

"Tell me," he went on, "what made that wad of Turkish Delight fall in love with you?"

"She didn't love me at all, sir," I answered.

"No?" he enquired.

"She was making fun of me," I explained.

"There's something in that," said he seriously, and went back to his office.

I had been expecting to be sacked that day. I was sacked the next day, but that was about a horse.

I had been given three letters to post, and told to run or they'd be too late. So I ran to the post office and round it and back, with, naturally, the three letters still in my pocket. As I came to our door a nice, solid, red-faced man rode up on a horse. He thrust the reins into my hand—

"Hold the horse for a minute," said he.

"I can't," I replied, "my boss is waiting for me."

"I'll only be a minute," said he angrily, and he walked off.

Well, there I was, saddled, as it were, with a horse. I looked at it, and it looked at me. Then it blew a pint of soap-suds out of its nose and took another look at me, and then the horse fell in love with me as if he had just found his long-lost foal. He started to lean against me and to woo me with small whinneys, and I responded and replied as best I could—

"Don't move a toe," said I to the horse, "I'll be back in a minute."

He understood exactly what I said, and the only move he made was to swing his head and watch me as I darted up the street. I was less than half a minute away anyhow, and never out of his sight.

Up the street there was a man, and sometimes a woman, with a barrow, thick-piled with cabbages and oranges and apples. As I raced round the barrow I pinched an apple off it at full speed, and in ten seconds I was back at the horse. The good nag had watched every move I made, and when I got back his eyes were wide open, his mouth was wide open, and he had his legs all splayed out so that he couldn't possibly slip. I broke the apple in halves and popped one half into his mouth. He ate it in slow crunches, and then he looked diligently at the other half. I gave him the other half, and, as he ate it, he gurgled with cidery gargles of pure joy. He then swung his head round from me and pointed his nose up the street, right at the apple-barrow.

I raced up the street again, and was back within the half-minute with another apple. The horse had nigh finished the first half of it when a man who had come up said, thoughtfully—

"He seems to like apples, bedad!"

"He loves them," said I.

And then, exactly at the speed of lightning, the man became angry, and invented bristles all over himself like a porcupine—

"What the hell do you mean," he hissed, and then he bawled, "by stealing my apples?"

I retreated a bit into the horse—

"I didn't steal your apples," I said.

"You didn't!" he roared, and then he hissed, "I saw you," he hissed.

"I didn't steal them," I explained, "I pinched them."

"Tell me that one again," said he.

"If," said I patiently, "if I took the apples for myself that would be stealing."

"So it would," he agreed.

"But as I only took them for the horse that's pinching."

"Be dam, but!" said he. " 'Tis a real argument," he went on, staring at the sky. "Answer me that one," he demanded of himself, and he in a very stupor of intellection. "I give it up," he roared; "you give me back my apples."

I placed the half-apple that was left into his hand, and he looked at it as if it was a dead frog—

"What'll I do with that?" he asked earnestly.

"Give it to the horse," said I.

The horse was now prancing at him, and mincing at him, and making love at him. He pushed the half-apple into the horse's mouth, and the horse mumbled it and watched him, and chewed it and watched him, and gurgled it and watched him—

"He does like his bit of apple," said the man.

"He likes you too," said I. "I think he loves you."

"It looks like it," he agreed, for the horse was yearning at him, and its eyes were soulful.

"Let's get him another apple," said I, and, without another word, we both pounded back to his barrow and each of us pinched an apple off it. We got one apple into the horse, and were breaking the second one when a woman said gently—

"Nice, kind, Christian gentlemen, feeding dumb animals —with my apples," she yelled suddenly.

The man with me jumped as if he had been hit by a train—

"Mary," said he humbly.

"Joseph," said she in a completely unloving voice.

But the woman transformed herself into nothing else but woman—

"What about my apples?" said she. "How many have we lost?"

"Three," said Joseph.

"Four," said I, "I pinched three and you pinched one."

"That's true," said he. "That's exact, Mary. I only pinched one of our apples."

"You only," she squealed—

And I, hoping to be useful, broke in—

"Joseph," said I, "is the nice lady your boss?"

He halted for a dreadful second, and then made up his mind—

"You bet she's my boss," said he, "and she's better than that, for she's the very wife of my bosom."

She turned to me—

"Child of Grace—" said she—

Now, when I was a child, and did something that a woman didn't like she always expostulated in the same way. If I tramped on her foot, or jabbed her in the stomach—the way women have multitudes of feet and stomachs is always astonishing to a child—the remark such a woman made was always the same. She would grab her toe or her stomach, and say— "Childagrace, what the hell are you doing?" After a while I worked it out that Childagrace was one word, and was my name. When any woman in agony yelled Childagrace I ran right up prepared to be punished, and the woman always said, tenderly, "What are you yowling about, Childagrace?"

"Childagrace," said Mary earnestly, "how's my family to live if you steal our apples? You take my livelihood away from me! Very good, but will you feed and clothe and educate my children in," she continued proudly, "the condition to which they are accustomed?"

I answered that question cautiously—

"How many kids have you, ma'am?" said I.

"We'll leave that alone for a while," she went on. "You owe me two and six for the apples."

"Mary!" said Joseph, in a pained voice.

"And you," she snarled at him, "owe me three shillings. I'll take it out of you in pints." She turned to me—

"What do you do with all the money you get from the office here?"

"I give it to my landlady."

"Does she stick to the lot of it?"

"Oh, no," I answered, "she always gives me back three-pence."

"Well, you come and live with me and I'll give you back fourpence."

"All right," said I.

"By gum," said Joseph, enthusiastically, "that'll be fine. We'll go out every night, and we won't steal a thing. We'll just pinch legs of beef, and pig's feet, and barrels of beer—"

"Wait now," said Mary. "You stick to your own landlady. I've trouble enough of my own. You needn't pay me the two and six."

"Good for you," said Joseph heartily, and then, to me—

"You just get a wife of your bosum half as kind as the wife of my bosum and you'll be set up for life. Mary," he cried joy-fully, "let's go and have a pint on the strength of it."

"You shut up," said she.

"Joseph," I interrupted, "knows how to pronounce that word properly."

"What word?"

"The one he used when he said you were the wife of his what-you-may-call-it."

"I'm not the wife of any man's what-you-may-call-it," said she, indignantly—"Oh, I see what you mean! So he pronounced it well, did he?"

"Yes, ma'am."

She looked at me very sternly—

"How does it come you know about all these kinds of words?"

"Yes," said Joseph, and he was even sterner than she was, "when I was your age I didn't know any bad words."

"You shut up," said she, and continued, "What made you say that to me?"

"A woman came into our office yesterday, and she mispronounced it."

"What did she say now?"

"Oh, she said it all wrong."

"Do you tell me so? We're all friends here: what way did she say it, son?"

"Well, ma'am, she called it boozalum."

"She said it wrong all right," said Joseph, "but 'tis a good, round, fat kind of a word all the same."

"You shut up," said Mary. "Who did she say the word to?"

"She said it to me, ma'am."

"She must have been a rip," said Joseph.

"Was she a rip, now?"

"I don't know, ma'am, I never met a rip."

"You're too young yet," said Joseph, "but you'll meet them later on. I never met a rip myself until I got married—I mean," he added hastily, "that they were all rips except the wife of my what-do-you-call-ems, and that's why I married her."

"I expect you've got a barrel-full of rips in your past," said she bleakly, "you must tell me about some of them tonight." And then, to me, "Tell us about the woman," said she.

So I told them all about her, and how she held out her arms to me, and said, "Come to my boozalum, angel."

"What did you do when she shoved out the old arms at you?" said Joseph.

"I got under the table," I answered.

"That's not a bad place at all, but," he continued earnestly, "never get under the bed when there's an old girl chasing you, for that's the worst spot you could pick on. What was the strap's name?"

"Maudie Darling, she called herself."

"You're a blooming lunatic," said Joseph; "she's the loveliest thing in the world—barring," he added hastily, "the wife of my blast-the-bloody-word."

"We saw her last night," said Mary, "at Dan Lowrey's Theatre, and she's just lovely."

"She isn't as nice as you, ma'am," I asserted.

"Do you tell me that now?" said she.

"You are twice as nice as she is, and twenty times nicer."

"There you are," said Joseph, "the very words I said to you last night."

"You shut up," said Mary scornfully, "you were trying to knock a pint out of me! Listen, son," she went on, "we'll take all that back about your landlady. You come and live with me and I'll give you back sixpence a week out of your wages."

"All right, ma'am," I crowed in a perfectly monstrous joy.

"Mary," said Joseph, in a reluctant voice—

"You shut up," said she.

"He can't come to live with us," said Joseph. "He's a bloody Prodestan," he added sadly.

"Why—" she began—

"He'd keep me and the childer up all night, pinching apples for horses and asses, and reading the bible, and up to every kind of devilment."

Mary made up her mind quickly—

"You stick to your own landlady," said she, "tell her that I said she was to give you sixpence." She whirled about. "There won't be a thing left on that barrow," said she to Joseph.

"Damn the scrap," said Joseph violently.

"Listen," said Mary to me very earnestly, "am I nicer than Maudie Darling?"

"You are, ma'am," said I.

Mary went down on the road on her knees: she stretched out both arms to me, and said——

"Come to my boozalum, angel."

I looked at her, and I looked at Joseph, and I looked at the horse. Then I turned from them all and ran into the building and into the office. My fat boss met me—

"Here's your five bob," said he. "Get to hell out of here," said he.

And I ran out.

I went to the horse, and leaned my head against the thick end of his neck, and the horse leaned as much of himself against me as he could manage. Then the man who owned the horse came up and climbed into his saddle. He fumbled in his pocket—

"You were too long," said I. "I've been sacked for minding your horse."

"That's too bad," said he: "that's too damn bad," and he tossed me a penny.

I caught it, and lobbed it back into his lap, and I strode down the street the most outraged human being then living in the world.

The Man Who Was Going to Die

(1942)

I WENT to the cottage on the side of the cliff, knocked at the door and Mannin himself opened the door.

He said, "I'm glad to see you but I won't be able to stay with you today because I'm going over to the Breens'."

I said, "What are you going to do at the Breens' now?"

"There'll be a man there," said he, "that I don't want to see but I'm going to see."

I said, "I'll go with you as far as the Breens'."

And we set out over the cliff. As you walk along this path, or a sort of a path, if you look down to the right there's a drop of—here a thousand feet, and there fifty feet running from the rest of the bump—and it's very variegated.

At a point he said, "Do you see that place now?"

"I do," said I.

"I'd great trouble there one day," said he.

"What trouble was that now, Mannin?" said I.

16

"A cow that I owned," said he, "went down there."

"Egad!" said I, "that was a dead cow."

"Not a bit of it," said he. "I went out looking for my cow to milk her, and I looked down and the cow mooed at me. It was a great pet of a cow," said he; "that cow loved me and I loved that cow, and there she was nearly fifty feet down the cliff, standing on a rock and looking up at me and saying, 'Here Manninuck man, what are you going to do about me?'"

"Well, Mannin man," said I, "what did you do?"

"Gad," said he, "I went down after her."

"Ha!" said I. "Much good that would be. What would you do with the cow when you got down there?"

"Why," said he, "I took her under the crook of my left hand and I climbed up the fifty feet with her, and I put her here, where you're standing now, and I gave her a kiss and I said, 'Be off with you now and get lots of milk in your udder,' said I."

Well, we went a little bit along. He said, "Here's the Breens'—I'll be going in. Will you come in with me?"

"Well, of course," said I. "I like the Breens nearly as much as you do."

"Be damned," said he, "I don't like them at all."

"No?" said I. "They're nice people."

"Sure they are," said he, "but you don't have to like people; most people that I know," said he, "are dislikable. But there's a man going to be there, from what I've heard, and there's something I've got to say to him, and if I said it to himself by himself he'd take no notice of it."

"Oh," said I, "that's bad, Mannin."

"For sixty-four years," said he, "that man and me have fought each other once a week, or twice a week, or more as it happened. On Monday I'd lick the stuffin' out of him, and on

Tuesday he'd lick some of my stuffin' out of me, and we never could make out which of us was the better man."

"Who is he?" said I.

"Why, his name is O'Rourke," said he, "a bad man. We were born together, nearly the same age barring that he's five years younger."

"How old are you now, Mannin?" said I.

"Well, I'm eighty-eight," said he.

"Oh, you look as strong as a horse," said I.

"Well, whatever I look," said he, "isn't true, because I'm not as strong as a horse—well, unless it's a rather gone horse."

He knocked on the door and a voice said "Come in," and we went in. There were about twenty people present in a wide long room with sand all over the floor. And everybody that told a story, when they came to the point of the story, in order that everybody else would know that they'd reached the point of the story, they then spat on the sand and then reached over with the leg that was loosest and shifted the sand over the spit, and then everybody sat up and began to listen eagerly because they knew that the point of the story had been reached. Of course all the chairs were sat on by the men so that they'd feel free; and all the girls (there were about eight of them) sat on the table and held each other, so that they wouldn't feel free. For a free man is one thing, but a free woman is the divil.

And somebody was telling a story at the time. I stopped listening after a minute because I'd read the story a lot of times. It was in the Bible, that story. It was about a little boy, or a little girl—I've forgotten which it was now—being found out on the River Nile or thereabouts, floating about among bulrushes, and somebody carried the child home and it became a great child. So I didn't listen to that part because I knew it and could have told it myself. And I began thinking and after a while I noticed that people weren't listening any more to that story—they were talking.

And then somebody said, "And now, Manninuck darling, will you tell us a story?—sure, you're the greatest story-teller that ever lived."

And Mannin said, "Well, it's not exactly a story I've come to tell you. I've come to tell something for O'Rourke over there."

"Ay," said O'Rourke, a big broad man going on in years. "Ay, Manninuck, what do you want to tell myself?"

So Mannin looked around them all and he said, "Eighty-eight years of age I am, and I'm going to die this year."

"Oh, Manninuck!" said about fifteen voices. "Oh, Manninuck; there, you wouldn't tell us such a thing."

"I'm going to die this year," said Mannin, "and glad I'll be to get out of a world that has something in it that looks like O'Rourke."

"Manninuck," said the voices, "sure that's an odd thing to say to a man that's a visitor like yourself in a house."

"It has to be said," said Mannin. "And what I want to tell you is this: when I'm dead and ready for my grave, and when the people are gathered together at my wake, O'Rourke over there is not to be let come into my wake."

"Manninuck," said a voice, "you can't do that to a man that was born only a year or two after you and that's known you all his life and has taken part in everything you ever did. There's no doubt," said that voice, "that O'Rourke must come to your wake, the same way as you would go to O'Rourke's wake if it was he who died before you."

"All right," said Mannin, "I'll agree to that. It is but human and according to the religion. O'Rourke!" said he—and he turned and he looked at that other old man, who turned and looked at him—"O'Rourke, you can come to my wake. But,"

said he, "if there's any whisky going at my wake, everybody at
the wake is to get as many drinks as he likes except O'Rourke,
and O'Rourke isn't to get any whisky at my wake."

Well, there fell a silence that you could have listened to;
and then a voice came again, saying, "Manninuck darlin',
you wouldn't do a thing like that to a man that was born soon
after you and that has lived all his life beside you; you've been
out in the same boats together in the nighttime catching cod
and catching eels and catching trout, and indeed it's told that
once in one boat yourself and O'Rourke caught a shark and
hauled it in. You can't deny the wetting of his mouth to your
neighbour and the man who worked with you so long."

"All right," said Mannin, "let it be so. O'Rourke!"—and
he turned and looked at that bony man and the bony man
turned and looked at him—"O'Rourke, you can come to my
wake and you can drink my whisky. But," said he, "if there's
any snuff going around at my wake, everybody that's at my
wake is to get his share of the snuff but there's no snuff to be
given to O'Rourke."

So the same voice came again while everybody listened,
and they all looking at Mannin and they all whispering and
saying, "Oh, Manninuck darlin', you wouldn't say a thing like
that." And O'Rourke with his two elbows on the table and his
head stuck between them, and he looking with two eyes that
looked as if they were two pieces of bone; and he looking at
Mannin, and there was no hate in his eyes and there was no
love in his eyes, and there was only a competition in his gaze,
and he didn't say a word.

And then the voice said, "Manninuck darlin', if O'Rourke
comes to your wake, and gets his sup of drink at your wake,
sure you wouldn't grudge him the bit of snuff that he'd take at
your wake, for it's well known that the amount of snuff that

O'Rourke ever takes is so little that you could put it on a three-penny bit if you had one, and that would represent a year's worth of the snuff that O'Rourke would take in a year. And what difference at all is there now, Manninuck darlin', between a half-dozen good drinks of whisky and between not giving a man a pinch of snuff?"

"Ah-h-h!" said Mannin, "That's how it is. All right," said he, "I'm ready for death this very year and you'll all be at my wake and make my provisions that there'll be whisky at my wake and there'll be tobacco at my wake and there'll be snuff at my wake. And if O'Rourke comes to my wake and drinks my whisky, why, I should say there's no reason why he shouldn't sniff my snuff.

"O'Rourke, you can come to my wake. You can have whisky at my wake, you can sniff snuff at my wake, and to hell with you!"

Great joy went about the room. The girls on the table, about a ton and a half of them, fell off the table, and the men all spat carefully on the sand. Everybody was happy and O'Rourke, with a granite head and a bony eye, was happier than any of them.

The Story of the Goat

(1944)

LIFE can land you with a husband, or a wife or a goat, when you aren't even thinking of these things, and might be terrified of them. Mildred got landed with a goat.

Now, the idea "goat" had never got into her head from the day she was born until the day when she was close on, or even more than, seventy years of age. Seventyish isn't the age at which a lady elects to own a goat; and, for that matter, observing the two together, you couldn't be rightly sure if Mildred did own the goat, or if the goat owned Mildred. Love is that way—'tis mutual or it's nothing, and it was so between these two darlings; they loved each other like, as one might say, like billy-o.

Mildred had a lovely flat in town. There was no part of that flat except the floor which was not covered with marvellous photographs of stunning women. They weren't beautiful or chic, they were stunning. They were all *actrices,* mainly operatic, mainly sopranish.

There were Melbas and Pattis and Tetrazzinis and Bern-hardts. Everyone who could stun, or had stunned, was there stunningly. Each photograph was signed by the represented personage—to darling Mildred, to my beloved Mildred, and so forth. Mildred had been a Concert Agent in her day, and she had talked down, and stared down, and dressed down every Cleopatra of them all. But when I knew her she was grey-haired and rosy and active, and very fat.

She was very active on her feet. Off her feet was another matter. I once saw her off her feet. She had, incautiously, done something which she hadn't done for fifty years; that is, she sat down on the grass. I sat with her, and we talked.

She was a delightful talker, with a non-stop memory. Al-though she was very intelligent she rarely talked ideas; she talked people more willingly, and her head was stored with these. She had an odd habit of crying at the pathos of a story, and of, at the same time, laughing at what she considered her own sentimentality.

Her conversation was largely anecdotes about the marvel-lous women whom she had introduced into acting, even if they couldn't act, and kept singing even when time and tonsils had advised that they should skip it. Little stories about the unex-pected kindnesses that her stunning clients had done to some-one or other formed the main of her tales.

When she told a story of kindness, the kindness of the tale always made her cry, and the mournfulness of me listening both to and at her always made her laugh, so the tale would finish by her wiping the tears of love and pity out of one eye, and the tears of self-mockery and ridicule out of the other.

Well, you will remember that during one of these conver-sations Mildred had sat, incautiously, on the grass. She was as comfortable as only a monolith could dream of until the tea-bell rang, and she started to get up. She didn't start much. She gave two or three curious but quite stationary heavings of herself, and then she began to laugh with one eye and to cry with the other.

"Darling," said she, "I can't get up."

It was true. She could no more retrieve herself from the grasses about her girth than a hillside can retrieve itself from the grasses at its feet.

Her maid came to see why we didn't want our tea. She and I took a grip on both sides of Mildred, and we hauled and heaved. We could not budge her by an inch.

Then the maid, a lengthy, thin woman, went to the gate and gave view-hello's in every direction. She came back with two men. We got Mildred up a foot, but we couldn't hold it, and down she went again.

Then I had a brain-wave. I went to the wood-pile and got six or seven flat blocks of wood. We hauled again, and as she went up I slipped two blocks of wood under her. At the next haul I slipped in two more blocks. The next two blocks did the job. Mildred got up with no trouble whatever, and was as brisk as a bee.

It was in that exact place that Mildred got her goat. She had grown tired of her lovely city flat. She said, seriously enough, that she had no time in Paris to attend to her soul and also that she had so many visitors she couldn't get on with her Autobiography; so she took this little cottage about twenty miles out, and then what would happen did happen, the war came.

English soldiers were firing cannons over her cottage from the west, and German soldiers were firing cannons over her cottage from the east. Whoever came to her door, from whatever army, she gave them their tea, and left it at that.

When the German army retreated from the Marne Mildred bought a goat, for she loved milk in her tea. Melanie was the goat's name. She was a kind, slender, inquisitive goateen when I met her. She nudged you for sugar, she poked you for bread, she bumped you for some of your tea in a saucer, and she ate your newspapers with astonishing relish.

These were only snacks, of course; her real food, hay and lettuce and such-like, she would not eat except out of Mildred's hand. Mildred was sitting on a kind of sofa in the garden and had provided herself with lettuce leaves and a wad of hay. The goat saw the provender, got up on the sofa and ate her ration out of Mildred's lap.

That was the beginning of it. Next day the goat refused all food and wept bitterly about it—you could have heard Melanie weeping two miles away. But when Mildred sat on the sofa the goat got up on it too; so Mildred filled her lap with fodder and Melanie ate every bit of it. She also ate Mildred's batik apron and a sleeve out of her blouse. From that day on the goat refused to eat except from Mildred's lap.

At that point of the recital we went into the cottage for our tea—that is, Mildred and I and the goat went in, and we all sat down, I in a chair, Mildred in a chair and the goat on the sofa. Mildred had asked me to go in first in order that I might observe the Entry of the goat.

It was very pretty. There was a one-inch strip of lintel at the door. The goat did not step over this. She stood and looked at the tiny ridge; then she gathered herself and bounded three feet in the air. That bound brought her exactly inside the lintel, and that bound was a miracle of grace, a marvel of effortlessness. It was proud and dainty and powerful and precise, and it was of a self-consciousness that was just delicious.

That Entry was performed for us. Melanie jumped on to

the sofa, sat down, and said "Ma" to Mildred, and Mildred said "Darling" to the goat, and began to cry out of one eye at her, and to laugh at me out of the other.

Her maid came in with the tea; she looked very steadily, very silently at the goat on her sofa—a bleak look if one may say so, a bony and bodeful look, a look which could not have been bettered—worsened, I mean—even by a wolf.

I went back to Paris, thence back to Ireland, and I didn't get to France again until after the war. I went, of course, to see Mildred, and after we had laughed a bit and cried a bit, I asked about the goat. Mildred stopped laughing and stopped crying. Her face took on that removed look which only doctors and clergymen see much of, that look which is at once aged and empty and stern and desolate. I looked at that look—

"The lovely goat is dead," said I.

"Yes," said she, "I'll tell you about it outside, after tea."

After tea we lit our cigarettes:—

"About Melanie?" said I.

Mildred removed the cigarette from her lips and blew smoke at it; she nodded about ten times at the cigarette and smiled at it.

"It was my fault," said she to the cigarette.

"Would Melanie say so?" I enquired.

"I did like that dainty head in my lap," said Mildred. "Melanie," she went on briskly, "presented us, somehow or other, with three lovely little kids one day, and after a couple of weeks they all wanted to feed out of my lap, and they all learned their mother's way of jumping over the lintel at the door—the darling little jumps that they used to make!

"One of them was a little Billie goat, and Melanie used to teach him how to fight—she would swerve to the left, flash to the right, rear backwards, and then came the great thrust of the battling head, and then little Billie lodged his little brow into his mother's big one, and they stood so, locked in mortal combat. It was all done in very slow motion and it was the very poetry of motion.

"They all used to come into the parlour and nest on the sofa, and they all called me 'Ma.' I loved them to say 'Ma' to me," said Mildred, "and I loved them to eat anything they could eat. They ate the sofa right down to its springs; they ate the chairs right down to their legs; they ate my parlour right down to its mats, and they ate the mats—I shouldn't have let them. It was all my fault.

"One evening I came back, latish, from an official visit about papers. I wasn't met by the goats when I came in at the gate. Nothing bounded by me or skipped round me.

"I said to Valentine, 'Where are they?'

" 'They are down here,' said Valentine, and she brought me down to the cellar.

"That's where they were. They were all neatly quartered, and cleaned, and hanging up on hooks in the cellar. —Give me another cigarette, James, and say me a few poems."

"I have a poem," said I.

"Not a painful one," said Mildred. "Tell me a poem about girls or God or something."

A Story of a Good Dog

(1945)

A MAN I used to know very well told me this story. He was a very truthful kind of man, but he used to elaborate things more than a bit, and perhaps he elaborated a bit on this.

Everybody, said he, has a best cat or dog that remains in the mind when other very dear memories have faded, and one says with complete assurance: "That was the best dog." There were Fairy and Tommy and Guzzle and Spot, and they were all such good dogs that it is hard to believe there could be any better, but my best dog had not got a name at all; he answered to a very low whistle. He never barked; he never made any noise of any kind, except that, now and again, he gave a kind of whispered gargle away down in his innards—you could hardly hear it—and that indicated the top of his delight. Poor old fellow, he hadn't much to be delighted about: he was just delighted to be delighted.

This is how we met. It was evening, and I was going up a street and down a street. I was looking for something. Among other things I was looking for a job, but this time I was looking for something else—and suddenly I saw it. It was in a dog's mouth: it was nearly half a loaf of bread, and the dog was slinking up an alley with it. He was a large terrier kind of chap, and I was stalking him for my share of whatever was going. I got him to the end of the alley, and he whispered a few very low grunts of inquiry at me. "Drop it," said I, and he dropped it.

He sat down on his hunkers a few paces away, and he looked at the bread, and he looked at me, and then he scratched himself, and then he looked at the bread again. I broke the half-loaf into fairly even pieces, and I handed him the largest half. He looked at me, and he looked at the bread, and I could see that he was trying to work out where the catch was. Then he scratched himself with some fury, and when I began to eat he began to eat. He would stop every now and then to take a good look at me, and then he made that curious whispered gargle of delight away down in his innards, and then he started again on the bread.

How good that bread was! I remember thinking that cake was not half as delicious as bread, and that this bread was the best that ever was baked; I could have eaten a hundred loaves of it, and then I could have eaten the dog.

It was evening and darkish, so I humped myself up for sleep just where I was, and the dog, very cautiously, came to me, and at last tightened himself up against me, and he gargled a little and scratched himself nearly all night. I didn't care about anything. I had a friend; and he cared less, for he had a friend too.

In the morning I saw what all the scratching was about. He was covered from head to foot with mange. He was almost a solid mass of scabs. One of his eyes was blind. He was about three years younger than I was—that is, he was rather old, and he looked at me out of his goodish eye with the benevolent adoration that a good dog reserves for its best pup. He knew that I was an incompetent person, and he was very glad of that, for he had made up his mind that he would feed me by day and keep me warm by night. It was winterish, and rainish, and darkish, and we wandered together up a place and down a place, and we kept carefully out of everybody's way. I didn't want people because they wouldn't give me a job, and he didn't want people because they heaved rocks at him.

For more than two months, whatever I ate he brought me. He was marvellously skilful. He knew where bits of bread grew. Sometimes there wasn't any, but most days there was a bit. I should have been very hungry but in those days my mind moved around at about a mile a minute and it despised stomachs.

One morning my good dog set out hunting as usual. Then, having gone but a few paces, he stopped. He came back and pushed his head against me. Then he moved away again, and stopped again. And then, suddenly, he lifted his head to the sky and howled—the first sound I had ever heard him make! He howled and howled as though he were trying to howl himself dead. My heart nearly burst with terror. I ran to him and took his head into my arms, whispering love-words to him, and as I looked into his face I saw what was wrong.

His other eye was gone. He was quite blind. He couldn't go hunting. He wasn't howling about himself; he was howling because he couldn't nose out something for me to eat. He cared no more about himself than I, at that moment, cared about me. He did want to howl himself dead, but my arms coaxed him, and in a little he stood silent and shivering.

My mind had a small domain of its own, an aery, flighty,

fanciful place, where nothing stood still for more than a minute, but my mind knew nothing of practical matters; it didn't know how to do anything. How should I feed my dog who was old, and blind, and nigh eaten to death by his diseases?

I picked him up—he was not a light dog—and I walked and walked and walked. There were fields on one side, with a dull sky over them, over us: the world was a box, and we were two rats in a trap. I came to a small place, and saw a chemist's shop in it; the door was open. I put the dog down behind the door and walked in. There was a young man—perhaps ten years older than I—behind the counter, and I said to him, "Please, will you kill my dog for me, without hurting him?"

He was a hard-faced, tough Northman, and he looked me up and down with eyes that were like bullets.

"What will you pay me with?" said he.

"I have no money," I answered.

"I've no painless poison," said he.

I looked at the rows of bottles on the counter and on the walls, and my next words were inspired; they were even crafty.

"You are a very wise man," I said. "There is nothing of this kind that *you* couldn't do."

His eyes became eyes again.

"What's wrong with the dog?" said he.

"He is old and blind and dying of the mange."

"Where is the creature?"

I pointed and he strode to look.

"Good God Almighty," said he, as he stared at the crouching dog. "Take that thing away."

I followed him into the shop.

"Listen," said I, "that is the best dog in the world. He has fed me for over two months."

"You ate out of that thing's mouth?" said he.

"Yes," I answered. "He went blind this morning, and he is dying of horror because he can't feed me."

The man looked at me as if I were demented.

"You know how to do everything," I said. "Do this for the best dog in the world."

He turned briskly, took up a pile of papers and placed them on the floor. "Stretch him on that," he ordered. I picked my dog up—he was all one jelly of trembling terror.

The young man went behind his counter, and in about five minutes he came again, carrying a bowl.

"Good God!" said he, as he looked at the dog, and then his face went gentle. "There is warm milk and bread and sugar—dogs love sugar," he added, "and there is just enough of something else that will end his troubles in no time."

I put the bowl to my dog's nose. He smelled, and smelled again, and then, with an astonishing joy, he began to lap and eat while I petted him. He was tasting a kind of food that perhaps he hadn't tasted for six or seven years. Not since his master of long ago had thrown him out, and flung rocks at him till he quit.

"Take him down to the railway embankment," said the young man. "He'll be gone in less than half an hour."

So I sat among the bushes with him, and he began doing and undoing things; he began to go asleep and he began to waken up, and he began to gargle joyfully, and then he began to forget these things, and all things.

He forgot blindness and age and fear. He forgot hunger, he forgot me, he forgot to scratch himself, he forgot life itself. He stretched himself a little, luxuriously, and then a small shiver ran all over him, and he was gone.

I pushed him deeply into the bushes, and walked away,

pretty lonely again, but I think you will agree that when I say he was my best dog I am not making any mistake in that very important matter.

Shortly after that I got a job—said the man who told me this story.

St. Patric

(1946)

I T IS a good while now since St. Patric was with us. He was
born in the year 389, and the legend states that when he died
he was 123 years of age. He was a small boy one thousand five
hundred and fifty years ago, and after such a lapse of days it is
remarkable that we should know anything at all about him.

We know a lot; he is very well documented: we have his
writings and the records of contemporaries. Of course, much
legend has gathered about him, and there are certain questions
which keep on arising, and which will now never be settled.

There is for example the question of his nationality. Some
scholars claim that he was a Roman by birth, which is nonsense; some consider that he was a Frenchman, which is ridiculous, and certain others assert that he was an Englishman,
which is wicked. There are also a few, among whom I am
most, who think that he was merely and only and simply an
Irishman.

In the matter of his being a Roman, we have his writings

in Latin, and that might prove him to be a Roman but for the
fact that his Latin was so bad it was actually barbarous. Meanwhile, we have not one French word and not one Saxon word
left by him: had he been a native of either of these lands a
word or two of their lingo would have crept into his matter.
Finally, he wrote quite an amount in Irish, and his Irish is perfect: bog-Irish is a very different thing from bog-Latin, which
reminds me of the nice story of a certain Pope who never
opened his breviary for fear that it would spoil his Latin.

There is also the question as to where he got the name
Patric. At his date this was not a name; it was a title given by
the Senate; it meant something like Count or Marquis, and
this title was not given by the Church until a couple hundred
years after Patric died. His name is spelled on his tombstone
PATRIC. Had he been a Frenchman or an Englishman and taken
this title, he would have been in gaol in a very short time for
lèse-majesté. No Roman soldier ever set foot in Ireland, so an
Irishman could pinch one of their titles if he wanted it.

It is now St. Patric's Day, and there are two stories I'd like
to tell you. I've forgotten where I got them. Someone told them
to me long years ago, for I've never seen them in print, but
they pleased me so much that I've never forgotten them. The
old tale goes that the Saint first tried to land on the east coast,
just beyond Dublin, beyond the Hill of Howth: that he was
chased out of there by the inhabitants and sailed northwards
and made shore in Ulster.

Now there are two villages just beyond Dublin called Leix
and Offaly. It was at Leix that Patric tried to land. He did land
there, and his delighted seamen prepared and set up on the
shore the first stationary meal that they and the world's best
saint had eaten for a couple of weeks. They were just sitting
down to dinner when the inhabitants of Leix charged down

on them from the woods, drove them back to their ship, and then these same inhabitants sat down on the strand and ate the dinner that had been prepared for the world's best saint and his tarry sailormen.

So far for that. Time passed and St. Patric became famous, and in about the same time the people of Leix became famous too. They were especially famous to the people of the next village which was named Offaly. The folk of Offaly got into the bad habit of asking a certain question of their neighbours from Leix.

Suppose, for example, that there were a number of Leix people in an adjacent hostel and that some men from Offaly chanced into the same pub; an Offaly man—they were very rude people these Offalys, one might perhaps say that they were Offaly rude—well, an Offaly man would suddenly become very curious and would ask in a loud Offaly voice, "Who was it that ate St. Patric's dinner?" Thereupon, and naturally, the men of Leix would seize that pub in its entirety and would hit the men of Offaly with it. After a time the bad neighbourliness of these two villages became so famous that it was almost a joke.

Now the scene changes: we will leave Ireland and go to of all places in the world China. Well, one day there was one of these great storms that you only get in a China sea. It was a storm that was composed of one complete hurricane that was being assaulted by a tornado and then battered by a typhoon. It was, in short, stiff, bad, tough detestable weather and a ship was wallowing in it and shuddering in it and trying to sidle out of it. They had given themselves up for lost when they were wobbled into a harbour somewhere, somehow, and were safe at last.

The hardy mariners tied up and then went into town the way sailormen do. When they got to where they were going, a second ship slid and wriggled and bumped into the same harbour, and these seamen, as tarry as the others and as thirsty as they come, did the very same thing: they went looking for something to drink that didn't taste like salt water, and they got to the exact same place which the others had reached scarce ten minutes ahead of them.

They went into the hostel and were as polite as sailors who don't know the language can be. And then they pricked their ears, for they did know the language, and they looked at the roof and at each other, and they couldn't believe their ears, for they were listening to the very tongue and throttle that belongs to the people of Leix, and they themselves belonged to the people of Offaly.

A man of them remarked to one of his companions, only loudly enough to be heard across a couple of acres, "Now could you tell me, son, who was it at all, who could it have been that ate St. Patric's dinner?"

In the proper part of three seconds the men of Leix and the men of Offaly were seeking each other out with legs of tables, and in ten minutes a small Chinese army escorted them to the jug. In the morning they were brought before a gentleman whom they referred to as the Beak when talking to each other, and as Your Honour when talking to him.

This Judge was a noble and learned soul, and he was very curious indeed as to why two different sets of storm-battered sailors should assault each other and wreck a pub within an exact three minutes of meeting, so the whole affair was gone into and diligently explained to him.

"Tell me now," said the judge, "when was this notable dinner stolen and eaten by these pestilent people who come from Leix?"

"Pestilent they are, your honour," said the interpreter,

"and 'twas most foully done one thousand five hundred and fifty years ago."

"What?" cried the Beak.

"One thousand five hundred and fifty exact years ago," said the interpreter.

The judge was confounded, then he was incredulous, then he was delighted. He stood from his seat. He bowed first to the men of Offaly, then he bowed to the men of Leix, and then he told his own population, including the Army, that this was the most remarkable and lovely tale of Ancestor Worship that he had ever heard of, that these men had certainly come from a saintly country and were probably saints themselves, every tarry jack of them, and that this story should be an example to all China, and especially to the young people who only remembered their grandfathers when they were walloped for forgetting them. He ordered that the prisoners should be released, and he sent them back to their ships with presents of casks of beer and kegs of *saké,* and he ordered that they were to live happy ever afterwards, and never to forget St. Patric.

This is a shorter story and a better one, for 'tis about St. Patric and St. Brigid and all Ireland. By the way, Brigid is a remarkable personage—she is a Christian Saint; a thousand years before that, she was the goddess of war, and before that again she had been the goddess of poetry. Well, the last time that she died she went to heaven as usual, and she and St. Patric used to meet a good deal there. They both loved heaven, and why wouldn't they, but all the same they were always talking about Holy Ireland.

"Do you remember Connemara?" said Brigid.

"Did you ever see the cliffs of Clare, with the sun shining on them?" said Patric.

"Did you know the County Kerry at all well?" said Brigid.

One day as they were reminding each other of this place and that they came out on a suburb of heaven called Radstown. It was a part of the country that they weren't used to, and there was Rhadamanthus the Judge, and he cross-examining sinners and saints and sending some people one way and some people another way, and he without a care in the world himself except to be just and to give people what they deserved. St. Brigid, the good, the kind, didn't like one single inch of Rhadamanthus, and she told St. Patric so.

Then a dreadful thought struck her. "Patric," said she, "that man yonder, that Rhadamanthus man would send even an Irishman to hell."

"He would and all," Patric replied. "And why shouldn't he, if he deserves it?"

"No Irishman deserves it," said St. Brigid, "and I will not have it done."

So they went to the Son, her foster-child, and Brigid got this concession from Him that every person who came from Ireland should be judged by St. Patric and not by Rhadamanthus.

"You will be very careful," said Brigid to Patric.

"I will indeed," he answered.

"But," she insisted, "what will you do if a bad Irishman is brought before you?"

"I'll convert him," said St. Patric.

"And anyhow," said St. Brigid, "there aren't any bad Irishmen."

St. Patric's Day in the Morning

(1947)

THE phrase "Saint Patric's Day in the Morning" is a line from a fairly elderly ballad, and it intends that what we do in the morning is very different from what we do in the night. When the sun rises in the morning that's one thing, and one world: then the moon rises, and that's another thing altogether, and another world. But that we are so used to it we might even think that these arisings and settings are strange matters indeed; but we can't think about matters we're used to, and so we get along very casually in completely different worlds per every twelve hours of our time.

There are two odd days in the month of March for Irish people. One oddity is the first of March. Our poets tell that on the first day of March there is a light to be seen on the neck of the swan, as she balances on the wave, a light not before seen on sea or land, and not to be visible again for three hundred and sixty-five days.

And then there is the seventeenth of March, Saint Patric's

Day. On the morning of this day we go to Church; we praise Saint Patric and we bless the seamrog. But on the evening of this very blessed day we go *en carnaval;* we forget the Saint, and, in our phrase, we "drown the seamrog." That moonwoven operation is much more spirituous than spiritual. The day may begin in piety and it may end in poteen.

One day the rose leapt from its bush for England, so one day the thistle became a Scotsman, and so the seamrog came out of the grass for us on a day now long ago, in the year four-hundred-and-thirty-something. St. Patric was not then a Saint; he wasn't yet even a bishop; and he was stuck in an argument with a king.

"My friend," said the king, "we don't understand this Trinity you speak of. You say there are three gods, and that the three of them add up to one. This is contrary to nature and to truth and to proof."

The Saint happened to look down in the grass they were walking in, and there he saw the seamrog. He plucked the little clover and showed it to the monarch.

"Look," he said, "it is three and it is one, and, so, the gods are three gods and one Godhead."

So on that day there came into being the trinity of St. Patric and the seamrog and Ireland, and they are one religion. I wonder what strange need or kink in the national being enables Ireland to praise and bless in the morning the seamrog, which it drowns the same night. I am not quarrelling with this—so it has come, and that is the way we have it. The person who would change a Law is a Progressive, but the person who would change a Custom is a Rascal.

I suppose that in more ancient days the most adventurous profession in the world was that of a clergyman; a young man of that trade had to go wherever he was sent, and had to be

prepared to take whatever came on the journey and on the job
—and in those times a journey was a real job. One moved on
one's own feet, or on the feet of a horse, and one took a personal jolt for every pace of the way. The young clergyman
had to stand up to warrior kings and their queens and their
warriors, and he had to prove to stubborn fighting men,
trained plunderers, that peace, if diligently regarded, could be
as honourable as war, and that it could also be much more
lucrative, and that in peace a better time is had by all. Every
fighting caste has, sometime or other, to re-learn these facts.

A young clergyman, a Patric, had to be the master of
many subjects. Naturally he had to know more about the spirit
than the next man, but as certainly, and as profoundly, he had
to know all that may be known about the world, the flesh and
the devil; he had to know philosophy and history; and, in
especial, genealogy, as well as did the very masters of these
subjects in the lands he was ordered to. More often than not he
was priest and poet and physician: he had to meet all comers
on all subjects, and, by whatever means, he had to prove that
he was better at every subject than the very men of the trade
itself. To be a clergyman then was a full-time job. I am inclined to think that now it is not quite possible to be a clergyman in the older acceptance of that term.

A Patric, coming to Ireland in the year four-hundred-and-
thirty-two, was not coming to an uncultivated country, nor to a
completely unchristian land. Before him, and contemporaneous
with him, there was the Order of the Druids and the Bardic
Order. These, from time immemorial, had ruled the roost in
Ireland. The Druid System was the religious system of the
country. It was a system of magic and spells and other now
forgotten matters, and so important was it, that the High King

could not speak publicly until the chief druid present gave him permission to do so.

The Bardic Order was another matter. It was powerful indeed: the bards were the historians, poets, musicians, teachers and physicians of the country. All secular learning was in their keeping. Learning was, until this century, knowledge of the past; national and spiritual history; and in St. Patric's day the Bardic Order went over almost in a body to the new religion, and to the new age which it conditioned—after all, our St. Patric was a poet, and a pretty good one too.

But such a change is a revolution indeed, and is the sign of an extreme disagreement between the old order and the then emerging new one. The druids were, of course, discouraged and destroyed and obliterated. Magic went away and labour took its place! That peace should take the place of war is always to be hoped for, but that labour should take the place of magic is a disaster indeed.

It should be noted that St. Patric did not conduct his mission in a completely Pagan country; nor did he disbelieve in magic. He prayed indeed to be delivered from "the spells of women and blacksmiths and druids." There were at that time among the peasantry and the nobility those who still held to the old modes. These were in decadence and had to die, as later, and as at the stroke of the clock, Elizabethan England had to die, and John Milton became the Patric of England.

But there was also a very great number of people in Ireland—and in England—who had already accepted Christianity. This was so much the case that Ireland had already produced certain heretics and their heresies which had to be dealt with by Rome itself. Palladius, who preceded Patric as first Bishop of Ireland was one such, and had to be recalled. Part of

Patric's mission was to destroy the teaching of his predecessor.

Palladius held that God was good and that, consequently, the world was good and all else was good. This theory had to be rooted out of Ireland, and out of wherever else it had spread to, for it conflicted with the official teaching of a necessary Mediator between God and man, and the forgiveness of sins.

There were certain other Irish heresies that had to be silenced and destroyed. Elsewhere in Europe there was a curious opposite to this heresy. Some Irish people, after St. Patric's time, spoke of themselves as "Patricians." They had to drop this name because in Eastern Europe there was a sect also called "Patricians." These believed that everything that came into life was invented or created by the devil, and that God had nothing to do with us dirty rascals, and possibly didn't even know that such inconsiderable creatures as we existed. This creed can, of course, be discovered in the East even to this day. Certain Vedantic Sects say as much; Buddhism says it too, as in the phrase, "Nothing comes into this world but evil; nothing leaves this world but evil." So the term "Patrician" had an Irish significance that was a good one, and a world-significance which the Church could not approve of.

Meanwhile, St. Patric's early life, or the legend of it, was romantic and adventurous. There are a number of things we don't know about him. His birthplace is claimed, on literary evidence, for England and Scotland and France, and perhaps for other places. He must have "lisped in numbers" indeed. When he was quite a boy he was voyaging somewhere. His ship was attacked by Irish pirates; he was taken captive and sold as a slave to some northern chieftain. He endured that slavery for several years; then he escaped. It is an odd thing that by this slavery Patric endured the tonsure before he sought for and accepted the tonsure from the Church. In the Ireland of his time, and possibly in most other countries, the heads of slaves were shaven. In this way a crop-headed man was known everywhere as a masterless man, and so as an escaped or escaping slave. If this custom was universal in Europe then we have the reason why Christianity adopted the tonsure for her priests; they were taking over the very sign and seal and clip of the slave, and were professing the lowest human humility itself, and redeeming it.

St. Patric travelled and studied Latin and prepared himself for the priesthood. Then he returned to Ireland, and became, with St. Brigid, the first and best-beloved of our saints and scholars. His life was thereafter a full one, spreading the gospel of Christ, and perhaps in especial, spreading the authority of the Latin Church. Both of these he did do with unswerving resolution.

A number of questions may be raised about St. Patric. There is no doubt whatever that there was such a person. There is no doubt that he was a determinedly able man, that he could face and outface any and every opposition, and that he is the most significant figure in our modern annals. But we are uncertain of his nationality, of his native language, and we are even uncertain of his name.

In his day the word Patric was not a name: it was a title of nobility given by the Roman Senate to those whom the Nation delighted to honour. It was many years after Patric's death that the Church took over the right of giving this title. Where did our Patric get it? Was he knighted by the Senate? The Saint has left literary remnants in Latin and in Irish: his Irish is perfect: his Latin is not very good. His poems in Irish are perfect: there is the "Cry of the Deer" and the famous "Breastplate" which, in Mrs. Alexander's translation, is perhaps the most remarkable hymn in the English Protestant Hymnal. But the Saint has left nothing to remind us that he was an Englishman, a Frenchman or a Scotsman, or that he knew any tongues except bog Latin and the good Gaelic of the bog.

FRIENDS AND OTHERS

Arthur Griffith

(1922?)

MR. GRIFFITH was born and educated in Ireland. Some years of his early manhood were spent abroad, and he had considerable experience in the actual handling of men on the Rand. I think the native people who served under him must have met in Mr. Griffith a type of master that they had never met before and could never hope to meet again.

Even in these young days his will was already set into something of the granitic quality that later became, not by any means his chief, but one of his most noticeable characteristics.

I remember that some years ago we were talking together, with something of the wonder with which young men who have never been ill in their lives consider sickness, about the illness of a friend. Mr. Griffith said, in a reminiscent way, that once he had very nearly been ill. It was while he was in Africa. There had been an outbreak of fever, and all his responsible assistants and many of his men were down with it. He awakened one morning with a feeling that he did not want to get out of bed, and while lying in a fuzzy and wuzzy condition he was able to tabulate a number of symptoms which made him practically certain that he also had the fever that was epidemic. But he did not intend to be sick, and he did not intend to have any kind of fever that he had not personally selected or arranged to have. He took himself with some difficulty out of bed, marched to a neighbouring ball-alley, and for some six or seven hours he played a solitary game of hand-ball until even he could play it no longer. It must have been a grimmish kind of game and quite devoid of anything in the nature of entertainment. At the end of his "game" he went back to bed and fell asleep. He awoke in the morning without any fever, and, indeed, fever never dared to threaten him again.

This was the young man who returned to Ireland with his mind quite made up that if nobody else could free her, he would do it himself, and the story is illustrative of him in quite a number of ways. The night on which that story was told to me is memorable also because of an incident which throws light on some other aspects of Mr. Griffith's personality: his forbearance, for example; his readiness in action; and, in particular, his more than masterly grip of the subject that happens to be interesting him.

For some time it had been a habit of ours to see each other home up to quite a late hour at night. We were marching down Grafton Street, meaning to turn into Nassau Street, and so to my rooms in Mount Street. Arriving there we would turn about, and I would see Mr. Griffith back to O'Connell Street and the last tram. Mr. Griffith had launched a daily paper called *Sinn Fein*. He had seen it in the cradle, and he was at the moment attending it to the grave. We were discussing something in connection with the paper. He was a little grave, as befitted the occasion, but by no means unhappy.

"This is the first time in my life," he said, "that I feel a sort of regret, not a real regret," he emphasized, "a sort of regret that I have always insisted on being a perfectly honest man."

"Why should you crave to be a thief on this particular night?" I enquired.

"I could have been a fairly wealthy man if I had the luck in those days to want to be dishonest."

"So," I queried, encouragingly.

"In the Africa of those days," he continued, "men in my position were able to retire after a few years and buy theatres."

At this moment we had arrived at Nassau Street corner. Some young men, in the negligent manner of those days, were leaning against the doorway of Yeates' the opticians, and, as we swung around them, one reached out a hand and tapped lightly on my companion's hat. We looked round. Nothing was visible but three young men who were regarding space with melancholy absorption. We turned to resume our way, and, on the instant, this acrobatic hand tapped again on the hat. We turned once more, and the same trio were still dreaming on the death of kings. Mr. Griffith half turned and returned in the one movement, and on this occasion the guilty hand had not time to be withdrawn. His left fist shot out and caught the owner of the hand a blow that turned him upside down. He was addressing his right fist toward a second man, while I was energetically wrapping myself about the leg of the third, not with a really militant intent, but purely as an obstructive tactic, for this third man was in the act of discharging himself as a running kick at Mr. Griffith, when we all found ourselves surrounded as if by magic by a crowd and a policeman. This officer's experienced eye made a rapid discrimination between the washed and the unwashed.

"Will you give this man in charge, sir?" he asked.

Mr. Griffith was astounded at being invited to deliver any person into the hands of what he politically considered was rank injustice.

"Certainly not," he said, and we turned away.

On the second step he resumed, "Personally I have never wanted to buy a theatre, but our paper would have had at least a chance to make its way and win its public. I am thinking of you men also," he said.

"How do we set up a craving for dishonesty in you?" I marvelled.

There were hasty feet behind us, and, with the words, "Hey, there!" a gruff, sulky voice called on us to halt. It was the young man with the agile hand.

"You knocked me down a minute ago, mister," he said. "Let's see if you can knock me down again."

Mr. Griffith was slightly perplexed, for his interest at the moment was in South Africa, but he was mildly unpacking a disastrous fist out of his trouser pocket, when I intervened and made a short speech. The young man was quite unused to the eloquence of a person who on the previous night had written fifteen poems, and in sheer self-defence he offered to apologize to us both. He wanted to shake hands also, and he did outstretch the identical delinquent paw which had previously toyed with the hat of an innocent and preoccupied stranger. Mr. Griffith for the first time was truly alarmed, and plunged both of his hands precipitately into his pockets, but I shook hands with the young man, for I was very proud of the effect of my first public speech. We resumed our walk; and, on the second pace:—

"If I had taken the chances that were all around me," said Mr. Griffith, "I could have paid you writers a great deal more than I am able to pay you now."

Sadness fell upon my brow like a damp sponge as I realized that, with some bitterness, Fate had visited my friend with a horrible honesty that was destined to bring myself and my family to the workhouse. But my temperament, too, is philosophical, and I seldom complain except in verse. I asked him a question.

"If, by touching a button on that lamp-post, you could kill a person living in China and get all his goods without fear of detection or punishment either here or in hell, would you touch the button?"

Mr. Griffith laughed, but focussed the problem.

"I would not touch the button," he averred.

"Would O'Connolly?" I urged. "Would Russell? or Montgomery, or Gogarty?"

"Yeats would," said Mr. Griffith, for at that time he held that there was nothing good about Mr. Yeats except his poetry: but he would perhaps not now maintain these mutually destructive postulates. As I was re-seeing him home that night he told me the story of how he had once nearly been sick.

Reminiscences of J. M. Synge

(1928)

IT WAS not until late in his rather short life that Synge discovered his true ability to lie neither in philosophy nor music but in drama, and one may wonder how he came to make this discovery, for he was a painfully slow writer, and his very slowness might have led him to distrust an art-form that was so difficult to handle. To the end writing was a toil to him.

In this, however, he was not exceptional; for the majority of writers have assured us that writing is a labour from which one may really shrink a little. Synge occasionally got some reviewing to do for a literary weekly, but he had to discontinue this because the article, for which he might receive two guineas, always cost him six weeks to write; and these were six weeks of painful cogitation as to how possibly one can say anything whatever with a pen that will afterwards be readable.

Still later he confessed that if his day's work had actually resulted in the addition of two words to his manuscript, although he might not feel triumphant and inclined to celebrate the occasion, he did yet consider that the day had not been wasted, that his subject had been carried on, or was not absolutely stationary.

He lived in Paris for some years at the rue d'Assas, and his apartment was adequately furnished with a bed, an oil-stove, a book-case, and a yard of French bread, and while in Paris he really needed whatever scarce guineas might come his way. Possibly the philosophy he toiled after was sufficiently robust at this time to tide him over the bad days but, although he did not complain, he did consider that a meal which cost more than one franc twenty-five had been extravagantly paid for.

He was somewhat negative to ordinary human beings (the dramatist tends to be so), not that he disliked people, but he did not admire them. He certainly did not love his fellow-human-beings in the mass. With him more than six people could easily become a crowd, and he could consider that such a gathering would have neither wit nor looks. The dramatist will love the rare, the personal, the individual, but he cannot even be expected to love the multitude.

Dramatic qualities were to Synge more easily discoverable in the countryside than in the city. He thought that every country-bred person has a measurable idiosyncrasy: has each a distinct nose and hat and accent.

And in the country he found many another cherishable thing. Birds and beasts and plants are there. There the earth itself seems to be more manifest. Each rood of it is there observed to be utterly different from any other possible rood of space. Every slope and ridge and hill; every stream and tree and cloud is known as distinct from every other similar sight or bulk in the world.

A moor (or, as we should say in Ireland, a bog) was not

for Synge a place from which turf or peat is cut. A bog was an enchantment, as indeed it is to everyone who has become acquainted with or has lived nigh to a bog. To get well into an extensive bog is to leave all else behind; is to have left the world behind; almost to have left one's self afar and apart and forgotten. There is the bog and the clouds, and the rest merges to them.

The sea is desolate, but it is also, and unforgivably, a desolation; but the bog is not a desolation; it is desolate, but is habitable and inhabited. Birds and rats and bees and rabbits are there. An odd donkey or a goat is always, somewhere, ambling or frisking away from you; is always cropping an endless breakfast. For in a bog you could easily imagine that the breakfast of a donkey began before time began, and that it will continue while time has yet a second to draw on.

And over it all there is wind and space and cloud and silence; the wind always different, and the cloud never the same, the silence never monotonous. All these seem to live as it were one life, and one's own life participates into that, or seems scarcely to be sundered from it.

He loved some other matters also; that is, his mind went willingly to certain things. He loved music and occultism and a something that we shall call bleakness. Whatever might be authoritatively uttered on these subjects would be diligently hearkened to by him.

Music, where it is understood, is loved by most of us, for we may only love where we understand. Occultism, or the theory of magic, is delighted in by everyone who is sane enough to wish to be saner; to wish, that is, to be wiser. But bleakness is another thing, and touches only to the fine soul. It is the especial, perhaps the final, acquirement of a cultured person. At last nothing but it is beauty. That is, nothing but bleakness can definitely satisfy the true man that is in every man.

Had he lived longer Synge might have carved a bare, an unadorned, a lean bleak art to replace the lush and somewhat vociferous art that he has left us. His art is lush, but there is continually to be found in it the wiry line, the rigour, the sharp and bare and bleak that he truly loved, and which he would have further striven to.

His knowledge of the countryside was extensive and penetrating. He knew the call of every bird and the habit of most creatures that are to be found in our ways and pastures. His approach to knowledge was—to be silent; to look eagerly at all that came; and to listen intently to all that happened. And, in his approach to a knowledge of the human inhabitants of the countryside, he used the same approach and attitude.

As a boy he had wandered the hills of Dublin and Wicklow, and he knew these intimately. He could assure a thirsty companion that behind a certain folding of a certain hilly track there was a well. And, if one was thirstier still, he would tell behind how many hills-and-a-half a tavern lay: or that on sixteen rising turns to the left a slaty cottage was couched among slaty rocks and that there one could get a glass of milk and a cake from the griddle.

And he knew that in all these places, if one were well-bred—if, that is, one were silent and inconspicuous—there could be heard a fashion of speech which was not conned from books; which had no acquaintance with art or science or scholarship, and which was yet abundant and racy and of a remarkable texture—the wild, the exuberant speech of isolated people. People who are always as timid in action as they are bold in talk: being bold indeed in the only thing they have practice of. For from these people every adventure but the adventure of speech has been retired, and they must seek in conversation all of the change, all of the excitement that others win from travel, from theatres, from the press of men and affairs.

He was different from many of his countrymen in a number of ways. One, but of prime importance, was that he came of a Protestant stock. A stock that included bishops and canons and missionaries who, through generations, had been to and returned from distant lands and curious peoples. He grew in a house that was filled with the furnitures and curiosities of strange countries.

His true schooling was up in the mountain and out on the bog; it came from the shy but vital life that moves in solitudes. His professors were the mountainy men and women, themselves almost as humble in station, almost as sundered from change, almost as bereft of ambition, but as vital, persistent, self-centred as was the lowly animal life that throve about them.

From these teachers he learned to delight in the curious cadences that may be in speech. He learned the craft of packing a phrase until it is explosive with adventure; the art of lightening however tragic or despairing a concept with just the irony or humour or tenderness that brings it back to earth and to a human relation.

He loved the village tailor who said, "I will make you a suit, sir, that will go around and about you like a curtain."

And when he once lamented the ageing condition of his own hat he was comforted by the remark of the person to whom he was speaking:—"Let you not throw away the hat," quoth his companion, "for there is an art about an old hat that is not in a new hat."

And what might that art be? Synge enquired.

"The art of an old hat is to cock it, and 'tis known that no person whatever would care to cock a new hat."

He loved the simple human relation, and however fantastic a tale he may be telling, it is always human. Perhaps his limitation lay here. He is a folk-writer working on folk material. His fantasy does not attempt anything but the world we live in; does not bid for an extra world or a spiritual experience. His tales are wonderful indeed; but they are wonderful because of the bog and the mountain that are in them; because of the men and women that rage and riot in them; because of all the things that he knew and loved so well.

And in this he differs from the other writers of his quality. The quest after divinity that is the Irish writer's torment and his joy, brought to Synge neither joy nor torment. Perhaps he had no time for these. "Men and women and their delicious burdens" were what he sought and wrote of. The common physical and mental vigour of life was what he loved and would seek. He was for years a sick man, and perhaps guessing that he was a doomed man, he did not search for another world, and a greater being: divining that he must quit the habitual earth, the companionable sun, the comforting spaces ere he could really fathom these or savour this life to the full.

A silent, an aloof, a listening man! Listening to and watching all that which had never been completely his, and from which he should soon be parted. He would stand on a headland that jutted steeply on the sea, and he would look and look and look at the sparkling waters below. He would look at a meadow, a sunset, a man, as though he must satiate his eyes with their wonder, and, if it could be, saturate his very being with all that he should not carry with him.

He died in a Dublin hospital. A doctor who attended him told that when his end was nigh, Synge petitioned that he might be lifted in bed so that he should look from the window and see the Dublin hills. Twice he was so lifted, and he looked again on the shapes that he loved better than all other shapes of the world.

But when on the third morning he looked from the window, he looked on blankness; there was a thick mist without, and he could not see the hills. As he was lowered again he was weeping, quietly, forlornly, and in a little time he died.

Some Irish Books I Like

(1937)

Some years ago, when I was Registrar of the Irish National Gallery, Miss Purser said to me: "Our Gallery has the greatest collection of first-class works by second-class masters in the world."

That was not a devaluation of our Gallery, but a subtle appreciation of it, and, to this day, I find the Irish Gallery less great indeed but much more interesting than the London Gallery itself. The London Gallery is a great collection of pictures, the Irish a most original collection, and it can hold any intelligent artist astonished, and delighted, and packed with enquiry for a whole swathe of his artistic life.

It is so with our literature. In it also there is an astonishing collection of first-class work by second-class artists. The reader should not unreasonably deprecate the term "second-class." It is the next-closest to first-class, and often indeed there is but little distinction between them: the point, and the great thing, is not

61

that the artist is of the so-called second-class; it is that the art is first-rate.

When one looks over the names of those who have contributed to English literature from Ireland we may be both surprised and pleased by the variety and continuity of that contribution. After the Elizabethan writers, the Irish contribution to drama is the most important which the English language has known: Congreve, Sheridan, Goldsmith, Wilde, Shaw, Synge, Yeats. Each of these writers is the best dramatist of his type and period and were the Irish contribution excluded from it, English drama would be poor indeed.

In poetry Ireland has not done well. We have, perhaps, some claim to Blake, and, if that be allowed, we must admit that he is the only example of fine poetry which the Irish race has given to English literature—unto today, that is, and "today" means the later poetry of Mr. Yeats. This lack of fine poetry is the more remarkable in that, racially, Ireland has always set more store by verse than England has, and that more varied elements of our population have loved poetry than can be parallelled in the social castes of our neighbours.

Poetry is at once not our best and it is our best. It is our best although in latency. Ireland has never had a good poet; also, and more astonishingly, she has never had a bad one. As it is said that there is no such thing as bad whisky, perhaps also there is no such thing as bad poetry, although it is to be admitted that some poets are just merely not so good as others. Even though inadequacy be there, there is flame behind the smokiest of our bards.

There are three books I should like to say a few words on. One of these we already have, and although we have the other two they are not readily available. The first is Lennox Robinson's *Golden Treasury of Irish Verse*. This is an invaluable book, and in it is stored the bulk of our national poetical treasure, such as it is, and such as it has been passionately loved by how many generations of our people. It is our past and we have it in good metrical security.

Another anthology should now be prepared giving examples of the work of all our poets during the past fifteen years. This would be a more remarkable book than many might consider, and would be an index to our cultural and psychological position in the current world which nothing else could give. I would suggest that Seumas O'Sullivan should prepare this book, for, since A.E. has gone from us, no other person has so wide a knowledge of Irish verse—or English verse for that matter—as he.

The third anthology I should wish to see would be chosen from the various books of verse published by Mr. Yeats in the last twelve years. Such a selection would give a reader entry to the greatest body of fine poetry written by any man of our time. This would be a perfectly delightful book, and a perfectly Irish one, for, after long wandering by the way, Mr. Yeats has got home and in this very year of grace he is greater than he ever was before.

This getting better and better of Mr. Yeats is a very curious matter, for it is rare that a man gets better as he gets older. The Irish proverb *dul in age, dul in olcas* (to grow old and bad) seems generally true. There are important exceptions. Titian was painting better at ninety than at forty. Verdi wrote *Falstaff* in his eightieth year, and although Mr. Yeats is not adult in these splendid terms, he is the only living man of whom it may be said not only that he gets better as he gets older, but that he gets better per year.

Some ten years ago he recovered from his youth and became renascent all over again, and since then every book he has written has shown an increase in craft and in actual power which is unexampled in modern letters.

It took Mr. Yeats about three decades of years to get himself into his work, for his own self was his perpetually enigmatic theme. His unceasing effort to do this dissatisfied many critics, but he has done it. It is rare that any writer manages to include and convey himself in his work but whoever can do so is a great writer, in the full meaning of that term.

Mr. Yeats is singular in many ways, and not least in this, that one must talk about him if one is to talk about his poetry at all. This is unusual, for good poetry is in general anonymous, as it were; but both he and his work are as unusual as were the person and the work of Blake, the only other poet who matches him for passionate and enigmatic verse. He is the only poet living who is capable of a passionate utterance.

The Tower, published in 1928, and *The Winding Stair,* published 1933, mark important phases in Mr. Yeats' renaissance. These books contain lovely poems, and both are emotionally connected with the entire of the writer's past. Mr. Yeats has let nothing go. He has never renounced a thought because it was a bad one, or because other people considered it to be intellectually or artistically unimportant. He has carried all his baggage of ideas through the years, and has brought even his most elusive matters to the perfection which, almost as by instinct, he had postulated of or for it.

In *The Winding Stair* the old and the new Mr. Yeats are seen in juxtaposition. In "Blood and the Moon" he says:

And God-appointed Berkeley, that proved all things a dream,
That this pragmatical, preposterous pig of a world, its farrow
    that so solemn seem,
Must vanish on the instant if the mind but change its theme.

And in "A Dialogue of Self and Soul" he asserts in the old manner, immediately followed by the new:

> I am content to live it all again
> And yet again, if it be life to pitch
> Into the frog-spawn of a blind man's ditch,
> A blind man battering blind men:
> Or into that most fecund ditch of all,
> The folly that man does
> Or must suffer, if he woos
> A proud woman not kindred of his soul.
>
> I am content to follow to its source
> Every event in action, or in thought;
> Measure the lot; forgive myself the lot!
> When such as I cast out remorse
> So great a sweetness flows into the breast
> We must laugh and we must sing,
> We are blest by everything,
> Everything we look upon is blest.

Mr. Yeats is reborn. He has dropped nothing by the way, but is transforming all that seemed passionate or petulant to its true loveliness, its true reality. So in two stanzas from "Vacillation" he carries the same thought further still, and perhaps will carry it yet further:

> My fiftieth year had come and gone,
> I sat, a solitary man,
> In a crowded London shop,
> An open book and empty cup
> On the marble table-top.

While on the shop and street I gazed
My body of a sudden blazed;
And twenty minutes, more or less
It seemed, so great my happiness,
That I was blessèd, and could bless.

I am inclined to think those ten lines the most original piece of verse of our time, and the top of Mr. Yeats' form.

There is a preoccupation with sensual love in all Mr. Yeats' books, and in this book also: but here it has undergone a curious change. Hitherto Mr. Yeats had written of love as a man. In *The Winding Stair* he is mainly writing of it as a woman. The whole section of "Words for Music Perhaps," and "A Women Young and Old," have this odd and powerful imagining for their theme. It is completely well done, but yet must be considered as a transforming process, and one wonders to what strange and beautiful thing his idea of love will transform when he has refined the sensual completely away, and nothing but love remains. His passions and angers have already come to the desire to bless others, his sensualities (and he is the most sensual poet we have ever had) must similarly lose and refind themselves in their own bliss of love and compassion.

This book, *The Winding Stair,* is a wonderful book.

W. B. Yeats

(1942)

I N THE last war quite a number of soldiers carried a volume of
Keats or Shelley or Wordsworth as very personal belong-
ings. Personally, were I packing a volume in such circumstances I'd choose Wordsworth against all comers, be it only
because he is so much more of his nation and its countryside.
The clay of England has got wonderfully into his verse. The
psychology of this people is very securely in his verse, and a
great deal of the manners and mannerisms of English people
is there also.

There is a sense in which one could hold that, of all the
English poets, the two who are most English are Chaucer and
Wordsworth, and, were I an Englishman, which I am for the
duration, I should carry Wordsworth with me to the war in
preference to any other poet whatever, and I'd learn from him
a lot about what one is prepared to fight for, and die for, or
live for. I should say that in prose the two most English writers

are, strangely enough, Anthony Trollope and George Borrow. *Lavengro* or *The Romany Rye* could make even a hide-out under a dust-storm seem like home.

If, however, I were asked what modern poet is best to be acquainted with, and best worth carrying, then I should plump for Willy Yeats. As Wordsworth was the most individual and personal poet of his time, so Yeats is the most individual and personal poet of our day. There are very few poets of whom it can be said, "Who touches this book touches a man": it can be said of Donne and Wordsworth, and curiously, Yeats. All other poets are, as it were, writing on another than the personal plane, and, very properly, forgetting themselves in a meditation on God and man and nature, so that one could easily conceive that in general, poets have no personal life at all.

Wordsworth in almost every poem is present, and is speaking personally to his personal friend, the reader, and there is more of the individual and communicative quality to be found in Yeats than in any other modern poet I know of. Shelley and Keats are not writing about you and me and themselves, and our own hills and vales and neighbours. They are writing about other and further and stranger matters. They are not good poets for hard, homeless times like ours. Yeats' poems often smell of the ground he walked on, and sound of the people he was interested in, or angry with, or hoping to get his own back upon.

I've had quite a number of meetings with Yeats in Dublin, in Paris, in London, and in Kentucky. Of course, I had met him many times with other people, and of course, those kind-of meetings don't count anyway. In his latter years whenever he came to London he formed a habit of ringing me up and asking me to go and see him. I always took a ring from another poet as a kind of royal command. And I always remembered that telephoning was one of the many things which Yeats didn't do very well.

Apropos of that, I was with him once in Dublin, but of that visit I only remember my departure. Yeats was seeing me out. We were walking down the stairs, when up the stairs came a maid carrying in her arms Yeats' son, then aged about three years. The huge-headed infant gazed very sternly at his father, and Yeats, thinking he ought to say something to his own baby, murmured a couple of lines from John Donne, in whom he was then greatly interested. He said to the baby:

> The Chapel wants an ear, Council a tongue;
> Story, a theme, and Music lacks a song:

The infant looked at him with no reverence, and roared in a titanic voice: "Go away, Man!" Yeats and I went abashed away.

In the hall the telephone bell rang. Yeats answered it. He listened very carefully, and then he said, "Yes, O yes, yes, yes," and he hung up. As he let me out he said sadly, "That was a message from the Government. I never," he went on, "can understand anything that the beastly machine says. I'll go round with you to the office and ask them what that message was about."

I asked him did he always take a taxi to a house that rung him up to find out what it was all about, but he answered that he usually did nothing about it, he just hung up, and left the sequel to be dealt with by Fate, Time, Chance, and Circumstances.

So when he rung me up I felt for him and listened diligently, for I also find some trouble in understanding telephone language, which often says nothing except, "Hello, are you there, don't ring off, hello, are you there. . . ."

On these occasions when I went to his hotel, or his club, we were always alone, and we always talked poetry. I should qualify that statement—Yeats' intention was that we should talk about his poetry, or, more closely still, that he would talk about his poetry, and that I should listen heartily, and interrupt as little as was possible.

But it never turned out that way, for I was as unstoppable a sayer of my own verse as he was of his, and quite unconsciously, the instant a man says a poem to me I say two quick ones back at him, and as I nearly always shut my eyes when I am saying a poem I never know whether my companion is asleep, or only yawning. No one, not even Yeats, can do anything to a man who has his eyes shut and is away in full flood upon no earthly sea.

Yeats and I, however, were very well-mannered with each other. There is always a point of distrust between two men who have any manners at all in private. Still, I'm inclined to believe that Yeats and I were the only poets with good manners that ever lived. When he had finished a poem I always asked him to say it again and when I had finished one he as scrupulously invited me to repeat *the last verse*.

Yeats was really only interested in his own poetry. He complained to me once that people kept writing to him about the work of new poets, pointing out that as he was "interested in poetry" he must read, praise, and help the new-comers. But, he said, almost angrily, "I'm not interested in poetry. I'm only interested in what I'm trying to do myself, and there aren't enough hours in days and nights for me to get through what I'm at. Besides," he went on, "out of any ten poets who are pushed on you by literary ladies, nine are no good, and the tenth isn't much good."

One day—this was in Paris—I asked him what he did

about books that were sent to him for signature. He became quite thoughtful about this, and then he became very happy. And then he told me this story:

He was dining once with Thomas Hardy, and as they were finishing their coffee he asked Hardy the very same question: "What do you do, Hardy, about books that are sent to you for signature?"

"Yeats," said Hardy, "come with me, there is something upstairs I want to show you." At the top of the house Hardy opened a door, and the two poets entered a larger room. This room was covered from the floor to the ceiling with books. Hardy waved his hand at the odd-thousand volumes that filled the room—"Yeats," said he, "these are the books that were sent to me for signature."

About a year before his death I went to his hotel, and was shown up to his bedroom. The great poet was in bed, with a dressing-gown about him and a writing-pad on his knee. We talked for a little, and then he said thoughtfully: "All my life I've been bothered as to how writers get on with their work in winter. If," he went on, "if you sit at a table you get stiff hands and frozen feet, and then the stuff you write can only be warmed by sticking it into the fire."

I agreed that, barring being boiled alive, being frozen to death was the worst torment of a literary life. "But," said Yeats triumphantly, "I've found out how to conquer cold feet. My feet are never cold now. Come over to the bed, Stephens," he said, "and I'll show you."

He threw the coverlets off. He was fully dressed under the bed-clothes, and had a dressing-gown on over his ordinary clothes. But it was his legs that delighted me. "There," he said, "you can't get cold feet if you wear these." He had on a pair of huge rubber fisherman's boots that reached to his thighs. "Inside these," said he cunningly, "I have on a pair of woolly slippers, and I'm as warm as toast."

He was anxious to know how I worked. I told him that I didn't work much at verse. Almost any of my books have been written in about a month: the verse comes in a rush, three or four pieces a day, and when it's finished I don't write any more for perhaps a couple of years, and I don't even try to, because I don't want to.

Yeats was astonished at this, especially at the not wanting to. "I," he said, "work at it all day and every day. I hunt poems the way a hound hunts rabbits. I prowl about poetry the way a hungry wolf prowls about a hen-run. . . . What is your best poem?" said he.

"I don't know," I replied, "I've a different best one every few days. . . . At the moment," I went on, "I'm in love with two of yours: 'Byzantium' and a little scrap that you seem to have written at a teashop table."

"I love that table-top poem myself," he said, "but I don't think it has the strangeness, the syntax, that makes a great poem." I chided him there—" 'Tis the highest movement you ever reached in your life, or that any man has reached in a century!" And thereupon I said ten lines of his own poem, "Vacillation," to him.

Yeats as Dramatist

(1943)

FUTURE criticism will have plenty to say about Yeats, for he was odd as a man, odd as a poet, and odd as a dramatist. One of these quiddities is, that he takes every opportunity he can find to talk about himself. You may think that there is nothing very strange about this, for we have all heard that a man has really nothing to talk about except himself, and that only the social conscience forbids it. But even in private life, the person who will talk about himself is considered to be a bore, and is known to be an ill-bred one.

In general, the thing called art is chary of touching any personal or autobiographical material. This is so, even in prose. There is almost no such thing as a good autobiography, for, underlying all such, there lies a deal of vanity and pretentiousness, and mere lying.

There are exceptions to every rule, and there are, at least, two exceptions to this one. John Donne was almost completely a poet of himself and about himself. Herrick also, that loveliest

of poets, would seem to be always autobiographical: but, towards the end of his life, he affirmed, nay, confessed, that all
these ladies of his—and how many they are! and are they not
the prettiest girls that ever bounced into verse?—he confessed,
alas, that they had never been in love with him, nor he with
them: that, in fact, they had never existed, except insofar as he
had invented them lovingly, and endowed them beautifully.
Sadder confession than this was never sanctified in golden
numbers. Except for John Donne, you can disbelieve almost
everything personal that a poet utters to the lute and soft re-
corders; and, except for him again, it can be said that personal
poetry is nearly always poor poetry; for the poetic talent is
too aery, and too incurious, to bother with any man's personal
hopes or fears or ambitions. Poetry doesn't answer any questions, and it doesn't ask any either.

Shakespeare's sonnets are, of course, personal poems. They
are not among the best parts of his work. The best of these
sonnets—which are also the best sonnets in the language—are
those in which he forgets both himself and herself and their
love-affair; but otherwise, and when the sonnets are personal,
they form a body of the most painful love-poetry in English.

Like Donne, Yeats has succeeded in being at once a person
and a poet, and he is, so, an oddity in verse. He is singular in
another way also. He is, at once, a poet and a dramatist, and he
is often a remarkable worker in these two almost antagonistic
arts: for poetry considers that drama is detestable, and drama is
assured that poetry is silly.

In general, it can be said that a drama written by a poet
makes a bad play (as to a poem written by a dramatist, no one
needs to say anything about it). There are many such bad
plays. Once every poet thought that he had to write a play or
two merely to show that he could do it if he wanted to. These

are rarely played, and very properly, for they are nearly always unplayable and are nearly always unreadable. The remarkable thing about Yeats is that many of his dramas can be acted, and can be read.

Poetic drama in English is a very curious thing. Curious chiefly in this, that, except for Shakespeare and Milton, there is almost no poetic drama in English of real worth. This, that, and the other poetic drama of the past may now and again be revived, but they all drop dead again immediately after the week of their revival, for the English language does not really like poetic drama, the English nation hates it, and the English actor can't speak it. Actually, the thing, Poetry, is debilitated by narrative matter, is scandalized by declamatory matter, and is vulgarized by personality.

Shaw and Yeats—writers, who, I think, had small admiration for each other—did each a curious thing in and to our modern drama. Shaw almost banished action from his boards, replacing it by an Idea. Instead of saying "Let's watch and drowse," he tended to say "Let's think and tumble." Yeats *did* banish action from his stage, and sought to replace it by speech. His success in this, the barrenest theatre the English language has known, is very great.

To an extent, he modelled his drama on the Noh Plays of Japan, wherein "significance" is matter of the first order, and the bustle of action is vulgarity. This drama is not confined to Japan: China and India have many examples in their own religious and ceremonial modes, of the same severe aristocratic art, wherein the voice that speaks is more important than the speaker, and the matter suggested is more attended upon than is the speech that half-utters it.

The best of Yeats' plays are, consequently, very short, and some of these masked and shrouded one-act dramas do attain to real beauty, and strangeness, and dignity. This is true of most of his poems also: but every poet's best poems are his shorter ones—only four poets could write longish poems and keep them good throughout.

There is yet another way in which Yeats is remarkable. There is a saying in Irish which is very unhappy, and terribly true. It is—"To grow old and bad": meaning that this is the natural inescapable progression of all things, and is the rule of life. There have been few exceptions to this law; but, of mercy, there have been some. In general, the later work of every artist is just habitual, formularized stuff. Spring-time, that should usher every soul to the tomb as to the womb, has long departed, and we do not leave life younger and gayer than we entered it.

The name of the habitual writer and painter and liver is Legion. But to this rule also, there are a few notable exceptions. 'Twas so with Yeats. With the publication of his book *The Tower* he started out all over again: and, right up to the very day of his death, he was perfecting his art; refining his ear, his mind, and his syntax in a way that is wonderful and reverend. He was recreating all these and was, artistically, in a condition almost equivalent to a reincarnation. He did not winter to decay, he died in a spring-time, and younger than he was born.

One rejoices when somebody goes out better than he came in, and one mourns a little that a few more seasons were not allowed him, so he might have proved that of the beginning, the middle, and the end, the end can be the best, which it ought to be.

"Byzantium"

(1944)

A<small>LMOST</small> every poet has one peculiar poem, and you find that
the whole man is involved in it. So "Lycidas" is Milton's,
and is Milton; the "Intimations" is Wordsworth's, "The Anniversary" is Donne's, "The Scholar Gypsy" is Arnold's, and
"Byzantium" is Yeats'. I am not now holding that these are the
greatest works of the various masters, but that these are works
which no one else but the given poet could possibly imagine:
they are his by a special proprietorship, a special accent.

The poem "Byzantium" is the strangest poem in English,
it is the most remote poem in English, and it is, even curiously,
constructed of Yeats' own idiom. Indeed, if one held that it is
created of Yeats' personal clichés, such could be held. There
is almost no line, no image, in this poem which an attentive
reader will not find to have been used before by Yeats, and
often many times. It is perhaps the result of an excessive devo-
tion to syntax that many phrases in Yeats' work come to
have a general character, a foreseeable flow and fall. Yeats had

discovered his own idiom, but he was not asleep to this fact, he was very practically aware of it.

A number of questions arise about this singular poem. One is, "Why did he write it?" "What is it about?" is another. "Is it well done? finally done?" is a third.

Yeats has been so recently with us that he is now a mysterious poet. He will become more familiar later on. We cannot imagine what future criticism will make of him, but this much is perhaps certain: that he will be reckoned among the "singular" poets, and the question of his being great or not great may not arise. "Singular" poets are Donne, Herrick, Blake, Coleridge, Hopkins, Yeats. Blake excepted, all of these artists finished up as disappointed, if not actually despairing creatures.

The singularity of these poets largely consists in the fact that they were too often writing about themselves. None of them is absent from even a page of their writings, and this accompanying ego obscures much of their work, and leaves us with the sense "two voices are there" where we had almost bargained to hear but one. As in saintliness you actually forgo a personal ego, so does the apparition of one in verse distort a certain innocency which poetry needs.

It is odd how carefully poetry excludes the writer of it. Ideally, every poem is anonymous, and the presence of a writer is felt as an intrusion, practically as a vulgarity. To every rule, of course, its own exception, and here is Yeats to be excepted. He has gate-crashed the Law and the Prophets, and, in a sense, he has gate-crashed Byzantium. He would live there, and truly he did not know its language, but, as truly, he was learning it.

Before Yeats composed his strange poem he had been moving steadily enough towards it. All his paths seemed di-

rected to that Graeco-Roman-Oriental bourne, whence truly no
traveller has yet returned.

His verse begins under the influence of the French Sym-
bolists. In his adult life he was endlessly interested in what is
indifferently called occultism or spiritualism. The Rosy Cross
also entreated him, and in later life he studied and pondered
the Hindu Upanishads. He loved certain words almost child-
ishly. Such words as Zoroaster, Pythagoras, Trismegistus, Byzantium. Byzantine art—which looks so primitive, and isn't—
that subtle, inhuman generalization, stylization, that simplifi-
cation which is more complex than complexity itself, that
loveliness which is always out of reach and almost out of
mind, captured his later imagination, and some quality of it
did get into his later art.

There is, of course, much of this strangeness and remoteness in all poetry. A man or a woman in a Byzantine drawing
is not a man or a woman: a man or a woman in a fine poem
is not a man or a woman: they suggest personality but do not
express it. Indeed, much that we call humanity has been ab-
stracted from them, and strangely enough, they are not less-
ened by this abstraction, they are even singularly ennobled
and beautified by possessing no recognizable being.

What girl is it that is for ever "Comin' through the rye"?
For a moment that is eternal she stands in the quivering field
and shall never leave it, and will be beloved for ever. She is
every girl or none. So, too, no poet's girl has ever existed, and
she, without even a rag or a bone or a brain, is all the better
for that lack, and is the more durable and the more adorable
for it. The poetic person is always an immaculate conception,
and disdains all that can be thought of as identity or reality.
"There is a lady, sweet and kind." That sweet and kind lady
is as Byzantine as any figurine of them all.

Yeats' "Byzantium" is not quite so. It is not immaculately conceived. It has unfortunate realities sounding and mourning through its brazen airs, and, while it is truly remote, it is not of that innocency, of that passionlessness, of that total non-violence and non-ego which, had he lived yet a poor few years, Yeats would certainly have carried it to, and crowned himself as a wonder, for he was the most determined seeker after what he did not understand, but did surmise, that has ever worked in verse.

This sense of a not-quite-completed life, a not-quite-compact comprehension, is one that troubles his reader, and makes it difficult quite to be his lover as well as his reader. You may love such or such a poem, and the Shelley or Keats or Blake or Herrick who wrote it—these, by the way, are the only "lovable" poets—but you cannot so love a Yeats poem and the poet who begat it, for he tends to be present, not so much creating a poem as producing it. Something, so, of drama and publicity is obtruded into his verse, and he is seen as having more petulance, more violence than is admirable in a poet; but he had not time to grow out of himself, his moods and his idioms.

There are three books by Yeats to which attention must be drawn in considering this famous poem. They are his three last books, *The Tower, The Winding Stair*, and *Last Poems*. Each a remarkable book. The first poem in *The Tower* is called "Sailing to Byzantium"; in his next book, *The Winding Stair,* there is the poem "Byzantium." These two poems are separated by three years of intense activity on the poet's part, and it is natural to consider that they are separate works. In reality they are only separated in a sense that a preface is separated from its volume, or an overture from its symphony.

I do not agree with Wordsworth's statement that poetry is emotion recollected in tranquillity, and especially I do not think that this statement can be applied to Yeats. His was an excitable nature, and out of some working excitement all his poems emerged. I think this is true of every creative artist, when they cease to live urgently they cease to work well, and until the day of his death Yeats did not cease from work.

In his later years, and in his very last work, he was more avid of personal experience than ever he had been in his youth. At the time he composed the first "Byzantium" Yeats was already an elderly man, but this is not the poem of an old man, nor are any of his poems of that stamp. Indeed as an old man he makes a curious reflection in his *Last Poems;* he says in "Imitated from the Japanese":

> A most astonishing thing—
> Seventy years have I lived;
>
> (Hurrah for the flowers of the Spring,
> For Spring is here again.)
>
> Seventy years have I lived
> No ragged beggar-man,
> Seventy years have I lived,
> Seventy years man and boy,
> And never have I danced for joy.

With the publication of *The Tower* a new Yeats, a new poet came into being, and it is worth considering how this came to be, and what kind of a person the new poet is.

After a curiously prolonged youth Yeats grew up. He came strangely of age when he had about reached his sixtieth year. In 1928, with the publication of *The Tower* he was forcibly parted from childish things. You will remember Milton's definition that poetry is simple, sensuous and passionate. Yeats' poetry till that date had been rather simple, rather sen-

suous, and rather violent, but now it began to fit the definition. Was he the only poet of our day capable of a passionate
utterance? I think he was.

He did not reach maturity: he was shocked into it by the
oddest personal realization that I know of. At almost sixty
years of age Yeats made a curious discovery. Every person of
sixty has made the same discovery before him, but they have
kept it dark—he discovered that he was growing old!

He regarded this Age that had stolen on him so quietly
with an astonishment that is almost comical, and he raged
against it with a fury that is extravagant. Last week he had
been young, this week youth had been raped from him, and he
was arrested, and sentenced to sequestration and hard labour
for all the small rest of his natural life.

There are things we all know perfectly well with the surface of our minds—that is, we don't know them at all—and
then, one day, we realize these things, and we know them with
a vengeance. Yeats knew, as you and I know, that "everything
grows old and withers and dies," but he didn't believe a word
of it: and then, with the poems of *The Tower,* he realized it
with a vengeance.

No one has left so angry a record of disillusionment behind him on this count as Yeats has. *The Tower,* and much of
the next book, is an almost frantic outburst of rage against the
indignities that Time was piling upon him—it was whitening
his hair, it was wrinkling his cheeks, it was bothering his ears,
his lungs, his bowels and his bones. What wasn't it doing! And
yet, at sixty digested years, he did not feel that the spirit within
him was one hour or one experience older than that spirit had
been when he was a careful thirty or a careless twenty. But he
could surmise, indeed, now he knew that Time had taken him
by the hair, and it would shake the life right out of his skin

within a measure of days which he could almost calculate. And yet, he knew himself to be more capable, more vivacious than he had ever been, and that he, who had never been young, was young at last; he had been born again. In "Sailing to Byzantium" he begs the Sages:

> Consume my heart away; sick with desire
> And fastened to a dying animal
> It knows not what it is. . . .

And again [in "The Tower" (I)]:

> O heart, O troubled heart—this caricature,
> Decrepit age that has been tied to me
> As to a dog's tail. . . .

[In "The Tower" (II)] he asks God or himself, this question:

> Did all old men and women, rich and poor,
> Who trod upon these rocks or passed this door,
> Whether in public or in secret rage
> As I do now against old age?

And in another poem he wonders what a mother would do if she could look into the future and see the son that is crowing upon her knee as he is doomed to be a little later on, "With sixty or more years upon his head." Would she imagine that such a grotesque had been worth giving birth to? Would such a young mother tip the water and the baby and the bath into the nearest puddle, and giggle insanely at the lot? In "Sailing to Byzantium" he says:

> An aged man is but a paltry thing,
> A tattered coat upon a stick, unless

> Soul clap its hands and sing, and louder sing
> For every tatter in its mortal dress.

He still wishes to dance, and continues [in "The Tower"]:

> Never had I more
> Excited, passionate, fantastical
> Imagination, nor an ear and eye
> That more expected the impossible—
> No, not in boyhood. . . .

And [in "From 'Oedipus at Colonus' "] thinking over all that he has lost and is losing he says:

> Never to have lived is best, ancient writers say;
> Never to have drawn the breath of life, never
>   to have looked into the eye of day. . . .

The first Byzantine poem ends like this:

> Once out of nature I shall never take
> My bodily form from any natural thing,
> But such a form as Grecian goldsmiths make
> Of hammered gold and gold enamelling
> To keep a drowsy emperor awake;
> Or set upon a golden bough to sing
> To lords and ladies of Byzantium
> Of what is past, or passing, or to come.

And in "All Souls' Night" he again revisits these reflections:

> I have mummy truths to tell
> Whereat the living mock, . . .
> Such thought—such thought have I that
>   hold it tight

Till meditation master all its parts,
Nothing can stay my glance
Until that glance run in the world's despite
To where the damned have howled away their
    hearts,
And where the blessed dance;
Such thought, that in it bound
I need no other thing,
Wound in mind's wandering,
As mummies in the mummy-cloth are wound.

He had come close to his later "Byzantium" and had not time to write the third and perfect one. Here then is his oddest poem, the famous "Byzantium." It is quite impossible to say anything about the meaning of this poem, for it disdains meaning. It is the strangest poem in the language. It is the most remote poem in the language. It is as though the writer had hearkened, with another than the physical ear, to a gong beating away on Orion or Neptune. Its meaning cannot be uttered, but it is, perhaps, possible to listen into its brazen and fuming climate, and to agree, that an unimaginable and inexpressible meaning has been drawn as closely to us as can be contrived.

The unpurged images of day recede;
The Emperor's drunken soldiery are abed;
Night resonance recedes, night-walkers' song
After great cathedral gong;
A starlit or a moonlit dome disdains
All that man is,
All mere complexities,
The fury and the mire of human veins.

Before me floats an image, man or shade,
Shade more than man, more image than a shade;

For Hades' bobbin bound in mummy-cloth
May unwind the winding path;
A mouth that has no moisture and no breath
Breathless mouths may summon;
I hail the superhuman;
I call it death-in-life and life-in-death.

Miracle, bird or golden handiwork,
More miracle than bird or handiwork,
Planted on the starlit golden bough,
Can like the cocks of Hades crow,
Or, by the moon embittered, scorn aloud
In glory of changeless metal
Common bird or petal
And all complexities of mire or blood.

At midnight on the Emperor's pavement flit
Flames that no faggot feeds, nor steel has lit,
Nor storm disturbs, flames begotten of flame,
Where blood-begotten spirits come
And all complexities of fury leave,
Dying into a dance,
An agony of trance,
An agony of flame that cannot singe a sleeve.

Astraddle on the dolphin's mire and blood,
Spirit after spirit! The smithies break the flood,
The golden smithies of the Emperor!
Marbles of the dancing floor
Break bitter furies of complexity,
Those images that yet
Fresh images beget,
That dolphin-torn, that gong-tormented sea.

Yeats and Music

(1947)

O NE day we were talking about music, and Yeats told me
that some people said he didn't know one tune from another. When I asked if that was true he hummed and hawed a
bit, he was a little grieved about this rumour, as anyone would
be.

I comforted him the best I could by asserting that, to my
very own knowledge, he knew two tunes perfectly. Yeats was
curious about everything that was about himself, and he would
listen to anybody's opinion about him till the cows came home:
so, in a little time, he asked what were the two tunes that he
knew, because he couldn't just remember what they were.

I replied, honourably and honestly, that to my certain
knowledge he knew the tune of "God Save The King"; and
that he also immediately recognized the tune of "God Save
The Queen," and I insisted that he never mistook these tunes
for "The Night Before Larry Was Stretched," or "The Wearing
of the Green."

He laughed a bit about this and we both took it for a joke, but he revenged himself a month later when I was saying a couple of verses of my own—I am inclined to sing-song when the poem permits it—"Stephens," he said gravely, "has a very original talent, he has discovered Gregorian Chaunt." I'll bet it took him three weeks to work that one out.

Around and About Yeats

(1948)

CRITICISM should be destructive, for only when it has destroyed all that is temporary and moody does the essence remain—and it is critic-proof.

The first thing that literary criticism must do is to look in any writer for his recurring motives. These should rigorously be questioned: for while the creative processes are unconscious, all recurring motives are unconsciously motivated also and are much more worthy of blame than of praise. To have subject-matter is one thing, and is a blessing; to have motives is another thing altogether, and is a curse.

Of pure criticism there is no such thing. We cannot criticize our own time, for the critic's own unconscious is engaged and embroiled there: we can only *review* time and period and person and technique, for these vanish as we look at them, and I am now merely recording discontents that can get into the mind, when we consider an artist of our own date, and look for his, and our, phobias.

There is the poet *and* the poetry. The one so ordinary, and the other actually incalculable. How these two ever get together is a mystery. There is the Milton who composed poetry, and the Milton who didn't. How enriched we should be if we knew nothing about Milton except what we know about Homer; they were both blind, and they both had dazzling insight; and as to their three meals a day and a job, who cares!

Then there is the Shakespeare who poked his own personal nose out-of-joint into half a dozen of the sonnets, discovering for us not that splendour of womanhood unparallelled in human history, but a doxy in the woodpile! Almost he spoiled the greatest outpouring of poetic loveliness that the world knows of.

There is John Donne, a first-rate poet, indeed, writing himself down, so skilfully, as third-rate—as a wit, as a cad, that is, for these two are the same lunatic one, and Donne is the wittiest cad that ever fooled himself in verse. There is no witty poetry. Then, of our own time and persuasion, there is Hopkins, and there is Yeats—poets indeed, both of them, odd enough to be original, nearly human enough to be great. But one needs to be odder than that, more human than that, and to be effortless into the bargain!

All of the poets that I've mentioned have got now and again into their own verse. Have they a right in the matter? Is it their own verse? Or is it ours? Wisdom fines down to a rule of life—it is to love your neighbour. As art it fines down to the same rule, and it is the rule that a poet should be talking about himself as little as can be managed. The man who talks about himself is a bore in prose or verse.

The poet's job is to talk to the reader about the reader. In prose, an astonishingly different art, you must introduce the reader to other people, other actions, and to all the tricks of the trade—for prose is piecemeal and informative, it is not revelatory. In verse you introduce the reader to himself, and to actions, emotions and thoughts which he did not credit that he was capable of; and you introduce him to no tricks, even to no trade. The man who gets a poem is twice the man he was before: indeed, so roundly is he introduced that, if he gets it, the poem is his poem.

This is a strange occurrence, and poetry is the only art that does this compactly, for the other arts are seldom of so essential an intimacy, being somewhat fuddled with a technique which is difficult to all those who are not of the Chapel. That picture which you bought is certainly in your possession, but 'tis only on loan: it is not *your* picture: it belongs for ever to its painter. But when the poet talks about himself, rather than about you, he is prosing in verse, and should be invited to be ashamed of himself.

Yeats so often does this one might be excused for thinking that he never does anything else. This is not true, but he rarely puts himself aside for the reader, that natural enemy! He prefers W. B. Yeats any minute, and so he is not impeccable. He breaks the rule. Has he a right in the matter? Has he the right to saddle carefree citizens with his politics, his aristocracy, his philosophy, his love-affairs—all his whatnots? I don't know, but Time will look into the matter; and may start psychologizing a man instead of lauding an artist.

That the poet goes personal at peril is not true of the minor poet. He, poor chap, has nothing else to write about: let his skin and his bones, and his no-brains be forgiven him, and his writing about these be taken as read.

For the poet and the poetry are very different things: they can be actual strangers: and you cannot get at the poetry until, by some means, you have got rid of the poor, secondhand bloke that wrote it: "Great men," said Lord Acton, "are almost always bad men." He didn't add that poets are worse, for when they are young they pile Pelions of egotism on Ossas of vanity. Usually they recover. Did Yeats? I think that his last book is yet more sinful in this respect than any of the others—and it is still astonishing!

Time, in general, weeds the plot. Even so, there are here and there poets whom time hasn't yet rubbed out of the work. There are of course many critics who consider that the presence of the artist in his art is a true hall-mark, and an indication of essential values. They are right in an essence, they are wrong on a surface. It may, however, be true of the painter, the musician, those wonderful muscle-bound labouring men who are shackled to a manipulative technique; but I consider that the presence of the poet in his poem is a vulgarity, and that, however interesting his personality may seem, the clear light is shadowed, and in time to come, the poem is brooded over by a repulsive ghost; for (which Lord Acton didn't say) all ghosts are bad ghosts, and the poetic ghost is a ghoul.

The offenders in this fashion are few in English poetry. John Donne and Byron were pretty continuously at it, but now and again they made up for it. So, now and again, the ghost of a Wordsworth in the rain, of a Browning in a fog, of a Hopkins in the dumps, becomes visible and audible and dreadful upon their pages. Did Yeats too often hang around in his own poems, clank about in his own rhymes? Time will tell.

We will suppose, although I don't believe it, that a poem may as readily be about the things that worry a man as about the things that please him. Yeats worried about certain matters: they bob, again and again, into his verse, and bump there.

He bothered, fantastically, about old age and death. He saw Death, that meddler and insulter, draw nigh and upon him; incredibly meddling and insulting him; not insulting you and me and the neighbour merely, but actually insulting W. B. Yeats. He felt that thing touch him and halt him and claim him, and he winced from it as the body winces from a pin or from a flame. Yeats said:—That damn thing will kill me! He should have known from the age of ten that all life is a preparation for the coming of that Angel who scatters her poppy, and scatters the Elixir of Life with it.

His notes on this matter are eloquent, for all that he did feel he could excellently transcribe—and often could transcend. . . . Yeats is of the band who can say or unsay as the mood goes. He will be mortal *and* immortal, a gentleman *and* a peasant, a lover *and* free, he will be passionate and sinless, he will be a hog and wise. Perhaps everybody wishes to be so, but Yeats is not talking of everybody. He is talking about the man that he puts to bed every night.

He worried about being an aristocrat, as one may worry about a thing that has been warned against by one's father and grabbed at by one's mother, but the person who spends time thinking that he is a gentleman is as silly as the loon who sits up in bed at one o'clock to tell himself that he is a poet. When you are what you are, be it crocodile, or cat, poet or gentleman, that is something you don't have to bother about any more, 'tis in the bank. (I never, by the way, met a she-cat that wasn't a lady nor a he-cat that wasn't a prince.)

He worried about Love, conceiving it as a passion, as a drama, and not as the simplest, the most abundant, the most natural thing in our otherwise bedevilled world: for love is undeviating trust, unremitting attention. The critic could conceive that this was an emotion which he had not securely adventured in, or perhaps adventured in at all, but which he thought he might plumb could he but pin it down, and rhyme it into reason. He and George Moore, and how many another, wrote much about an almost-crime called Love, a violent kind of thing that doesn't really brood about the chickens, but is passionately concerned about the mice.

I think it is certain that Yeats was the most considerable poet of our time, perhaps the greatest since Tennyson. Criticism will make up its myriad mind as to whether he is to be included among those the greatness of whom is now unquestioned. These, the great ones, through a long six hundred years of history, are still less than a dozen. There are seven great poets and, leaving lyrics aside, there are less than a dozen great poems. The present reviewer thinks that Yeats may not be worthy of so great a company. The great poet is everyman of his caste; and Yeats was too continuously in his own mind to be lost in his poetry, and securely found in its universe. He has left many works which the intellect approves: verse of a technical mastery which is admirable and creative: he had spendour and passion in plenty, but love and hate and pity were not so adequately at his hand, and so he has left few poems which our affections instinctively delight in, and state to be memorable for ever, and to be lovely for no reason: for if the poem be not irrational it is not lovely.

To be oddly irrational and to be, thereupon, even more oddly precise, that is the secret of poetry, and Yeats scarcely dared that secret thoughtlessness. To surprise and delight that, is poetry: it is the irrational that delights, it is an impossible precision therein that astonishes.

Did he somewhat lack also in the rich humanity of the great poets? for whether it be Chaucer, Spenser, Shakespeare, this "humanity" is effortlessly with them.

This, in Yeats' work, is not present often enough, or is not present often enough in the condition which poetry permits and demands.

The "humanity" I speak of is effortless and anonymous. Yeats is rarely anonymous: he is rarely effortless. Love and hate and pity were not absolutely real to him: he stares at them, and sees their shadows: he tends to use scorn instead of hate, and admiration instead of love, and instead of pity he invokes uncompassionate Nature and the aristocrat who is beautiful and merciless.

Donne and Browning, Hopkins and Yeats are difficult poets, in the sense that they win their poetry with a great diligence of labour, and that they are read in questionings. One feels that they had to work like hacks to get that which should *seem* to come easy as the unhurried wing in limpid air: a sense of "technique conquered" stays about them: they are all marvellous, they are not wonderful.

"Sir," I would say to whatever complaining poet, "why don't you sing? And, even tho' your breast be up till the thorn, why don't you sing?"

Yeats the Poet

(1948)

CRITICISM goes so far, and then there is a point at which criticism stops dead. It is that point at which true excellence has been come to. We can say with perfect certainty why and how a certain work of art is bad, for we can always discuss that which is inferior to us, but we cannot say why a thing is good or even how it has been arrived at. The knowledge of goodness is not absent, but it lies deeper than words can reach to: it is the basis and the urge of creation itself, and when this point of reality is discovered the critic becomes merely a satisfied person, and says, "This is the real thing, and here neither the artist nor the thing will abide our questioning."

And yet the poet himself uses merely well-worn words. The mysterious thing is, that only those words which he has used, and the form he has imposed on them can say the thing he has said in all its fullness, and an astonishing thing is, that this matter which he has stated has never been stated before, and that the alteration or misplacement of even one of these words will falsify or even nullify the statement.

When we hold that Yeats was the "finest" poet of our time—leaving the word "great" for the future to deal with—we intend that he stated certain matters with such certainty that no question arises as to whether the matter discussed is true or not.

Truth is not a thing, it is merely an intellectual aspect of the thing, and it is modified by every change the thing submits to; for change, or becoming, is the Law, and truth comes hurrying after with a bucket and a broom. So much is this the case that the idea "true" becomes quite as qualityless as is the idea "untrue." Truth goes out and a thing-in-itself stands in its own solitude and as its own proof. Here the critic merely says, "This is," and he rests from all probing.

That in his work Yeats did this more certainly and more abundantly than any of his brother and sister poets is, I think, accepted. But, and also, he raises many questions. The considerable poets who lend themselves most easily to destructive or ill-tempered criticism are Wordsworth and Yeats. They were both innocent egoists, and they both confounded their autobiographical commonplaces with the carefree thing which is poetry.

Poetry is the mind at play, and we can only play when we are in perfect security. And then, at their times, both of these poets leave the critic standing and astonished, for they both give him the extra term of the famous definition that poetry must delight and surprise. It is the word "surprise" which is the master-word of this definition, for we can be delighted easily enough, and almost with anything—how should we live if that were not so? But to surprise us takes quite a deal of doing, for as we moderns are now inoculated against a variety of ills so are we largely gadgeted against surprise, and are almost immune from even its expectation. Something or other called Life—a surprising thing indeed—is not being lived: it is just being carried on, and we seem to exist by mere force of habit as between the cradle and the grave. Poetry somehow considers that life is lively, and that even death is somehow delectable.

In poetry the intellectual statement can please us, but we are astonished indeed when this prose matter can simultaneously be made emotionally urgent, and even more surprised that it can, at the same moment, be made to sing; and, thereupon, we are astonished all over again by the fact that we don't care whether the matter spoken of be true or not. That is perhaps the great surprise. Yeats is a master of this passionate urgency, of this untroubled song, and of an irrational and effortless precision. He, who was practically tone-deaf, had that tolling and throbbing within him which is music's self, and when his poem comes off, its music is at one with the matter which inspires it.

Usually it is in his dramatic, and so non-personal works that the poet most easily escapes from his too-insistent self, and becomes the singer of his song and so carefree. Shakespeare's best lyrics are dictated by the play he is creating, and not by his own badgering memories; for the badger, memory, is always turning up old boots and buttons. So Yeats' dramatic lyrics are not compounded and confounded by memory. How excellent musically and temperamentally this short piece is. It is from his play *Deirdre*.

> "Why is it," Queen Edain said,
> "If I do but climb the stair
> To the tower overhead,

When the winds are calling there,
Or the gannets calling out
  In waste places of the sky,
There's so much to think about
  That I cry, that I cry?"

But her goodman answered her:
  "Love would be a thing of naught
Had not all his limbs a stir
  Born out of immoderate thought;
Were he anything by half,
  Were his measure running dry.
Lovers, if they may not laugh,
  Have to cry, have to cry."

But is Edain worth a song
  Now the hunt begins anew?
Praise the beautiful and strong;
  Praise the redness of the yew;
Praise the blossoming apple-stem.
  But our silence had been wise.
What is all our praise to them
  That have one another's eyes?

This certainty of music and matter is not always found in
his work, and it is a curiosity belonging only to Yeats that he
did not usually get his poem in one jet of inspiration. He knew,
with that knowledge which does not bother about an argument, that he had not got what he wanted, and very often
he had to rewrite a particular poem several times before he
came to the form which need never be written again. He was
not immediately aware of this, and he printed all his trials and
errors in perfect good faith, but his readers can be held up
by poetic repetitions in the general work, and by an apparent

duplication of contrivance and inspiration which is critically troublesome, for one should not give a thing and its versions, and there is a lack in the deep knowledge which we call "tact" when this occurs.

At one time I used to think that Yeats had to write every poem three or four times, at a couple of years' interval, before the matter would consent to come through in its own form, but the great thing is that, unconsciously, he did recognize that it had not yet come, and as unconsciously he conceived that a poem can be run down if one pursues it.

Will and obstinacy are not dissimilar things, and he was a very obstinate poet indeed. One example of the poem which he still had to write is the famous "Byzantium." He has left us two versions of this astonishing poem. He did not live long enough to compose the third, which would have been the real one.

Normally, an art tries, with all the skill which is in its power, to give us the thing in the round, in space, and in the dimensions. A realism is its guide and its star, but Byzantine art dismisses space, dismisses the round and the dimensions and gives us its findings in the flat. To my mind it is the world's greatest artistic effort and as near to magic itself as sensuous art can get.

A poem should be strange but it should not seem strange, and Yeats' "Byzantium" is perhaps the strangest-seeming poem in the language. But it is not written in the flat, and while it has its own straining after magic casements, it is not non-dimensional and of that unselfconsciousness which is evocation itself, and is the justification past reason.

Talk

(1948)

The strange thing about talk is that talk is almost the only
subject you can't talk about. I have known a few great
talkers, but not one of them could have given you a good talk
about talk. Then, there are the historically great talkers—you
won't learn anything of the art from them either.

I fancy that the least admirable would have been Macaulay. He had a cast-iron memory, he never forgot anything that
he had heard or read. I fancy that his mind would have been too
tightly packed with actual—real, that is—matter to be capable
of the playfulness that is the soul of talk.

On the evidence of Hazlitt and Lamb and Wordsworth,
and that is good evidence, Coleridge must have been the
greatest talker that time has told us about. I use the word
"greatest" instead of the word "best" but I imagine that
Coleridge's talk would *not* have been conversational; it would
have been a vast monologue, perhaps more wonderful than
satisfying; and it may be that a couple of sessions with Cole-

ridge could blank out the mind of any but the born listener.
A "born listener" is especially endowed with humility and an
ear, as the "born talker" is densely compact egotism and a
tongue.

Charles Lamb's conversation might be much closer to real
talk than the alarming set-to of these great men who sling a
culture at you with one hand and heave its history at you with
the other. It must have been very pleasant for Lamb to think,
as we may be sure he did, that whatever else he was, he wasn't
a great man, and that he didn't have to talk like one. He must,
every now and again, have felt a bit sorry for Their Nibs as
they tried to talk up to themselves, but he would certainly
crack his own particular joke into every conversation that he
was sitting with, and it may be that he could humanize a
Coleridge, a Wordsworth, a Johnson as nobody else could. I
am certain that at certain special phases of the moon he even
made them laugh. But I feel somehow that Wordsworth only
laughed when it was raining, and that Coleridge laughed
wildly when it wasn't.

Then there is the great Dr. Johnson. He also was not
extensively talked with, and he may have been more listened
at than listened to. There is a story about him that gave me
a deal of pleasure. His habitual hostess was, of course, Mrs.
Thrale. Every great man is in luck at last when he falls upon
his own peculiar, his only and original, hostess. She is his gift
from the gods as truly as his talent is. His life and his talent
are crowned by her: he has a roof to his fame at last, and is a
made man, and talked about.

Well, one day another lady borrowed Dr. Johnson from
Mrs. Thrale, and, as anyone could have predicted, it was a
fiasco. The doctor came in and sat down; his hostess and her
guests sat and looked at him admiringly, expectantly, and he

looked back at them, and began to wonder what he was doing in that gallery. As Wordsworth said on another occasion, "They were all silent and all damned."

Johnson went away after a bit, for they had nothing to say to him and he couldn't think of anything to say to them. You've got to give your cat, or your dog, or your conversationalist something to play with or they and he can't play. Mrs. Thrale was a perfect hostess, and she always had a nice ball to throw, or a slipper to worry, and her dear doctor always jumped to the game.

As for what lies at the back of the great talker, Francis Bacon, who defined so much and so sharply, has an aphorism on this matter also. He said: "Reading makes a full man, writing makes a precise man, talking makes a ready man." Your good talker is a ready man; but if he is not also as precise as a good writer and as full as a good reader, he can be as ready as he likes, but he is not listenable-to for more than his fair share of the time.

Learned talk can be depressing. It is known at once as derivative, where real talk is original: it comes from the Fountain, pure, shining, bubbling, stimulating. If it doesn't bubble over and chuckle under, the talker had better go home, and so had you.

La Bruyère once said, "We write as well as we can, but we can never write as well as we talk." That is so; no man's writing is ever half as good as his free chatter over the table and the glass. There is the strangest difference between the act of writing and the act of talking. Everything you write has to be halted down to the pace of the letters of the alphabet. Beauty and passion, despair and hope and knowledge, all have to be spelled very slowly with a pen, and the thing that you can talk in a minute will take you twenty minutes to think out and spell out and write out and somehow shuffle out and shape out until it is larger than life and twice as unimportant.

That is prose when it isn't prosy. Speech isn't prose, in spite of Molière; it is a much rarer, a much swifter, a very much more tangential thing than prose dares even attempt, for prose must not move at any angle whatever from its subject, and the talk that doesn't do precisely that is no good. The talk that is consecutive is no good. That is why a record of talk is useless, for the matter which is really free as air is cribbed, cabined and confined and ruined when its freedom to be wayward and inconsecutive is taken away.

I grew up in the middle of real talkers. They were all good, but there were a few who were special. I can't define a good talker; but we can talk about him. I should say that one sort of good talker is the genius who turns you into a good listener. Another, perhaps better, talker is he who forces you to hurl questions at him, and who takes these questions on the wing and replies to them without any real halt in the matter that he is actually set upon. If everything in talk isn't on the wing 'tis on the ground, it has become pedestrian, the nightingale is dead, and instead of the Bird of Arcady, the good old clumping donkey is braying great sesquipedalian he-haws. After ten of no-matter-who's eloquent brayings you yawn your head off without making him yawn his head shut.

The oddity about talk, good or bad, is that it dies immediately upon its utterance. We have scraps from, say, Sydney Smith, or who not else, bits of comical or witty interjection that could be remembered; but the talk itself, from which these witty streaks wasped or butterflied away, has disappeared forever, and it disappeared upon the very instant of its utterance.

On the whole, a witty person is rarely a good talker. The

wit is a gate-crasher, who sits at the edge of a conversation and throws small bombs at it until he blows it to blazes. You've got to start talking about something else altogether when a wit has passed, for that conversation is dead, murdered by him. The real talker is witty in lightning-like tangents from his matter; but the wit has only a tangent; it has nothing whatever to say on any subject.

If someone asks what is it that makes a good talker, I'd answer very simply: that a good listener makes a good talker. And what then is a good listener? A good listener is one who likes the person that is talking. This listening with affection is creative listening. No person, however gifted, is talking at his best unless he likes the people he is talking to, and knows that they like him; then he is inspired, almost as the poet is. Without this unexpressed affection, something can occur—a solid, informative, good-enough pudding of stuff—but not memorable, not on the wing and the bubble and the moon, and that transfiguring into play of dense, dreadful, detestable life; for that is the transformation which good poetry and good talk undertake, or somehow manage. Prose can rarely do it.

The talkers that I especially remember were Yeats and Russell and MacKenna. Yeats was not the best of these, for his mind was always more at work than at play. He could surprise and inform you critically, but not creatively; for the creative act is always fantastic and flighty and almost unconcerned. If whatever is forward isn't effortless it is not quite worth any but practical attention. Yeats in his poetry, in his prose, in his talk does not always give this sense of the effortless deed. There is, be it only somewhat, a sense of striving after his matter, and that sense stays, almost imperceptibly, with a good deal of his matter. Russell was a better talker, for he had a sense of fun which Yeats did not quite possess. Yeats

knew jokes that had been told him when he was young, but
he didn't make any himself.

The thing we call tact and the thing I call fun are in very
near relation: if tact isn't as effortless as fun is, it is very dread-
fully remarkable, and the instant you notice that tact is present
you also notice that vulgarity isn't far away.

MacKenna (the translator of Plotinus) was the best talker
I've ever met. He had all the gifts, all the readinesses. He was
the full man of Bacon's aphorism, the precise man, the ready
man; he was philosopher enough, and humourist enough, and
fantastic enough to take on anybody whatever on these matters,
and both Yeats and Russell went silent when MacKenna
chose to talk. But his remarkable and never-absent great
quality was that he not only made his listeners listen, he made
his listeners talk. When you were with MacKenna you discovered that you were talking just as much as he was, and that
you were talking just as well as he was. For the first time in
your life, perhaps, you found that you also were a philosopher,
a wit, a lover of the moon, and an intimate of Eve and the
dragon, and the donkey and the duck.

Once I interjected to MacKenna:—"The prettiest sight in
the world is the sight of a woman loving her baby."

"Nonsense," he replied, "the prettiest sight in the world is
the sight of a baby loving its mother."

I did see that particular sight later on, and I saw that this
was true. A woman loving a baby is happy and careful and occupied. But a woman who is being loved by her baby knows at
last that she is the hen that laid the golden egg: she squawks:
she is tranced and entranced away in a valley of this restless
mind: she is strayed into a lunacy of delight that no man has
ever given her hint of, or imagination of, or desire for. Mac-

Kenna knew corners and oddities of life and letters that no one
else had spotted and that he was always awake for.

It is odd to sit in a conversation and watch it. A novelist or
a painter has to do that sort of sitting-away-from all through
his day and his life. A musician never listens to anyone, and
can't whistle—'tis an unhappy art. You can watch how a talk
is accelerated, furnished, deflected, and how it affects this, that
and the other of its party. How one fellow has the talk and
loses it; and how, now and again, the winner doesn't know
what in heck to do with the conversation he has stolen: he has
it, and it next-door-to-chokes him. You will see a man lying
in wait, attending the psychological moment when he can
slink in, or dart in, and pinch the neighbour's subject. And you
can also see the most curious, wordless, withdrawals from some
matter that is forward.

G. W. M. Sullivan was a very good journalist. He was also
a pleasant talker and listener on dozens of subjects. He could
take you up and set you right about money and beer and biology and motor cars and music, but when the word "poetry"
was mentioned, right upon that instant a film came over his
eyes like the film you see sliding over the steady stare of a
vulture when it's bored, and he refused to speak one word
about it, or even listen to one. Painting-talk he could stand; but
he'd sit up all night about music, or quantum theory—Beethoven, Newton, Dostoievsky and gadgets, these irradiated
him, and upon all of these he wasn't only informative, he was
delightful.

But how a man can love music and hate poetry leaves me
goggle-eyed and pancaked. Or how a man can love social-
science and hate religion leaves me dilapidated, for poetry is
the very soul of music, and religion is the essence and actual of

every science whatever; and that this can happen flabbers one
and ghasts one, than which two nothing worse can happen. To
ghast I understand and wince from, but to flabber beats me.

I have noticed people remove one complete prairie and a
half when certain subjects took the floor. I have seen those who
shied like startled horses when the word religion was uttered;
others who went to sleep if you happened to say the word
woman, or sport or politics; while for others these same words
are like the depressing of a spring—the light leaps on and they
are jodelling upon the mountain, all agog and aglee, and only
to be stopped by force.

"Is there bad poetry?" said MacKenna to me.

"No," I answered, "if it's poetry, it's good, and if it's bad
it's not poetry."

"You are only saying and etcetering out of you," Mac-
Kenna complained. "Give an example of what is and what
isn't."

"The poetry of a wit," said I, "climbs up a tree and falls
out of it. One of those wits wrote—

> Be she sweeter, kinder than
> Turtle dove, or pelican . . .

—That's poetry."

"So it is," said MacKenna.

"But," I continued, "the brute goes on—

> If she be not kind to me
> What care I how kind she be? . . .

—That's
wit: the second-thought in poetry is always witty and dreadful."

"Yes," MacKenna admitted, " 'tis pure wickedness, 'tis a sin that the Holy Spirit would never forgive."

"Why don't you talk English when you're not talking Irish?" I complained. "Holy Ghost is a better and a lovelier and a more understandable term."

"Jamesy," said MacKenna, "your poetry is the worst in the world, and your prose is getting to be nearly as good as that."

A.E.: I

(1942)

Now and again we all take five minutes off from living and have a look at life, and we can then wonder what we made of it and what we got out of it. I got a couple of friendships out of it, and a neat bit of a talent. My bit of a talent often bored me, but my two friends never did, and I wish they were both hanging around still so that I could tell them what I think about the war, and combat violently what they think about it.

George Russell (A.E.) was from twenty to twenty-five years my senior. . . . A.E. was the most remarkable man I have ever known. To a young man he was alarming, inspiring, astonishing. He was, professionally, a seer, a painter, a poet, an essayist, a journalist, an economist, and with one exception, he was the greatest conversationalist I have ever met.

In all of these pursuits he was just one boundless torrent of energy. In any and every week he would write practically the whole of his weekly journal, *The Irish Statesman*. In the spare time of that week he would also compose from ten to twenty poems, paint from five to ten or more pictures, address a number of business or occult gatherings, add so many chapters to whatever prose book he was engaged on, and would then talk to anyone who would listen from eight o'clock at night to four o'clock in the morning of every night in the week. I have never known him to be intellectually or artistically weary.

It has also been said of him that outside of India he was the greatest living authority on the Advaita philosophy and the Vedas. With all this there was not one scrap of the pedant in him, and if he bored many people, which he did (but so do you and so do I), it was because these were very bore-able people. We are all bored when we meet a mind that is slower than our own, and we are exactly equally bored when we meet a mind that is faster than our own—that is the whole natural history of boredom, and there is no cure for it except perhaps some form of Yoga exercises.

To all the activities which I have just mentioned A.E. added yet another accomplishment. How he found time to squeeze it in is a real conundrum. No day passed in which he did not tuck his long legs under him, squat in the Eastern meditation posture, centre his mind into one point and visualize beauty, or truth, or power, or God. He was a practising Yogi.

He told me once that he had given up the meditation on power as being too dangerous for a mere man until he had become more than something of a saint. Only the saint, he said, can handle power and be unharmed by it.

I asked what had happened to make him quit. And he answered very simply that he found himself turning into power. That is, he was turning into fire. He was already a pillar of flame about twenty feet high, and he could hear himself as a rushing roar like the dreadful grumbling of half a Niagara

—so he switched himself off in sheer terror lest he should in another second be just one calcined cinder which someone might carry away with a tongs.

I blamed him there and then for not having dared the deed, and held that to be a cinder of that ilk was a far far better thing than to be the editor of a barely wanted Irish weekly.

He told me a number of stories about creatures and beings that he had seen while wide-awake but in the Yoga mood. He had painted some hundreds of pictures of the type we call mystical—winged beings, plumed and glowing creatures. They were not very well painted, perhaps, but they were wonderfully well conveyed, and he assured me that he had never drawn one of these other-dimensional beings without having actually seen it as plainly as if he had seen it in the flesh. This condition he spoke of as Vision.

He was a firm believer in the interrupted immortality which is called Reincarnation, and claimed that he remembered pretty well seven of his previous existences on our Earth. When I asked why he didn't pursue his memories further back, he answered, simply enough, that there would be no sense in doing that, for until one became Illuminated, life in every incarnation is only a matter of knocking three meals a day out of it, going to bed every night and getting out of bed every morning. When you remember other lives, he went on, life becomes one continuing boredom of eating and sleeping and slanging the neighbour.

I was very pleased, however, when he remembered that he had known me well in at least four of these lost visits under the moon. I asked did he or I ever make any cash out of this reluctant planet. He thought that we never did, and believed—morosely, I imagined—that we never would.

It was his belief that we travel through life and time with our own company of friends and enemies. That there is a small clann of personages, and that this is the real family. The wives, husbands and children of such a person are almost unimportant, almost accidental. The clann is treading the Path seeking whatever they are seeking for of power, or beauty, or deity. They are almost bound to find it together, or be still delayed in the quest.

I once listened to him and Yeats discussing, if the choice lay with them, in what walk of life they would choose to be born in the next life. They were both, by the way, perfectly certain that there is a next life. They agreed that they would never again be public men, or have more than the most restricted and intimate acquaintanceships. For this reason they elected to become peasants, living in some remote hilly region —Mountainy-men was the term they used. They would come down from their hill once every month to sell a pig or a dozen chickens, and would then return to their lean wives and sparse acre of rock to think life out, and think themselves out of it.

They both held the opinion that to be a poet is a private thing and has almost no public significance whatever, and they warned me against expecting any special audience for work in verse, A.E. holding that the number of people who are interested in poetry is infinitesimal. Yeats named a figure, however, asserting that in our forty-odd millions of people there is a constant audience for poetry of about one thousand souls.

I had the impression that A.E., who feared no one, was almost terrified of Yeats. Yeats certainly lorded it somewhat over him, and was the only person who could abruptly halt his conversation. They were discussing one Lady Something whom A.E. liked and Yeats didn't:—

"A.E.," said Yeats, "you know nothing about women, and should not even speculate about them."

Yeats had not half the reading nor, perhaps, half the intellectual power of A.E., but being easily the greater poet he had easily the greater authority, and A.E. instinctively bowed to this as in painting he would have bowed to the opinions of Augustus John.

He was at his best in religious and artistic generalization. So good, so fertile was he in these fields that it did not matter in the least whether what he said was right or wrong. Right or wrong he was profound and disturbing and inspiring to the listener. He was a miraculous critic, particularly of poetry. I think, however, that he preferred Shelley to any other versifier, and that, in the highest sense, there is much of weakness in such a preference. Yeats also loved Shelley, but preferred John Donne.

What was strange was that A.E. could not criticize immediately and subtly his own work in writing. He would not observe that fairly early in life he had evolved his own mannerisms, formulas, clichés, and would not cease from over-using them. In verse or prose or painting his status is really that of a wonderful amateur, not that of a great professional. Yet there are a certain dozen or so of his poems, and some dozens of his pictures, which only he could have composed and painted. I give one verse from a poem of his, "The Voice of the Waters," which is, I think, the slowest measure in English verse:

Where the Greyhound River windeth through a loneliness so deep,
Scarce a wild fowl shakes the quiet that the purple boglands keep,
Only God exults in silence over fields no man may reap.

I have said much more about the man A.E. than A.E. the artist because the man was truly an inspiring personal and individual being. While that is perhaps true also of his work, it will only be true to those who live after him and had not the great privilege of knowing this very great person.

I would advise anybody interested in his literature to get his *Selected Poems,* which he read to me only about a fortnight before he died; of his prose, I would suggest *The Candle of Vision, Imagination and Reveries* and *The Interpreters.* A.E.'s poetry is singular because there is only one other poet in the English language who did the same thing—George Herbert and A.E. always wrote about God and the soul, and you might say that these two great artists had no other subject but the soul in relation to Deity.

"Reconciliation" I consider to be the finest prayer in the English language:

I begin through the grass once again to be bound to the Lord;
  I can see, through a face that has faded, the face full of rest
Of the earth, of the mother, my heart with her heart in accord,
  As I lie 'mid the cool green tresses that mantle her breast
I begin with the grass once again to be bound to the Lord.

By the hand of a child I am led to the throne of the King,
  For a touch that now fevers me not is forgotten and far,
And His infinite sceptred hands that sway us can bring
  Me in dreams from the laugh of a child to the song of a star.
On the laugh of a child I am borne to the joy of the King.

A.E.: II

(1948)

A.E. DIED only a few years ago, so there must be a lot of people who remember him—not that you can depend on that, for while memory is the most personal thing we've got, it is also the least trustworthy item of our equipment. Ten people remembering someone may be recollecting ten different persons, not one of whom ever existed, for memory is oddly specialized in each of us, and we tend to recall people and events according to our own temperamental selection among these. We are, helplessly and hopelessly, remembering ourselves in everything we remember and we tend to disengage whatever isn't us from all that is forward.

All the same I wonder what those who knew A.E. remember him for. I asked this very question of Oliver Gogarty the other day, and was impressed by the one second's pause, and the considered finality of his reply—"I remember A.E. for his goodness," said Gogarty.

And I found myself reflecting that something to be called

goodness was an almost secret though pretty continuous activity of Oliver himself. There is a goodness among men and women which they rarely betray, and which they never publicize. A.E. was that unfaltering goodness certainly, but also he was such a lot of other things that it is difficult to remember him in his total.

A.E. was editor of *The Irish Statesman*. . . . His journalism was first-rate. Lloyd George sent for him for consultation on the national economic situation. About the same time, Mr. Balfour and A.E. had been exchanging a fairly regular correspondence on philosophy in general, and on the artistic and spiritual idea of beauty in particular. One would like to read such a correspondence between two such men.

He was also the leading travelling lecturer on the Co-operative-Trade idea in Ireland. He went everywhere and talked to everyone about this. Dairies and cows, pigs and hens and horses poured from his mind as if they were stabled there, and if the horse didn't lay eggs as well as the hen it wasn't A.E.'s fault.

It is evident that he was a busy man. . . . He was a gifted and original painter. The word "original" doesn't mean "great"; it means essentially personal—and A.E. could turn out, or knock off, a picture a day for ever.

Most pictures are not worth praising, not worth blaming. Praise and blame are the extremes of appreciation, and the painter who isn't worth blaming for something is scarcely worth praising for anything. You could praise A.E.'s pictures for being irrational or even loopy, and you were justified in blaming them when they weren't precisely that. Very often an innocent gaiety got into his canvas, and he was one of the few artists of our time who could be gay without being funny.—

The good old word "funny"—on what evil days it has

fallen! You will get an "innocence" in Italian painting that is captivating, you get a "gaiety" in French painting which goes deeper than that, and old Chinese beats each of them in both. The top of being, or of art, isn't high seriousness, it is gaiety. Gaiety isn't humour—it is a kind of happiness, it is the infancy of happiness, and like every other art, it is a lost art.

Furthermore A.E. held a class twice every week in which he discoursed tirelessly on the Meditation of Divinity, and on the Yoga of anything else that you pleased to call for. . . . MacKenna held that A.E. was the only man living who could pray at you, pray with you, or pray for you, and whichever way it was, you were stuck.

Then, he was the most famous talker in Dublin. A humorous Englishman—alas, all the others were invented by Dickens!—once said that one went to Dublin to see the Phoenix Park and A.E. He added that he didn't know which of these two was the more wonderful, the more extensive. A.E. talked nearly as well as the Phoenix Park looked. Tea and talk could delight him every night for as many hours as you could stand it. You yawned yourself away, around two o'clock in the morning, but he was as fresh as Chaucer's daisy, which is fresher than any daisy that ever grew in a field. That's where poetry beats life: whatever it grows is fresher than life can manage, and it never withers. It dies at last of extreme youth, as the gods die.

I asked him where he got all the energy from, and he answered that he got it from a sinking of himself into that meditation which is known in every system as "The practice of the presence of God." He said that as a boy he had been as scatterbrained as any other youngster. Then he fell in with certain religious-philosophical writings, and he began to discipline himself along the lines they suggested. Some deep memory had awakened in him. He began to train his mind, his memory and his will, and within a couple of years these three were his obedient servants. He just said to them "Do it," and they did it.

I watched him at work many times. First he filled his pipe—half coltsfoot for the lungs, half tobacco for the nerves—then he lit the pipe. Then he reached for the pen; then he began to write, and didn't stop until that article was finished. Then he re-coltsfooted the pipe and was ready to begin another article.

The way he came to be called A.E. isn't generally known. For the first article of his accepted by a paper he had chosen the nom-de-plume of Æon, but his handwriting was so bad the printers couldn't make out the word, and just printed what they could decipher of it, the first two letters.

That name became his. I never heard anybody call him Russell except Yeats, who had an odd kind of love-and-not-love for him. Love that is also not-love is called jealousy. Yeats in a bulk was dramatic; moody so, and inclined to anger. A.E. as a bulk was gay; he inclined to sit on the top of the morning all day. Each of them slightly lacked what the other abundantly had. They were both tone-deaf, and each had a divine inner ear. So with Beethoven—the deafer he got the better he heard. One could wish that a lot of musicians were deaf. Most of our poets are.

Nearly every picture by A.E. contains angelic or semi-angelic creatures. Wings and haloes are common in his art, and there is a sense of beauty in his brush that doesn't derive from plain bread and butter. Sometimes winged and haloed animals of his are chewing the cud of content in heavenly pastures. There is nectar about—that taste a child gets off its thumb, and never tastes again, is nectar. Now and again, indeed, his landscape itself seems to have wings, and to be stuffed to the gizzard with haloes. Happy is the donkey that browses there! Thrice happy the goat! So I asked him about wings and haloes.

He told me that he never painted an other-world figure unless he had actually seen it; so I enquired into that also. A.E.'s way of seeing things wasn't everybody's: he would shut his eyes, and look at them in a darkness that he lit up for himself. He held that the light and colour you awaken *inside* your head is much more vivid than the same happening outside your head. Many people will consider that this is not vision, but rather imagination or fancy. A.E. asserted that this was not so; that he saw with real insight, and that these extra-terrestrial beings were there, were most truly visible to the inward eye and could, altho' inadequately, be followed with a pencil— "They have more colour than our eyes are used to," he averred. He usually referred to this third eye, which is between the brows, as "The Eye of the Centaur."

Incidental to this, he told me that he remembered seven of his previous incarnations, and held that he always travelled with his own crowd.

"Who are your crowd?" said I.

"One's own friends and one's own enemies are one's crowd," he replied—and then he was away on the inverted love that is hate, and the perverted hindrance that is truly helpful: and how, perhaps, your enemy is dearer to you than ever your friend can be.

"But now," he continued, "we are densely overpopulated, active friendship is rarer among human beings than it used to be, and," he admonished me, "when you come to my age, if you can claim that you have had six friends in your life you will be a luckier man than anyone has a right to be."

"I am one of your six," I boasted.

"You are one of my four," he replied severely; and something like desolation fell on him for half a minute.

"What about the enemies?" said I.

"At a certain point," he answered, "enemies cease to be enemies, and become plain fools. . . . I have been in Ireland three times," he asserted.

"And you don't know the Gaelic yet," said I.

"I have forgotten more and better Gaelic than Osborn Bergin ever dreamt of," said he. "I have even," he continued sadly, "forgotten Chinese and Sanscrit!"

"So have I," said I, and we both spoke so sadly that we nearly laughed ourselves into a fit.

A.E. painted too much and too quickly to be our best painter—he could have been so. He wrote too much and too quickly to be the best prose-writer of our time—he might have been so. He produced poems almost as though he conjured them out of a hat, but at its best his poetry has only been bettered by one other poet, by Yeats himself.

It is curious how certain writers have one general subject: they depart from it in order to return to it, and they are all glad to get back from fruitless wanderings. Nearly all Chaucer's poems are about people—they are the nicest people in poetry, as Chaucer is the nicest poet in poetry. Spenser sings a lot about "lady gents," which is his odd way of putting it, and these ladies are among the best gents in English. The best gent in English is, of course, Milton's Devil. Herrick's poems are rarely about love—they are all about making love, and they are lovely. Too many of Wordsworth's soliloquies are about "human nature's daily food"—he tends to conceive that a piece of meat and two veg. is a kind of woman, and who are we to disagree with him!

A.E.'s poems are all about God. It is perhaps unusual that a recurring motive in his poetry is the idea of God the Mother; he departs here from the Old Testament and from most mythologies. He once said of one of my books that he preferred my tinkers drunk to my gods sober, but I think he was mixing me up with Milton, whose God is soberer than total abstinence.

Unlike Milton, A.E. held that there is laughter in heaven. He explained that the joke from which all other jokes are derived, the primeval joke, is now only effective in Heaven and in the English House of Commons, whence Heaven perhaps borrowed it. So when, after perorating a bit, an Archangel sits down on his own hat, Olympia is convulsed, and business has to be suspended for half an hour. A.E. asserted that foreigners do not get this joke, for all foreigners burst into tears when they hear of a ruined hat.

Stephen MacKenna: I

(1948)

"HAVE you ever met a great man?" said I.

MacKenna answered that he had only met one in his life, and that the brute treated him like a slave.

"That great ass makes me shave him every morning," said he.

He added that he had also met Tolstoi and Rodin and a host of painters and things and thought them a whole handful of goods and bads and unknowns, expert only in every uncertainty.

Still I think that a certain greatness can hang around, unsuspected, and be surmised, though not manifested. It is not easy to imagine Shakespeare as great in any sense of the world and its ways. And yet one is pretty certain that, to those who met him off stage, Shakespeare would come through in some way or other, and an awareness might be about that this man wasn't summed by being described as a ham actor, or an author with a grievance; that he was also a rum bloke with a way of his own, and that anything he said on any subject had sharp corners to it and sly slopes: that in fact he was worth listening to if you had the time.

The Genghis Khans, the Henry the Eighths, the Cromwells and Napoleons, and the who-nots-else of a queer lot were greatly authoritative persons; had they also hinterlands of self-consciousness and places of retirement and dismay? Or were they just bored bumpkins when they were left to themselves?

The top men that I was acquainted with—Yeats, Russell, Joyce, MacKenna, and some others—were all talented men, but they were only about as great as you and I and the neighbour and Shelley and Keats. The way in which MacKenna stands away from my other friends—leaving out that he and A.E. were closer to me than the rest—is not easily told. He was more varied in a way. This life and some of its problems interested him nearly as much as did the next life and its satisfactions. These were all deeply religious men, and he was as deeply concerned there as they. But MacKenna could not meet any of these others on their common ground of writing. They could all write rings round him with half a pen.

He had a well exercised pen indeed, but it refused to run away with him or to run away from him. "Damn it," said he, "I don't know how to write! What's the good of philosophy if a tailor can't tail, if a carpenter can't carp, if a writer can't write?" Indeed, he had journalized in London and Paris and Moscow and New York as well as in Dublin itself.

But he could criticize any of those others: he could review them historically, and linguistically, and, saving the term, philosophically. Also, if the whole four of them were sitting together they would all be listening to MacKenna and looking at him.—He was very good to listen to: he was very nice to look at.—They would all, I think, rather be dead than to listen to each other, and they would all rather listen to MacKenna than be dead.

MacKenna would hold that if you aren't listening to something you are dead. He was more widely travelled, as widely read, more densely acquainted, more gracious, and twice as witty as the rest. A.E. was, I think, as humourous; MacKenna was more comical.

A.E. and MacKenna were the greatest talkers that I have known, and if one praises one's masters, and one does, they both taught me something or other in some way or other.

But there is a distinction to be drawn.

A.E. was a monologist. When he was speaking everyone else shut up, or they merely cheered him along his radiant way with an apt question or a look of love.

MacKenna was a conversationalist, and he would insist upon his vis-à-vis talking nearly as much as he did. After a chat with him you felt that you were a witty man, and a well-packed one. In fact you could get the odd idea from him that what you didn't know wasn't worth knowing. I asked him how it came that he was able so equitably to distribute his chatter. So he told me the story of how he stopped being a monologist.

"One time," said he, "I was in a car, with a man. The man was driving. We were triumphing up into the hills, and marvelling down into the valleys, and I was cheering this lad on with the best chattering I could work up.

"Really," said he earnestly, "I was marvellous. The jokes I made at that man were of the brand that you sometimes dream you are gladdening heaven itself with, and the subject they were festooned about was exciting and beautiful and unforgettable. I had come to the hub of my wonderful matter when suddenly a bull, a cow and a calf, who were happy as the day is long, trundled and tramped into the mountainy road, and my driver became a pair of inspired hands and a mind that was alert on nothing whatever except a five-foot of swerving and stamping and snorting beef, and a nine-foot width of bumpy road.

"I shut up, of course, and left him to God and the steering-wheel and the cows. 'Get the hell out of here,' said he to the cows. 'Come along, love,' said he to the steering-wheel, and 'God, love a duck,' said he to me.

"We got past them very skilfully at about one inch and a bump a minute, and I was just going to take up my marvellous talk again, when a preposterous thought struck me. I thought, 'I'll let him ask me for the next part of that story just to see if it interested him.'

"Well," said MacKenna, "he never asked me one word about it. He never recollected that the wittiest, the brainiest, the most exciting bit of literature that was ever passed from man to man was only half finished. He had said 'Ah' and 'Oh' and 'Ha Ha' at the proper spots of my talk and he hadn't listened to a single word of it.

"In a few more minutes I spotted that what he really wanted was to talk himself. So I led him to it, and in another few minutes again I was saying 'Ah' and 'Oh' and 'Ha Ha' at the proper places, and he was telling me about cars and cows and mountainy roads. He also told me what to do with a stomach-ache that you didn't want, and the best way of curing the pip in a hen. He warned me that if your boots were too tight you should take them off no matter who was there, and that one drink over the eight was bad for the car and the cow, the pip and the boots.

"When he left me he must have talked most of his teeth

loose and he was the happiest man on earth. So now when I'm among people, I make them talk if they can talk at all, and I only talk myself if I notice that their ears are bigger than their mouths. The woman or the donkey who don't look at you with their ears are no good.

"Now and again," he continued, "you meet exciting listeners. They are exciting because you know they are listening —nothing more exciting than that ever happens in life—and you know they are listening because they inject the proper questions into the proper places. The listener who doesn't question isn't listening," said he.

MacKenna was a man in love. He was inconstant too, and marvellously lighthearted, and there was a very serious something or other behind everything that he said. He was wildly in love with everything that he couldn't do. A man once objected to a statement of his on some Biblical matter, saying, "But you don't know Hebrew, MacKenna," and MacKenna started taking lessons in Hebrew the next day. He told me that Hebrew was nearly as good as Irish but not as unexpected.

"A joke in Hebrew is very emphatic," he said. "It has to be led up to via the Red Sea and the Promised Land. There is also an odour of sanctity about a Hebrew curse that dehydrates it."

He was a great linguist. He knew Latin, Greek, German, French and Irish. He held that Latin was a marvellous language to speak, but that its literature wasn't worth bothering about; and that Greek was a marvellous literary tongue and not worth speaking. He knew modern Greek as well as the ancient. In fact he had joined the Greek Army, and fought with it against the Turks. The Turks were, he thought, the finest gentlemen he had ever met.

"But when," said he, "I heard a Greek woman yell at her offspring 'Come over here, Socrates, till I wipe your nose,' something Greek—divine—left me."

German, he considered, had been invented on the devil by a bull: it moos and bellows, and it bellows when it ought to moo. French, he thought, was a fruitful speech, and if it had kept more of its Celtic roots, you could have grown potatoes on it. It has the world's worst great poetry and the world's best great prose. English, he held, had the world's best great poetry and the world's worst great prose.

"We have no prose literature," said he. French and English, he held, make two languages and one literature. Those two countries, artistically and imaginatively, are closer together than anyone knows.

He loved excessive opinions. "The world's greatest utterance," said he, "is Blake's sentence, 'Too much, enough!'"

He took to music very suddenly. He happened to notice that his wife could read music and he couldn't. He was surprised, he was outraged. He began, on the advice of somebody, with a piccolo, and he explained that machine to me, and gave me one.

"It is heavenly but babyish," said he. "It is the oddest contrivance invented by music or man. All the time you play it, it spits on your knee," he lamented. "Then you change your trousers and it ruins your only other next pair. I took," he explained, "to playing the piccolo over a bucket. One sole man," he continued earnestly, "one sole man with a piccolo could irrigate the Sahara desert in a week."

He removed from that instrument to the concertina, and gave me one. Then he switched from that to two guitars—one for me:—

"Only an octopus can really play the guitar," he complained sadly. "You need four hands for the top of it and four hands for its bottom."

But he was in love with it for life. "I played Handel's *Largo* last night," he wrote me joyously, "and it was as though the *Largo* were being hummed before the Lord by a bee-hive."

He had a marvellous talent musically; that is, he could play four wrong notes in every bar, and never spoil that tune by the accidental entry of even one correct note from beginning to end.

He and I had been to a Wagner opera one evening, and as we went home I asked him:

"How did the famous Kiss Motif strike you?" He replied with cautious enthusiasm:

"It made me think of an almost perfect Prelude to the love-affair of elephants. You know, Seumas," said he, "where you and I merely get ants in our pants that Wagner man used to get elephants in his trunks."

He moved about a lot intellectually and spiritually.

"The man," said he, "who dies in the system he was born in has wasted his life unless he comes back to it by the round-about."

He had been a Catholic, and loved that sacred pageant. But at one time he became a Vedantist; although he once halted A.E. by saying, "It's all in the Penny Catechism, A.E."

A few years after that he was a Buddhist. Thereafter he became a Unitarian. Then he died in the bosom of his primal church. I'll bet that the clergyman who listened to the last confession of Stephen MacKenna had to laugh so much at Mac-Kenna's detailing of it that he could have forgotten there was anything sad about the passing of that odd genius of the good, the precise and the comic.

He is remembered now, and will be remembered, by his

great translation of Plotinus, five big volumes of it, a life's work, and a fine one. But those who knew him remember a man whom you could like and love, whom you could listen to and talk to, who could surprise you and delight you, who was wise and wayward and witty, and was each of these at the right time, and in the companionable spoken tongue. Whatever he thought he said, and whatever you thought he made you say.

Stephen MacKenna: II

(*Undated*)

THERE came a day when I met MacKenna, and I said:
"You've met everybody and you've done everything, Monsieur MacKenna."

"I've been done by everybody," he said, "and if everything can do you, everything has done me—but I don't mind little things like that."

"Who's the greatest person you've ever met, MacKenna?"

"Well now," he said, "I don't believe I've ever met any great person. I meet all kinds of people, but it's strange how, sitting in front of those people, the greatness evaporates—it just isn't there."

I said: "Who was what the world thought the greatest person you've met?"

"Oh, undoubtedly," said MacKenna, "Tolstoi would be considered the best man that anybody could meet.

"And," said he warmly, "he *is* the greatest man that anybody could meet. I was unfortunate," said MacKenna, "or rather, Tolstoi was unfortunate on this particular day.

"I was working," he said, "for the New York *Sun*, or the New York *Times*—I forget which exactly—for a great New York paper.

"And they suggested to me that as I was in Russia and wanted to see Russia and was doing something in Russia, I should try to get an interview with Tolstoi."

He said: "You know I am a courteous bloke. When I'm going to interview a person I write to them about it and I say, 'Dear Old Bean'—or whatever man it is—'I want to interview you for a certain paper. It's a good paper; I am a good interviewer. I won't say a single thing that you don't say. You can be sure that in an interview with me the matter will come as you want it, without any fantasies thrown in from me.'

"And so I wrote to Tolstoi:

My dear Count Tolstoi,

I am the greatest admirer of yours that lives in my native country, which is not England, but is Ireland, the land of saints and angels, as you might have heard if you have ever read anything about it; and I would like to interview you, not for Ireland but for America.

I have read all your books; I have admired all of your books, some much more than others. I should like to just talk about your books with you and to get your ideas as to the position of the artist not only in life itself but in the social life that is about us.

"So I sent off my letter, and then I got a note from that place where he lived—I've forgotten it—saying would I come on such and such a day. And the date he put was a month ahead because, he added apologetically, he was very busy.

"So," said MacKenna, "I set off and I stopped in that place for three or four days to get the atmosphere.

"And then on the day stated I went to see Tolstoi.

"I came to his great estate, and at the hour appointed there was nobody to meet me, and it struck me that in a month Tolstoi had forgotten all about me—all about the appointment.

"And I stood outside the gate because I simply didn't dare to go in.

"The gates—very wide gates—were open and sitting in them were about ten monstrous dogs. And they all looked at me and they all showed fangs at me; and then they all set up a tremendous hullaballoo.

"There was a party inside at tables. It was summer time. They were sitting chatting, a party obviously of ladies and gentlemen.

"I looked among them trying to see Tolstoi, looking for a man in blues and perhaps moleskins—a man dressed as a peasant—but there was no such person.

"After a little, however, I did see—because the howling of those dogs caused everybody to look—I did see Tolstoi; and he was dressed exactly as people would be dressed who could stay in France or in England taking their leisure on the lawn.

"And I saw that gentleman remove himself from the party and go towards the house; and then some people came and held the dogs while I came in.

"And I sat at the table and we were talking French, because they all understood French, and French—after Irish—is the language that I am next best at.

"And I waited for some twenty minutes, and then Tolstoi came from the house and walked to me, and he apologised to me very graciously. He said:

" 'Mr. MacKenna, I had unfortunately forgotten the exact date on which you were to come—I thought it was tomorrow.'

"And I," said MacKenna, "was very angry. I very rarely get angry, and I stood up and said: 'Monsieur Tolstoi: you have put yourself to the trouble of going into your house and changing from your ordinary clothes to the clothes of a peasant.

" 'I am not impressed, Mr. Tolstoi, by this rapid change of garments you have made.

" 'I find what you have done, personally, detestable, and I refuse to have anything to do or any interview with a person who can be guilty of so filthy an action.' "

I can see MacKenna saying those words. He was a man about six-feet-one, slender as a rake, with a most singular nobility of carriage; and I could see his face and the bleak look that would be in it when he spoke these horrible words.

"What did you do, MacKenna?" said I.

"I turned," said he, "and I walked away from that table and out through that gate with the ten bloody dogs all yapping at my heels. And I went away feeling sad at the pitiful exhibition which a great man can make when he thinks somebody is coming to interview him for a modern newspaper.

"Then the newspaper," he went on, "threatened to sack me because I didn't give them the interview, but I gave them an excellent article wherein I showed that the parts of Russia I was in were exactly like parts of Connemara or the County Cork; that the landscape looked exactly the same only ours is better; and that the people were almost exactly the same except, of course, there are no people in the world who are half as good as we are."

Bernard Shaw

(1943)

I HAD left Paris a few months earlier, and had now a job as Registrar of the National Gallery in Dublin. Mrs. Shaw came to me at my office and we had a long talk about France and mystical philosophy and many things. Nigh the end of our chat she said, "As you haven't met my husband I'll get him to call at your flat tomorrow evening, about five o'clock: your wife can give him tea, and in that way you can all get acquainted."

Knowing how wildly occupied a great man must be when he visits his native parts, I replied, "Don't do that. Mr. Shaw will have more than enough visiting to do while he is here, without bothering about someone he has probably never heard of. Let the poor great man have a bit of a rest."

Mrs. Shaw smiled at that. I think now that she was smiling at the idea of her husband having anything to do with the idea "rest," for that is something he has never needed, and mightn't quite know what to do with. He is not restless, but I think he never rests. After some more conversation about the war (this was in the second year of the 1914 war) she went away, and I considered the matter was settled.

The consequence was that I didn't go home to tea at five o'clock the next day. I turned up at six o'clock, and found a very lofty, slender gentleman on the door-step thanking my wife for his tea, and saying good-bye to her. We shook hands on the door-step, he peering away down at me and I staring away up at him. And he moved down the stairs.

About ten steps down he stopped and looked back at me. Very mildly and thoughtfully he said: "I don't like French Irishmen."

And I, gently and thoughtfully, replied: "I don't like Cockney Irishmen."

And that was the entire of our conversation at our first meeting.

Next day I met George Russell, the poet-painter—who was and still is perhaps better known by his pseudonym "A.E."— and I told him of my unfortunate meeting with Mr. Shaw. He had a follow-up story to tell me.

After leaving me, Mr. Shaw went home to dinner. He was staying with Sir Horace Plunkett. The only other guest at that dinner was A.E. himself. Now this is to be remembered— people who lived in London held, very firmly, that Mr. Shaw was the greatest conversationalist in the world. On the other hand, people who lived in Dublin, where conversation was the only form of exercise that our people ever took, held that A.E. was the greatest conversationalist in the world.

I cannot imagine which of these great men was the greatest in that respect, but I am certain that when either of them was in a house nothing but the house going on fire would stop him from talking. (Talking is, of course, sometimes referred to as conversing.) I fancy, myself, that either of these remarkable artists could have talked Coleridge into a fit, and if you know your literary history, you will know that nothing but an endless gramophone record run by a perpetual-motion engine could halt or jolt or disjoint the conversation of Coleridge. Maybe Coleridge did not talk in his sleep, but that is improbable.

A.E.'s talk was packed and overflowing with wisdom, humour, criticism, and with the visions which he had had that same day of the gods and demi-gods, the elementals and the faery-folk. If you dared to doubt him upon the actuality of these visions, A.E. would seize a pencil, and in ten strokes he would draw you the identical divinity, or what-not, that he had been telling you of. There was just no doubting him upon such a matter. He saw it, he told it, he drew it, and he made a poem on it. He was tremendous, his conversation was wonderful, and I am told that Mr. Shaw's was better.

I said to A.E.: "It must have been the great talk between the pair of ye."

"It was," said A.E. "Shaw," he went on, "is the best talker I've ever met."

"I wish I'd been there," said I, enviously, and went on, "Sir Horace must have thought he was in heaven."

Here A.E. commenced to laugh.

"What's the joke?" said I.

"Well," said A.E., "after dinner Shaw and I got going beautifully. I dare say," he went on, "that there was more fun and knowledge going on in that drawing-room at that moment than in any other house in Ireland. Shaw was crackling thunders and lightnings at me, and we were both set on hours of frolic when a curious sound halted it all. Shaw looked round to see where that strange noise was coming from. I looked round, and then we looked fixedly at Sir Horace Plunkett. There he was, fast asleep, and snoring contemptuously at the pair of us.

" 'He has been lulled peacefully to rest,' said Shaw, grimly, 'by the wittiest chattering that ever happened on earth.' " And from that story and that instant I seemed to know Bernard Shaw nearly as well as I knew A.E. himself.

But there are a great number of Bernard Shaws, and you have to work a lot to know any of them. The mere work that he has done in this world is literally colossal. He has written about sixty plays. Not one of these has taken the edge off him. After he had worked he was as full as ever, and nearly all of them got a Preface: not the modest little half-dozen pages that you and I would consider a proper introduction to a play, but an overplus of thought and energy so generous that three of these prefaces put together make a large book.

In a way, it is a pity that these prefaces cannot be acted, or chattered, or got over to the audience somehow, in the intervals between the acts.

His plays alone would be a generous life's work for from three to five ordinary dramatists—and how famous all of these men would be! His prefaces would reward and glorify three other literary men. This does not exhaust the tale, for the man is inexhaustible. He has written five novels. And there is his journalistic work; say, ten volumes if collected. Add his astonishing art of musical and pictorial criticism, four more volumes; his socialistic and economic work, ten more books; and his lectures, public speeches etc., perhaps a dozen more books. There are then the interviews he has given to a couple of hundred press-men from all over the earth, who have published these interviews, mainly all his own work and making some dozens of volumes. Nor is all said—there are his letters to the press; not mere letters, but real expositions, models of wit and urbanity and, when he wished them to be so, deadlier than bombs. And finally (perhaps) there is his mere conversation, effortless, continuous, rewarding; so profound you might miss the wit, or so witty you could escape the profundity.

A vast work, and a vast worker. If the old Faery-God-mother had appeared at my birth-bed, and prophesied that I should have had to work as hard as Shaw, I should have considered that I was being bound apprentice in Purgatory, and that I had a lot to howl about.

If you ask people what they think about Shaw, a majority of them would answer at once that he is a great humourist. Naturally they would be right: he is that: but they would be wrong also. They would be wrong in failing to recognize that his is the most serious mind that has been at work in the literature of our day. In his prefaces certainly, he wastes no time cutting capers. If a joke is needed he has a Golconda of them ready and willing to slip anywhere and do anything; but the whole vitality of these great Essays is spent in saying the thing he wants to say, and in making the reader think, and think again. He is not trying to make the reader laugh, and it is this so-cogent, so-persuasive seriousness that makes his non-dramatic writings the wittiest and most human writings of our time. The person who reads Shaw's Prefaces is up to and ready for every question that is a reality and compulsion in our days and times; and that goes for this minute of talking.

Every cultivated English-speaking person now between the ages of twenty and seventy has come under the ruling of Shaw's mind, and has taken more direction-of-thought from him than they could have got any way else, and from anyone else. I think that to be so eminent as he was, and is, was no easy matter, for there was much competition from his first day to the present day. There has been an enormity of competitive talent about him all through his life: he was not born into a second-hand generation, but into as intellectually vivified a race and period as has ever been. The London of his early and middle years was richer in literary talent than all the rest of the world put together could equal—there were Meredith and Hardy, Wilde and Barrie, Yeats and Synge, Pinero and Wells and Bennett and Chesterton—and a couple of dozen more. Any one of these names would be an honour to any period of any country; and I think of George Bernard Shaw as being the best among the lot.

Legend already grows about Shaw thickly as the late August blackberries are growing in the hedges round about me here. I think that, with one other, he is our greatest living man, and I think that his work will outlast even his legend. Of course, the writer himself is responsible not only for all that he has written, but even for all that has been written about him. His legend becomes real after him and, no matter who assisted in its fabrication, he, the artist, is implicated and is present in every truth, in every lie, and in every guess-work and patch-work that grows as out of his brain, and his heart, and his ground.

The Great Man

(1944)

GREAT men do go out of date pretty fast. Young people tend to imagine that everybody over forty-five years of age died a couple of years before Columbus discovered America, but in the case that I now have in mind, everybody knew about him, and I, even, had an idea or two about him myself. For example, I thought he was dead.

I was lecturing in America, and a lunch had been given for me in Cincinnati. We were about twenty people in a long room, at a long table. My host was at one end of the table and I was at the other.

A waiter came to me and whispered that a gentleman would like to speak to me for a few moments. I asked him to go and whisper about it to my host. My own idea was that the gentleman who was after me was a newspaper-man, and that I was going to be interviewed between the entrée and the sweet. My host nodded to me enthusiastically, and I bade a fond farewell to the rest of my lunch and hoped, pessimistically, that my dinner would make up for it.

In about three minutes the door opened and the waiter introduced a gentleman as if he were ushering in royalty. He was a tall gentleman. In fact he was taller than that. He was about six feet three all up and down, and although he was slim and elegant, he yet had a carriage to his shoulders that made him seem even taller and even more elegant. He made everybody in the room look a bit sloppy. Barring the Indian poet, Tagore, I had never seen so immediately "taking" a figure. My host led him to my end of the table and introduced him to me.

"Mr. James Corbett," said he.

In another moment Jim Corbett was sitting down just back of me, and not one of the twenty guests who were assembled to do me honour were taking any notice whatever of me: they were looking at him. In two more minutes I had switched my chair so that my back was turned upon my host and his guests and my lunch, and Corbett was being interviewed. I think he is the only man I have ever "interviewed": and I think I made him recite every good punch that he had ever given or gotten. He corrected me upon the idea of a "good punch" much as I might have corrected him upon the idea of a good poem.—

"Mr. Stephens," said he gravely—it was rather curious that he and I mistered each other scrupulously all through that hour of chattering—"when a man gets a good punch he gets knocked out. But a man whose feet are as good as his shoulders never *gets* a good punch. Boxing is dancing," he went on. "You dance too far away for the punch to be more than a tap, or you dance too close in for the punch to be more than a bump. A boxer is far too busy to be thoughtful during a combat, his feet do all his thinking for him, and he wins or loses on his toes."

He told me that in his last famous battle with Fitzsimmons he was the winner, and that Fitz knew it. But that would make another story, and I wish now to tell the tale of the greatest punch that Corbett ever got.

It all came out of his statement that he loved England, Ireland and Scotland next best after his own country, and that he loved his own country next best after his own wife (but she is another story also). He was very proud that he had once met the greatest man in England, the greatest man in the world he amended.

"Who can that have been?" quoth I, in great wonderment.—

He answered reverently:—

"Jem Mace," said he.

And he went on: "I had a hundred reasons for wanting to go to England, but one special reason was that I wanted to see Jem Mace before he died. He was then about eighty-five years of age, and I thought to myself: 'If I don't see the greatest champion that ever lived now, I'll never see him at all.'

"So I wrote from London asking might I call, and he wrote back to come any time that was convenient, and, as in honour bound, I went that same day. He owned a public-house somewhere outside London, and I was Mr. Mace's guest that night.

"There were a dozen others at our dinner, all men, all bruisers, and all heavies. I don't think Jem Mace would have let a light-weight in his house. Every one of the bruisers managed to confide in me that he personally could have licked Sullivan in half the rounds that I took, and each managed to convey also—very pleasantly, of course—that he would lick me in from three to five rounds if someone or other would put up the purse. We had a most interesting professional night.

"Next morning at breakfast I said to Mr. Mace: 'I'll be getting back to London now, for I'm off to Ireland in the morning.'

" 'Don't go for an hour or so,' said Mr. Mace, 'I want you to come into the gymnasium to show me a few of your new tricks. 'Tis rumoured,' he went on, 'that you have invented more tricks in your few years than boxing itself has invented in fifty years, and that you are the cleverest fighter the ring has ever known.'

"Well, that embarrassed me a bit, but I laughed it off, admitting that I had thought out a few bits of technique, and adding that I'd be very glad and very honoured to show him anything he might be interested in. When we got into the gymnasium he locked the door.

" 'I hate being interrupted in important matters,' said he, 'and if it got about that we were here there'd be a crowd around us in ten minutes and we wouldn't have any comfort.

" 'Now, Mr. Corbett,' he went on, 'just show me some of the new ways that you've brought into the game, and then I'll show you a few things we used to do about forty years ago.'

"That seemed about the funniest thing I had ever heard in my life, but I didn't like to laugh, for after all, Jem Mace was over eighty years of age—eighty-five I think—and he was a great man. Also, he was taking off his coat. I wasn't bothering about my coat, but he begged me to oblige him, for, as he said, when men box with their coats on that's a row, but when they box with their coats off that's business.

"We stood facing each other with our hands hanging down, and that special negative look in our eyes that fighters give as they measure each other. During that look of about five seconds we know more about each other than a doctor could find out in a month, and one knows in those few seconds exactly which foot to start off with, and almost exactly how the game should go.

"What Mr. Mace was thinking of as he looked at me I don't know. What I thought was that he looked almost exactly like a very kind elephant.

"I gave him a particular stance, and asked him to lead at me. He led, and, on the instant, I was away, and back, and tapped him twice, on the stomach and on the chin.

" 'Very pretty,' said he.

I showed him half a dozen of my ins and outs, and he complimented me on every one of them.

" 'Now Mr. Mace,' said I, with a chuckle that he could neither see nor hear, 'you promised to show me a few of the things that we've forgotten.'

" 'Well,' he said thoughtfully, 'what is your favourite stance?'

" 'Why,' I answered, 'I naturally fall into this one.'

" 'Very well,' said he, 'you would naturally lead from there with the left, and follow up.'

" 'Yes,' said I.

" 'Well, lead,' said he.

"I led.—

"Mr. Stephens," said Mr. Corbett, "I wakened up in about five minutes. I don't know where Mr. Mace pulled the punch from. I don't know what he packed it with. I went out for all the counts that a boxer has ever dreamt of in a nightmare; and, in an intellectual sense, I must have really stayed knocked-out for the day, for the next thing I really and completely remember is being on the boat to Ireland and being remarkably sick on that little journey.

"Mr. Stephens," said Mr. Corbett, "Mr. Mace was a very great man."

The James Joyce I Knew

(1946)

I F I TALK about James Joyce I find that I *must* talk about my-self: the reason for this will become clear in a minute or two.

The first time that Joyce and I met we disliked each other by what is called instinct, which is always very misleading. We were introduced by a perfect stranger to me.

I was walking up Dawson Street, thinking of nothing, which was and is my favourite form of thinking, when I noticed that two men were coming towards me, and that one of them was deliberating upon me as if I were a life-buoy spotted suddenly in a sea of trouble. Suddenly they stopped, and that one said, "Stephens, this is Joyce," and then, turning to his companion, he said, "I've got to run"—and he ran.

There stood Joyce and I, he stuck with me, and I stuck with him, and the other drowning man was swimming to a reef two streets off. Joyce looked at me without a word in his mouth, and I looked at him with nothing in my mouth except vocabularies. We halted upon each other. We were very different-looking people. Joyce was tall, which I wasn't; he was thin, which I wasn't; he wore specs, which I didn't; he looked down at me, which I couldn't; he rubbed his chin at me, which I wouldn't.

Suddenly I remembered a very cultivated remark which I had once heard a gentleman in a tall hat make to another in a straw hat whom he didn't know what to do with, and I repeated it to Joyce:—"Come and have a drink," said I.

He turned, and we walked back toward Grafton Street, and I regaled him with the gayest remarks that I could think of about what is known as the weather and this and that:— "An American," said I, "holds that it never rains in Ireland except between the showers."

"Ah," said Joyce.

"But a French lady," I continued, "told me that it rains in Ireland whether there are showers or not."

"Ah," said Joyce.

"This is Pat Kinsella's," I continued, as we halted outside the first tavern that we came to.

"Ah," said Joyce, and we went in.

The barman brought the refreshment that I ordered—it was called a "Tailor of Malt." It was larger than a single, and it only escaped being a double by the breadth of a tram-ticket, and it cost me three pence. When Joyce had silently dispatched one-third of a tailor into his system he became more human. He looked at me through the spectacles that made his blue eyes look nearly as big as the eyes of a cow—very magnifying they were.

"It takes," said I brightly, "seven tailors to make a man, but two of these tailors make twins. Seven of them," I went on, "make a clann."

Here Joyce woke up: he exploded moderately into conversation. He turned his chin and his specs at me, and away
down at me, and confided the secret to me that he had read
my two books; that, grammatically, I did not know the difference between a semi-colon and a colon: that my knowledge of
Irish life was non-Catholic and, so, non-existent, and that I
should give up writing and take to a good job like shoe-shining
as a more promising profession.

I confided back to him that I had never read a word of his,
and that, if Heaven preserved to me my protective wits, I
never would read a word of his, unless I was asked to destruc-
tively review it.

We stalked out of Pat Kinsella's; that is, he stalked, I
trotted. Joyce lifted his hat to me in a very foreign manner,
and I remarked, "You should engrave on your banner and on
your note-paper the slogan, 'Rejoyce and be exceedingly bad.' "

"Ah," said Joyce, and we went our opposite ways, and
didn't see one another again for two years.

Our next meeting was in Paris. One evening my concierge
told me as I came in that a tall, beautiful, blind gentleman had
called and had left a note for me. It was from Joyce, and it
asked me to meet him the next day. After that we met several
times a week for a long time.

I discovered that he approved of me in the most astonishing fashion, but it took me a little time to find out why.
Then, as the Dublin newsboys used to yell at customers, the
whole discovery was found out.

How Joyce had made this discovery I don't know, but he
revealed to me that his name was James and mine was James;
that my name was Stephens and the name he had taken for
himself in his best book was Stephen; that he and I were born

in the same country, in the same city, in the same year, in the same month, on the same day at the same hour, six o'clock in the morning of the second of February.

He held, with a certain contained passion, that the second of February, his day and my day, was the day of the bear, the badger and the boar. On the second of February the squirrel lifts his nose out of his tail and surmises lovingly of nuts; the bee blinks and thinks again of the Sleeping Beauty, his queen; the wasp rasps and rustles and thinks that he is Napoleon Bonaparte; the robin twitters and thinks of love and worms. I learned that on that day of the days Joyce and I, Adam and Eve, Dublin and the devil all shake a leg and come a-popping and a-hopping, yelling, "Here we are again! We and the world and the moon are new! Up the poets! Up the rabbits and the spiders and the rats!"

Well, I was astonished. I was admired at last! Joyce admired me: I was beloved at last: Joyce loved me. Or did he? Or did he only love his birthday, and was I merely coincident to that? When I spoke about my verse, which was every waking minute of my time, Joyce listened heartily, and said "Ah." He approved of it as second of February verse, but I'm not certain that he really considered it to be better than the verse of Shakespeare and Racine and Dante. And yet, he knew the verse of these three exhaustively!

Now in order to bring this birthday to an end, let's do it in the proper way. If I were Joyce's twin, which he held, then I had to celebrate this astonishing fact in my own way: so upon our next birthday I sent him a small poem:

> As bird to nest, when, moodily,
> The storm-cloud murmurs nigh the tree,
> Thus let him flee,

Who can to sing,
Here hath he calm, and sheltering.

As bee to hive, when, with the sun,
Long honey-gathering is done,
Who can to sing,
There let him flee,
This is his cell, his companie.

As child to mother running, where
The thunder shudders through the air,
Thus let him flee,
Who can to sing,
Here hath he ward, and cherishing.

Fly to thy talent! To thy charm!
Thy nest, thine hive, thy sheltering arm!
Who can to sing,
There let him flee,
This is, naught else is, certainty.

Joyce reported back to me that he was much obliged. He practically said "Ah" to my poem, and I could almost see him rubbing his chin at it.

As well as Dublin and the second of February, there were certain things that Joyce loved. There was, for example, a little Swiss wine called Riessler or Reissler, or thereabouts; its name was like that, he loved it. There was another imbibement called Champagne Nature, and he loved that with a critical contentment that he never gave to either prose or verse. And then there was music. Joyce loved music.

Perhaps that is not a precise way of putting it: he loved operatic music, the music that you can sing—Verdi, Puccini,

Donizetti. Any opera that elevated the tenor voice above all other voices was adored by him. He had himself one of the most musical tenor voices that I have ever heard, and had he trained to be a singer he might have been renowned in that art also. He *could* sing. He also loved folk-song. He took his hat off to English and German and Italian folk-song, and said "Ah" at them, but he adored Irish folk-song in Reisslers and Champagne-Natures and Napoleon Brandies.

One day we were in that Café which is half way up the Champs-Elysées on the left-hand side—very famous, and I can't remember its name—and he told me at table that he was the only person living who knew a certain folk-song. He had learned it from his grandfather, and his grandfather had asserted that it was, one, a lost song and, two, that it was the best love-song in the world. He sang it to me in his careful tenor voice, while three devoted waiters listened in and bowed respectfully at the end of each verse. All waiters loved Joyce: he gave millionaire tips and, better, he always asked the waiter's advice. He would ask a waiter which was best, the *sole chose,* or the *gigot quelque-chose;* and would as eagerly ask whether the waiter preferred Racine to Corneille, or the other way about. They loved him.

At that time I had a gift which has since deserted me. If I heard a song that I liked, thereupon that song, its music and words became mine. Because of that small talent, here is the song that Joyce sang to me on the Champs-Elysées, in a lovely tenor voice:

> I was walking the road one fine day,
> Oh, the brown and the yellow ale,
> When I met with a man who was no right man,
> Oh, Oh, Love of my heart!

And he asked if the woman with me was my daughter,
Oh, the brown and the yellow ale,
And I said she was my married wife,
Oh, Oh, Love of my heart!

And he asked would I lend her for an hour and a quarter,
Oh, the brown and the yellow ale,
And I said I would do anything that was fair,
Oh, Oh, Love of my heart!

So you take the high road, and I'll take the lower,
Oh, the brown and the yellow ale,
And we'll meet again at the ford of the river,
Oh, Oh, Love of my heart!

I was waiting there for a day and a quarter,
Oh, the brown and the yellow ale,
When she came to me without any shame,
Oh, Oh, Love of my heart!

When I heard her tale I lay down and I died,
Oh, the brown and the yellow ale.
And she sent two men to the wood for timber,
Oh, Oh, Love of my heart!

A board of holly, and a board of elder,
Oh, the brown and the yellow ale,
And two great yards of sacking about me,
Oh, Oh, Love of my heart!

And if it wasn't that my own little mother was a woman,
Oh, the brown and the yellow ale,
I'd sing another pretty song about women,
Oh, Oh, Love of my heart!

To end on the difficulty that is Joyce. All writers who are hatcheting out a route for themselves in a wilderness are bent on avoiding the tradition and the tone that is their inherited art and their language. All such are difficult. So Proust, in France: there is a sense in which Proust is almost not French: but, and as against that, he is not anything else either: he is an oddity and an enormity, and you can read him if Heaven will expand time into eternity, and so give you the chance to mark and digest him.

So it is with the Joyce of *Finnegans Wake*. You need all the rest of your life to read it, if you are going to read it, and you will then need a life after that again to understand it. We use the word "pure" in curious and subtle ways: we speak of pure music, pure mathematics, pure poetry. We rarely speak of pure thinking, although in religion there is such a thing; but we never speak of pure prose.

In a sense the thing which we term pure would have little intellectual or emotional value: it should have gone beyond the relative exchange which we call value. There is an Eastern phrase which says: "Cherish thoughts that depend on nothing whatever." That is pure thought. There is a lot of pure poetry. As to pure prose, who shall define it?

In *Finnegans Wake* Joyce was trying to write pure prose. When we have said all that we can say about this book we will make two statements only: we shall say, "It is unreadable," and we shall add, "It is wonderful." Upon these two conflictions James Joyce may sleep in peace until his second of February comes round again.

Here is the end of the episode called "Anna Livia Plurabelle." Night is falling, the river and the landscape is obscuring, and the words that describe it are obscuring also; the river, and the landscape, and the words have almost gone to sleep.

You can't see and you can't hear, and you can't bother. A stone is muttering drowsily to an elm tree:

Can't hear with the waters of. The chittering water of. Flittering bats, fieldmice bawk talk. Ho! Are you not gone ahome? What Thom Malone? Can't hear with bawk of bats, all thim liffeying waters of. Ho, talk save us! My foos wont moos. I feel as old as yonder elm. A tale told of Shaun or Shem? All Livia's daughtersons. Dark hawks hear us. Night! Night! My ho head halls. I feel as heavy as yonder stone. Tell me of John or Shaun? Who were Shem and Shaun the living sons or daughters of? Night now! Tell me, tell me, tell me, elm! Night night! Telmetale of stem or stone. Beside the rivering waters of, hitherandthithering waters of. Night!

I'll just say that it's wonderful, and there is an endless much more of it, in every mood that can be imagined.

Ulysses

(1948)

J OYCE was strangely in love with his own birthday and with
mine. He had discovered somehow that he and I were
twins, born in the same hour of the same day of the same year
in the same city. The bed it seemed was different, and that
was the only snag in our relationship.

He held that if there were any kind of heavenly twins
knocking about he and I were those twins and were heavenly,
for we were second of February beings, and he sang to me,
"Two, two for the lily-white boys clothed all in green-O" and
he promised to buy me a green Tyrolean hat with a white
feather in it, the twin hat of one he already had and loved.

"Let us," said he, "be green for Ireland, and let us show the
white feather to prove that we aren't heroes or anything like
that. The only heroic writer literature knows of," he went on,
"is one Penny Dreadful, Esquire, but Homer always got under
the bed when a Greek came into his room with gifts."

All this is apropos of the fact that two Joyce books have

appeared, one a reissue of his *Ulysses,* the other a book about *Ulysses* by Richard M. Kain, called *Fabulous Voyager.*

This last book is a commentary on Joyce's *Ulysses.* I don't quite know what to think about a writer who has to be interpreted so extensively: but a newish literature was getting about at the time Joyce wrote his great book. Freud and Adler and company had come along around these times, and had made literature a bit more medically conscious than it used to be. Perhaps the time is not distant when we shall fall in love with lunatic asylums: whereon, of course, literature will go a shade more medical still, and will be written entirely in prescriptions.

The plan of Joyce's *Ulysses* is excellently elucidated by Mr. Kain. The entire action of this very long book takes place in one day—eighteen hours, to be precise, for even Penelope has to go asleep sometime.

The day is the 16th of June 1904. The chief characters are Ulysses, Telemachus and Penelope, the hero's wife; but these three have got switched into modern Dubliners: Leopold Bloom, his wife Molly and their friend Stephen Dedalus. Bloom is a solicitor, his wife is very easily and abundantly solicited, and their friend Dedalus, as well as being a school-teacher, is Joyce himself. Dedalus is packed with ideas about science and art and sex and religion, and he is packed all over again with dubiety on all these subjects and on every subject whatever.

In addition to these principal characters, there are a couple of hundred others—'tis a crowded book. All these personages are popping into and out of the famous "stream of consciousness" and they are all popping into and out of offices and churches and banks and pubs, race-courses and shady dens; in fact they are weaving in and out of Dublin's fair city. This is no dead book and this multitude of people are curiously emphatic. I think Joyce put into this book every soul that he ever knew, and however they be likeable or dislikeable, they are alive all right, and they each talk his or her own lingo, of course rejoyced a bit.

This long day and long book is divided into four periods. Each period has its own tone, and in especial its own colour. The morning of the narrative is young and gay and pink. The noontime of it is hopeful and joyous and golden in colour. The third period grows twilightish, and its colour becomes steadily grey and greyer. The last period is black. This black period belongs very properly to Molly Bloom (chaste Penelope, if you please) and in all good black sobriety it has to be read to be believed.

Ulysses is still an astonishing book.

The fact that it now has a past abates nothing of its challenging quality. When a writer dies much of his work dies right there with him. There are, say, five thousand writers with us: they all die, and within a week of the death not three of them are read any more: and within a year, perhaps not one of them at all will be read, or even remembered again.

Joyce has not died in that way. He wrote a great number of pages, but he did not write a great number of books. There are the *Dubliners,* the *Portrait of the Artist, Ulysses,* and the even more famous *Finnegans Wake.* He wrote a tiny book of verse too, called *Pomes Penyeach.* They are not good, for his poetry is all in his prose.

When his *Finnegan* was finished, I asked him what he was planning to follow it. He grew curiously excited, and replied that he had a wonderful idea, and thereon he shut right up. He was sparkling with expectation, but would not utter one word about it.

He was a strangely discreet man. His *Ulysses* is a secret

kind of book. His *Finnegans Wake* is that self-same secrecy carried even further, and his next projected adventure is truly as secret as the tomb. What was it that he would tell and would hide? and would still tell and hide again? The poet and novelist live by being open as the day upon every subject under the sun. Joyce is the only example of a reticent writer that I know of, in our literature anyway.

Finnegans Wake

(1947)

I WOULD call *Finnegans Wake* Joyce's autobiography: factual, imaginative, spiritual, and all curiously disguised; for Joyce was a secretive man, as we all are, and we all tell what we do tell with some precaution.

Sometimes I think that when you are discussing a book you had better get rid of the author. Where would Hamlet be if Shakespeare was hanging around? Or if you read *Pickwick* and have Dickens in mind, you are at home with neither of these curious extremes of each other. Every soul in that book is Dickens and Every Man.

There are a number of things to say about Joyce, for he was always a little different from what he was—that is the definition of an author. One says of him that he was an Irishman, a writer, a Catholic and a linguist; but these permit of a narrower definition in each case. He was a writer; that is, he was a prose-writer. He was a Catholic; that is, he was trained in the Jesuit System. He was an Irishman; that is, he was a

Leinster man—which is, of course, the top of the world and the only animal worth being. And he was a linguist; that is, he preferred City of Dublin English to any other lingo or pigeon that ever came his way. He loved the City of Dublin with a passion which was both innocent and wicked, the way that every passion is; for if it isn't both of these, it is just animal and stupid; and that Dublin love-affair is responsible for this book.

And then there is a curious fact about *Finnegans Wake*. Every other prose book is written in prose. This book is written in speech.

Speech and prose are not the same thing. They have different wave-lengths, for speech moves at the speed of light, where prose moves at the speed of the alphabet, and must be consecutive and grammatical and word-perfect. Prose cannot gesticulate. Speech can sometimes do nothing else.

Finnegans Wake is all speech. Now it is soliloquy; now it is dialogue; it becomes at times oration and tittle-tattle and scandal, but it is always a speech, and however it be punned upon by all the European and a few of the Asiatic tongues, it is fundamentally the speech that used to be Dublin-English.

Consecutiveness and such-like doesn't quite matter to this speech; it hops and skips and jumps at its own sweet will; it is extraordinarily varied and sportive, and even when it is serious it isn't as serious as all that, for it easily makes up in abundance and exuberance for all that it lacks in meaning. The meaning isn't lacking, but it isn't meaning as the crow flies; 'tis, rather, meaning as the bee bumbles: honey here and honey there and heather-honey on the mountain.

Where he liked he disliked a bit; where he disliked he liked also. He rather dislikingly liked everything that happened. This extraordinary prose-poet, Leinster Jesuit, and Liffey linguist loved Joyce and Dublin. He was so almost a pessimist by limitation, but the English language doesn't permit more than a spoonful of pessimism—to be well shaken before taken—for it isn't built that way; and we can only be pessimists before breakfast.

First Meeting with George Moore

(1946)

I was Registrar of the Dublin National Gallery at one time. My man came in and said: "Mr. George Moore to see you, sir."

"Ah," said I to myself, "the famous novelist that everybody talks about but nobody reads, and of whom I've never read a word either! . . . Show him in," said I.

In ten more seconds George Moore stepped into my lovely office. There were three or four pictures on each of my walls, and a beautiful fire in the grate. Moore looked very carefully at all my pictures before he looked at me, and said: "Ah, copies, I presume."

"I think not," I replied, "but you are more of an expert than I am."

Moore sat down. "You are an expert, ex officio," said he.

"Oh no," I answered, "I am merely a very superior official. My Director is Quattrocento and my Board is Byzantine. They are our experts."

An odd thing happens when two writers meet. Without a word being uttered on the subject each knows in thirty seconds whether the other has ever read a line of his work or not. Neither of us had, and we were both instantly aware that life is not perfect, but while I was full of patience and hope, Moore was scandalized.

"What are you working at now, Stephens?" said he.

"This morning," I replied, "I translated 'The County of Mayo' from the Gaelic."

"That is my own county," said he, "and so I am interested. But, my dear Stephens, that poem has been translated so many times already that you are wasting your—ah—talent, yes, perhaps talent, on a job that every literate person in Ireland has done before you."

"Why, Moore?" said I.

Here he broke in: "Don't you think, Stephens, that I have come to the years in which younger men should address me as 'Mr. Moore'?"

"Certainly, Mr. Moore," said I—and he smiled a grave, fattish and reprobating smile at me.

"You were going to say," he prompted, turning on me his pale, fattish face and his sloping, thinnish shoulders, and his air of listening to me almost as through a keyhole.

"Only, sir, that a translation is never completed until it has become a piece of original verse in the new tongue."

"That is an excellent and beautifully impossible definition," said Moore. "Perhaps," he went on, "you would like to say the verses to me. How many are there?" he added hastily.

"Only four," I answered, "and as it is about your own county, sir, you should be the first to hear them."

"Thank you, Stephens," said he, unnecessarily, for I intended to say that poem to someone. So I said the little poem, and he praised it highly, mainly, I think, because I had called him "sir."

"I must leave you very soon," said he, "for I have a lunch engagement, but if you ever need literary advice, I hope you will write to me. In fact, I beg that you *will* do so, for I have a proposition to make to you."

"I am in need of advice right now, Mr. Moore," said I, "and although some might think the matter not literary, I consider that everything that has to do with a speech problem has to do with literature."

Moore agreed. "Psychological problems," said he, "are women and religion and English grammar. They and all other problems are literary. Tell me the matter that is confusing you, Stephens."

"Well, sir," said I, "I have been invited to the first formal dinner party of my life."

"Your first dinner party?" he queried.

"I have eaten," I explained, "with every kind of person and at every kind of table, but I have never 'dined' with anybody."

"At a dinner," said he, "formal or informal, you just eat your dinner."

"Oh no, Mr. Moore," said I, "the problem has nothing to do with mastication and is quite a troublesome one. I shall be sitting at a strange table and on my right hand there will be a lady whom I have never seen before and may never see again."

"Quite," said he.

"On my left hand," I continued, "there will be another lady whom I've never seen before. In the name of heaven, Mr. Moore, what shall I say to these ladies?"

"Why," said Moore thoughtfully, "this is a problem that never struck me before. It is a very real one," said he, sitting up at me and at it. "If you were an Englishman," he went on, "you could talk a little about the weather, vaguely, you know, a number of Dirty Days and How Are You's, and then you could say a few well-chosen words about the soup and the meat and subsequently about the pudding—pudding, Stephens . . ."

"Dammit," said I.

"An Irishman," Moore said, "can always find something to say about the cattle, and the crops, the manure, and the . . . No, no," he continued energetically, "no manure—ladies think it is very strange stuff; they prefer to talk about theatres—actors, I mean—and hats. I'll tell you, talk to the first woman about how pretty her dress is; say that you have never seen so lovely a dress in your life. Then turn to the other hussy and say that she is the most beautiful person in the room. Admire her rings: don't ask her where she got them: never ask a woman where or how she got anything whatever; questions like that often lead to divorce proceedings. In short, Stephens, talk to them about themselves, and you are pretty safe."

He enlarged on this matter:

"You may talk to them about their hair and their eyes and their noses, but," he interrupted hastily, "don't say anything whatever about their knees."

"I will not, Mr. Moore," said I fervently.

"In especial, Stephens, do not touch their knees under any circumstances."

"I will not, Mr. Moore."

"Restraint at a formal dinner party, Stephens, is absolutely necessary."

"I quite understand, sir."

"Moreover, Stephens, women are strangely gifted creatures in some respects; all women have a sense akin to absolute divination about their knees."

"Ah, sir?" I queried.

"When a woman's knee is touched, Stephens, however delicately, that lady knows infallibly whether the gentleman is really caressing her or whether he is only wiping his greasy fingers on her stocking. But formal dinner parties are disgusting entertainments anyhow. Goodbye, Stephens."

"Goodbye, Mr. Moore," said I fervently, "and thank you very much for your help. I shall never forget those ladies' knees."

Moore smiled at me happily, almost lovingly. "Write to me about this dinner party, Stephens."

And that was our first meeting.

Poets on Poetry

(1946)

(*with Gerald Bullett*
and Dylan Thomas)

BULLETT: Now of course poetry can't be defined: it can only be pointed at. But, just to start the ball rolling, let's begin with something easier. The relation, if any, between poetry and verse. The popular idea has always been that all verse is poetry and all poetry is verse—in fact that the two words are interchangeable.

THOMAS: That of course is nonsense.

STEPHENS: There's some truth in that. A very large part of the produced verse that we have is just prose, shaped and quickened and vivified. A good deal of rhetoric passes for poetry, because it is written in verse-form: "Roll on thou deep and dark blue ocean, roll; A thousand fleets sail over thee; Man marks the earth with ruin; The something-or-other that thunder strike the walls Of rock-bound cities, bidding nations quake And monarchs tremble in their own dug-outs" and all the rest of it—it's just excellent prose, no secret about it, no music, just measure and vehemence.

Or the Macaulay ballads:—"But with a noise like thunder fell every loosened beam, And like a dam the mighty wreck lay stretched athwart the stream" and the rest of it. It's magnificent, said the Frenchman one time, but it isn't war.

So with a vast area of our printed verse: verse, some of it is jolly good indeed, but it's prose, disguised in the cast-offs of verse. Get a copy of the longer poems of the English. More than three quarters of these are prose, and bad prose at that.

THOMAS: *Paradise Lost? Ancient Mariner? Don Juan,* which is nearly all good *verse?* But anyway, we want to know what poetry is. All I know is that it is memorable words-in-cadence which move and excite me emotionally. And once you've got the hang of it, it should always be better when read aloud than when read silently with the eyes. Always.

STEPHENS: Poetry does two things, according to Keats: it must astonish and delight. If it doesn't do both, it does neither.

BULLETT: It doesn't consist of fine sentiments or great thoughts. It's something existing in its own right, something made out of words, a new creation—and the magic of it has something to do, hasn't it? with elements that are inherent in human speech —measure and cadence and so on. I don't expect an answer, but I should like to ask whether the *lyrical* quality is or is not the very essence of poetry?

STEPHENS: The poet is a fellow who can take hold of a thought and make it *sing*. Anyone who can compose to the measure of some kind of a dance is a poet.

THOMAS: I hope you're listening, Tin Pan Alley.

> O Soo
> I'm blue as blue
> baby
> I love yoo

Maybe

Maybe

oo

love me. . . .

STEPHENS: Nevertheless, I repeat, anyone who can compose to the measure of some kind of dance is a poet. All who write epics, and elegies, and lyrics and epi-and-prothalamiums, the wise-guys who write songs for music-halls, verses for Christmas cards, and mottoes for crackers—all these are poets, unless, of course, you can point out that they are just disguising prose in verse. Some of them are good, some not so good, and some are not good, but they are all of that Mystery, they are of that Licence. They are poets, which those Macaulays and people are not. The bits of things they give cannot be given at all in prose, or in any other form than even the "bad" poet has given it. Not even Shakespeare could tackle "Twinkle, twinkle, little star"; he could not rewrite it, or improve it, or do anything whatever to it except, perhaps, to deplore it. Lots of poetry is poetry, but is also no good.

THOMAS: I'm not going to argue with all that. Sometimes I just sits and thinks. I agree that music-hall songs can be good poetry—so can limericks, drawing- or tap-room—but I don't think cracker-mottoes etc. ever have been. I think, Stephens, you must be pulling my (comparatively) young leg. The younger generation used to be called, by their elders, flippant. Not any longer. It's we now who deprecate their flippancy. I feel rather like the little pedantically reproving girl addressing Matthew Arnold in Max Beerbohm's picture: "Why, Uncle Matthew, oh why, will not you be always wholly serious?" I'm all for taking the *serious* nonsense out of one's appreciation of poetry; I hate, as much as you do, the hushed-voice and hats-

off attitude, but I don't like the double-bluffing approach either
that pretends to think that "I'm one of the ruins that Cromwell
knocked about a bit" is better poetry than, say, the serious, un-
fashionable work of Cowper or Francis Thompson. It's just
very different poetry.

BULLETT: As Chairman, I'm not supposed to have any opinions
on anything. But I feel bound to say at this point that I think
it's very perverse—and very confusing for the ordinary listener
—to call such things poetry at all; such things as "I'm one of
the ruins that Cromwell knocked about a bit" and the like.
I'm not being snobbish about it either. I'm merely asking that
words should be used in their common meaning. Auden, I remember, some years ago brought out an anthology in which—

> I have no pain, dear mother, now
> But OH I am so dry;
> Connect me to a brewery
> And leave me here to die—

was put next to an exquisite lyric by W. B. Yeats, the idea being, I suppose, that both equally belonged to the category of
poetry. That, I think, is not only nonsense but pernicious nonsense, because it confuses people. One may enjoy music-hall
rhymes, now and again you get something very entertaining
in that line, but why muddle the man in the street by pretending that they belong to the same category of art as Keats'
"Nightingale" and Milton's *Paradise Lost?* Things aren't poetry just because we happen to like them. One may like ginger
pop, but that's no reason for pretending it's the same thing as
Sauterne or Montrachet. Poetry, I suggest, is something that
happens when language is used with so high a degree of exact-
ness as to express something otherwise inexpressible. A bit

pompous perhaps, but I shall stick to it till someone gives me a better definition.

THOMAS: Almost anything one says about poetry is as true and important as *anything* else that *anyone* else has said. Some people react *physically* to the magic of poetry, to the moments, that is, of authentic revelation, of the communication, the *sharing,* at its highest level, of personal experience; they say they feel a twanging at their tear-ducts, or a prickling of the scalp, or a tickling of the spine, or tremors in what they hope is their heart. Others say that they have a kind of a sort of a vague feeling somewhere that "this is the real stuff." Others claim that their "purely aesthetic emotion" was induced by certain assonances and alliterations. And some are content merely to say, as they said of the first cinematographic picture, "By God, it moves." And so, of course, by God it does, for that is another name for the magic beyond definition.

STEPHENS: Let's get more to it. Yes, there's a transforming that takes place in poetry. It is transformed right away from prose. A.E. (George Russell) once said to me, "Poetry is written on the Mount of Transfiguration." Fine poetry sometimes subsists on nothing. When Chaucer says, "The barren isle standing in the sea," he is next door to saying nothing, but I want to keep that line for ever. Or Marvell, with his "Annihilating all that's made To a green thought in a green shade." When Blake says, "Oh sunflower, weary of time," I'm satisfied that he is where he wants to go. Or "Speak silence with thy glimmering eyes, and wash the dusk with silver." There is nonsense in it, but who wants sense when he can get poetry instead? So, also, "Brightness falls from the air, Queens have died young and fair, Dust hath closed Helen's eye." Anyone can say, well, what about it? Why there's nothing about it, except that something or other, quite unnamed and unnameable, has transformed, and is only here by grace.

THOMAS: In other words, the magic in a poem is always accidental. No poet would labour intensively upon the intricate craft of poetry unless he hoped that, suddenly, the accident of magic would occur. He has to agree with Chesterton that the miraculous thing about miracles is that they *do* sometimes happen. And the best poem is that whose worked-upon unmagical passages come closest, in texture and intensity, to those moments of magical accident.

BULLETT: Let's have a few more examples, shall we?

STEPHENS: When the Abbé Bremond wrote his famous book, *Pure Poetry,* he gave seven examples of pure poetry from the French, and all the other examples, millions of 'em, were from the English. "And through the glass window shines the sun, How should I love, and I so young? The Bailey beareth the bell away, The lily, the lily, the rose I lay." The most exciting and incomprehensible verse in English. "Is she kind as she is fair? For beauty lives with kindness." "By shallow rivers, to whose falls Melodious birds sing madrigals." "Fair love, let us go to play: Apples be ripe in my garden," and in one line love is switched from Piccadilly Circus to the Garden of Eden. But there are so many, and every line of them original, and unique, and properly inexpressible.

THOMAS: And there's this to be said too. Poetry, to a poet, is the most rewarding work in the world. A good poem is a contribution to reality. The world is never the same once a good poem has been added to it. A good poem helps to change the shape and significance of the universe, helps to extend everyone's knowledge of himself and the world around him.

BULLETT: And a man who is himself a poet, people like you,

Dylan Thomas and Stephens, have a double interest in poetry. They make it and they read it. They're at both ends at once, the giving end and the receiving end.

STEPHENS: Let me tell you a story. It's a true one, but good, for all that.

BULLETT: Go ahead.

STEPHENS: I called on Yeats one day: He was in a bad temper. He pointed to a pile of books and explained that he wasn't going to read them, or do anything about them. He waved his arms, "People think," he complained, "that I love poetry, and that I must be very glad to get some. I don't love poetry," he went on, "why should I? It's the hardest work in the world, the most exacting, and the least rewarding that any intelligent person can undertake. Moreoever," he went on, "I am not interested in the least in other men's verse, I've trouble enough with my own. It's like those love stories in novels: as if we all didn't get misery enough out of our own love-lunacies without having to weep and wail about the fictitious love-yowling of people that never existed. I can't conceive," said Yeats, "how any working poet can take the smallest interest in anyone else's verse, and besides, out of any hundred poets ninety nine and a half of them are no good, and the whole hundred of them despise, and even loathe, every other poet that lives."

BULLETT: Just a minute, Dylan Thomas wants to cut in.

THOMAS: I can only believe those were casual, throw-away remarks, little spurts of annoyance never intended to be remembered. Anyway, he contradicts himself in his essays and letters, any number of times, and in his rather erratic *Oxford Book of Modern Verse*.

STEPHENS: Yeats was in a very bad temper: "Besides," said he, "England, Ireland and Scotland hate poetry and hate poets, and they only buy the stuff as table-ornaments anyway. Do people buy your stuff, Stephens?" he enquired. "Oh, yes," I answered, "the whole forty-two millions of 'em clubbed together and bought nine of my books last year. In fact," I went on proudly, "no year has passed in which I haven't made from seven and six to twelve bob, beat that if you can, W.B.! There was," I continued reminiscently, "one marvellous year in which I knocked fifteen shillings out of my fellow men." These intimate truths put Yeats into a wonderful good temper.

THOMAS: I think there's an inverted snobbery—and a suggestion of bad logic—in being proud of the fact that one's poems sell very badly. *Of course,* nearly *every* poet wants his poems to be read by as many people as possible. Craftsmen don't put their products in the attic. And contempt for the public, which is composed of potential readers, is contempt for the profound usefulness of your own craft. Go on thinking that you don't *need* to be read, and you'll find that it may become quite true: no one *will* feel the need to read it, because it is written for yourself alone; and the public won't feel any impulse to gate-crash such a private party. Moreover, to take no notice of the work of your contemporaries is to disregard a whole *vital* part of the world you live in, and necessarily to devitalise your own work: to narrow its scope and possibilities: to be half dead as you write. What's more, a poet is . . .

BULLETT: I don't want to interrupt but we have about two minutes to go.

THOMAS: What's more, a poet is a poet for such a very tiny bit of his life; for the rest, he is a human being, one of whose responsibilities is to know and feel, as much as he can, all that is moving around and within him, so that his poetry, when he comes to write it, can be his attempt at an expression of the summit of man's experience on this very peculiar and, in 1946, this apparently hell-bent earth.

On Speaking Verse

(1937)

We haven't yet invented a term for the uttering of poetry. Nobody likes the word reciting. It has certain village-hall, school-girlish associations, pleasant enough in their modest, amateurish place but not indicative of harmonious speech, or of matured artistic intention.

In general we may say that the utterance of poetry, private or public, is unsatisfactory. People who recite poetry seem to be a little ashamed of doing so. 'Tis as though they were thinking —this is pretty odd stuff, and is rather more she-man and he-woman than we quite care to seem at home with. They think that the voice should go neuter while repeating it.

Consequently, and in defence of the national artistic shyness of these islands, those who approve of verse have adopted an almost uniform system of speech for it, and they use this speech for every poem so that all poetry whatever seems to have been written by one universal tongue-tied author. Many singers do the same thing. Too often they lift up their voices without lifting up their hearts. They present their dreadful lungs to the public and call it song: so do many reciters of verse, and they call it poetry.

Spenser, Milton, Wordsworth, Shelley. How different they are! The space separating any one of these poets from every other, in matter, form, tone, is so great as to make them seem psychological strangers to each other, inhabitants of widely separated lands, and heirs to utterly alien cultures.

Not so are they to the speaker of their verse. He resumes them all into his grave, comely, unemphatic modesty of locution; he levels all the diversity out of them, and serves them up, tepid, with bread-sauce and no veg. and he seems, while doing so, as though he were apologizing to his nation and his Maker for having mentioned them at all. Soaring verse, pedestrian speech!

It is not easy to speak in verse. It is certainly the most difficult form of speech which the English tongue can attempt, and it is difficult for everyone. One might think that trained actors would speak verse well. So they do, they speak it, and poetry is not spoken. We want some other name than speaking for the saying of poetry. The actor fails in this form of speech because he has to fail, and because his training is against it.

Underlying all music is tune: underlying all poetry is song. Poetry is not dramatic, it is lyrical. Even dramatic poetry is lyrical: and the dramatic attack can ruin six out of every seven poems which are so approached. Actors are trained to dramatic speech, and I have never known an actor, on the stage or off it, who was capable of any lyrical utterance whatever, or who even knew what lyrical utterance means.

Poetry, moreover, is not fundamentally emotional, which the actor's art is—it is passionate, and the actor does not live who is capable of passionate speech; scarcely does the poet now live who is capable of that speech either. Passionate does not mean loud or angry. It means intense, and wise, and effortless. The word "effortless" is the master-word in every artistic matter, in every creative matter. The actor's training is entirely in dramatic and comic idiom, and outside of these, actors are not good speakers—artistically, their training is parochial.

It is of the essence of the actor's art that he should be presenting, publicly and to others, everything that he says, or thinks, or feels, or does. Poetry is not a public utterance at all. It is inviolably private. It is a self-communion. The speaker of it, even in public, even especially in public, should be, as it were, talking to himself, and only overheard as by inadvertence.

And, speaking of readers of poetry generally, the worst has not been said. Underlying inability of diction in verse is an even worse intellectual inability. Too often the chosen poem is imperfectly understood by the speaker of it. The words and phrases are understood, but that open and expressed secret which *is* a poem, is in general not even suspected by the reciters of it. They say these words and phrases, but the voice, and tone, and pace, give no indication of that which is the poem, and of which words and phrases are merely the carriers and carters. They think, unconsciously of course, that poetry is not essentially different from prose, and they make of all poetry just rhymed prose. This central incomprehension lies behind all poor speaking of verse, and it lies behind all bad writing of verse also. There is a mort of this.

In order to bring this point out more fully I will state, shortly, the duties of verse as against the duty of prose. For every one thing which prose does poetry must do four completely separate things, and poetry must do these four effortlessly, unnoticeably, and must also do them in a much shorter time than prose takes for its one job. To further simplify this—

an immediate, intelligent statement is mainly what is demanded from prose. This too is generally conceded by poetry, but to that necessary thought there is added the emotional equivalent of the thought, the pace of the thought, and a musical addendum which unifies the three. This done, the whole must yet be shorter by half than prose.

The speaker of verse consequently must be taking care—of a thought, its emotion, its pace, and its music. He has nothing but a voice to do all this with, and he must do all this effortlessly.

There remains the question of gesture. Three words only need be added as to this. They are: Don't do it. Poetry has no need of gesture, and is vulgarized, is denatured, by its use. Whatever gesture seems as indicated in the verse must be conveyed by the voice alone. A poem, a voice, and a true ear—that is the outfit. In order to sing a song, first, lift up your heart, and then cut loose. In order to say a poem, first, lift up your soul, and then carry on.

I have chosen four poems. Each is, in its way, a masterpiece, and each is completely different from the others in matter and technique. The only idea which unites them is the idea of complete tonal difference.

I hold that tonally there are three different kinds of verse, and that each of these demands a different speech-adjustment and attack. There is a form, generally the epic, which is to be uttered in a fashion approximating to gravely-modulating speech. There is a form, the lyrical, which, without being sung, approximates to singing. And there is an intermediate form which is come to by a subtle balancing of phrase against phrase. The first example of these forms, Campion's "Rose-Cheeked Laura," is in the balancing form.

Though not the earliest, it is the most exquisite example

of consonance and harmony which has come to us in this form.
As well as being an accomplished poet, Campion was a practical musician. Many of his poems were composed for lute-
accompaniment, and this is an example of his musical com-
position. The measure he uses here was never used before in
English, and it has never been used again. This poem is one of
the loveliest things in lighter English verse.

> Rose-cheeked Laura, come;
> Sing thou smoothly with thy beauty's
> Silent music, either other
>   Sweetly gracing.
>
> Lovely forms do flow
> From concent divinely framèd;
> Heaven is music, and thy beauty's
>   Birth is heavenly.
>
> These dull notes we sing
> Discords need for helps to grace them;
> Only beauty purely loving
>   Knows no discord;
>
> But still moves delight,
> Like clear springs renewed by flowing,
> Ever perfect, ever in them-
>   Selves eternal.

Our next poem is quite another matter. It is by an artist
whom I should rank as second among the four most curious
poets who have written in English; the four curious poets being Blake, Gerard Manley Hopkins, Christopher Smart and
Charles Doughty. The present example from Hopkins' work

is his famous "The Leaden Echo" and its pendant, "The Golden Echo." If I were to give you a sustained examination of this poem alone it would result in a complete criticism and evaluation of Hopkins and all his works. One could write a Hopkins book on this one poem.

It was the effort of Gerard Hopkins never to write anything at less than the tension of ecstasy itself. Ecstasy should be, of course, the wing of every poem. Hopkins wished his poem to be all wing, all poise, all flight, all width and air and urgency. In this poem he came as close to that difficult ideal as it is possible to get without artistic disaster.

Every technical treatment has its own special artistic danger. Ecstatic treatment has the tendency to over-run its subject-matter by sheer pace or by uncontrollable intensity. Over-running by exorbitant pace is known to any athlete who has out-run his legs, and gone head-over-heels along the earth he should be spurning. Every rider has known his young horse do it. This accident happens as easily and eagerly in verse as in sport. Shelley is the splendid, occasional, example of this danger.

This poem is a marvellous example of ecstatic adventure, and of superb lineal control. It uses all the tonal forms, speech-verse, balance-verse, and song-verse. The person who can say it can almost say anything in verse-form.

The opening line of "The Leaden Echo" is, I think, the longest line in English poetry and some of the central lines are even longer than that.

I must make one point in criticism of this poem. There is a simple, or simply-to-be-expressed rule, in poetry. It is this: the beginning of a poem should be good, the middle should be better, and the end should be best.

The end of this poem does not fulfil the most important

of these rules. The end is not the best part of the poem. Critically, the end of this poem is of great interest, and is elucidatory of that Hopkins who so eagerly wanted to go, but did not always quite know where he was going, or even where he ought to be going. The end of this poem, poetically, goes nowhere, it gesticulates instead. Here is Pegasus refusing the fence:

The Leaden Echo

How to kéep – is there ány, is there none such, nowhere known
    some, bow or brooch or braid or brace, láce, latch or catch or
    key to keep
Back beauty, keep it, beauty, beauty, beauty, . . . from vanishing
    away?
Ó is there no frowning of these wrinkles, ranked wrinkles deep,
Dówn? no waving off of these most mournful messengers, still
    messengers, sad and stealing messengers of grey?
No there's none, there's none, O no there's none,
Nor can you long be, what you now are, called fair,
Do what you may do, what, do what you may,
And wisdom is early to despair:
Be beginning; since, no, nothing can be done
To keep at bay
Age and age's evils, hoar hair,
Ruck and wrinkle, drooping, dying, death's worst, winding sheets,
    tombs and worms and tumbling to decay;
So be beginning, be beginning to despair.
O there's none; no no no there's none:
Be beginning to despair, to despair,
Despair, despair, despair, despair.

The Golden Echo

    Spare!
There ís one, yes I have one (Hush there!);

Only not within seeing of the sun,

Not within the singeing of the strong sun,

Tall sun's tingeing, or treacherous the tainting of the earth's air,

Somewhere elsewhere there is ah well where! one,

Ońe. Yes I cán tell such a key, I dó know such a place

Where whatever's prized and passes of us, everything that's fresh
   and fast flying of us, seems to us sweet of us and swiftly away
   with, done away with, undone,

Úndone, done with, soon done with, and yet dearly and dangerously
   sweet

Of us, the wimpled-water-dimpled, not-by-morning-matchèd face,

The flower of beauty, fleece of beauty, too too apt to, ah! to fleet,

Never fleets móre, fastened with the tenderest truth

To its own best being and its loveliness of youth: it is an everlast-
   ingness of, O it is an all youth!

Come then, your ways and airs and looks, locks, maiden gear, gal-
   lantry and gaiety and grace,

Winning ways, airs innocent, maiden manners, sweet looks, loose
   locks, long locks, lovelocks, gaygear, going gallant, girlgrace —

Resign them, sign them, seal them, send them, motion them with
   breath,

And with sighs soaring, soaring síghs deliver

Them; beauty-in-the-ghost, deliver it, early now, long before death

Give beauty back, beauty, beauty, beauty, back to God, beauty's self
   and beauty's giver.

See; not a hair is, not an eyelash, not the least lash lost; every hair

Is, hair of the head, numbered.

Nay, what we had lighthanded left in surly the mere mould

Will have waked and have waxed and have walked with the wind
   what while we slept,

This side, that side hurling a heavyheaded hundredfold

What while we, while we slumbered.

O then, weary then whý should we tread? O why are we so haggard
   at the heart, so care-coiled, care-killed, so fagged, so fashed, so
   cogged, so cumbered,

When the thing we freely fórfeit is kept with fonder a care,
Fonder a care kept than we could have kept it, kept
Far with fonder a care (and we, we should have lost it) finer,
    fonder
A care kept? — Where kept? Do but tell us where kept, where. —
Yonder. — What so high as that! We follow, now we follow. —
    Yonder, yes yonder, yonder,
Yonder.

Each of the poems, so far, has been a curious poem. The
next is also curious. It is the work of a highly intelligent mind,
playing gravely and beautifully with its subject. Its subject is
love, seen as romance. This poem is well-known to the adepts
of poetic art, but many lovers of verse have insufficiently loved
it, or have not sufficiently praised it. It is truly beyond praise,
and its seriousness is a most elaborate and cunning piece of
learned play. It will never be bettered.

The title of this poem is "As ye came from the Holy Land
of Walsinghame." Some earlier critic attributed it to Sir Walter
Raleigh, but it does not lie within Sir Walter's splendid occasional talent, or his non-adventurous technique.

There are two especially great English poets:—one is
Shakespeare, the other is Anon. This poem was written by
Anon, and it was written at the best of that great poet's form.
It is in dialogue-form, for there is an interlocutor and a re-
spondent. Some of these stanzas are very famous. Two are
especially so. They are, singularly, and at once, the most pes-
simistic and the most beautiful utterances on love in English.
This poem is worth learning by heart.

> "As ye came from the holy land
>   Of Walsinghame,

Met you not with my true love
　By the way as you came?"

"How shall I know your true love,
　That have met many a one
As I came from the holy land,
　That have come, that have gone?"

"She is neither white nor brown,
　But as the heavens fair,
There is none hath her form divine
　In the earth or the air."

"Such an one did I meet, good Sir,
　Such an angelic face,
Who like a nymph, like a queen did appear
　In her gait, in her grace."

"She hath left me here alone,
　All alone, as unknown,
Who sometimes did me lead with herself,
　And me loved as her own."

"What's the cause that she leaves you alone
　And a new way doth take,
That sometime did love you as her own
　And her joy did you make?"

"I have loved her all my youth,
　But now am old, as you see,
Love likes not the falling fruit,
　Nor the withered tree.

"Know that Love is a careless child,
    And forgets promise past;
He is blind, he is deaf when he list,
    And in faith never fast.

"His desire is a dureless content,
    And a trustless joy;
He is won with a world of despair,
    And is lost with a toy.

"Of womenkind such indeed is the love,
    Or the word love abusèd,
Under which many childish desires
    And conceits are excusèd.

"But love is a durable fire,
    In the mind ever burning;
Never sick, never dead, never cold,
    From itself never turning."

Another poem that should be learned by heart is the loveliest poem ever written in our tongue by a man born outside
the British Isles. It is the "Helen" by Edgar Allan Poe.

This poem is one of the small masterpieces of the English
language. It falls within the definition of "pure" poetry, as
against great poetry, and a real examination of it might assist
the reader and student to realize what the obscure term "pure"
really means when it is used to define a certain class of artistic
effort. A poem is "pure" when it succeeds in saying very little
so marvellously it seems as though very much had been said.

Poe could be included among the strange poets whom I
mentioned before. He is odd enough for the oddest company.
He occupies an honourable position in verse, but with some

insecurity. Neither his life nor his work was completely integrated. He was man at odds with himself, at odds with life, at odds even with his art. Were it not for "The Raven" and this poem to "Helen" he might be thought of as among the singularities of literature rather than as among its achievements. "The Raven" is a splendid poem. Of "Helen" this is to be said—it is divinely lovely, and to have written such a poem is to have been, be it for only four stanzas' duration, in the very lap of the gods.

> Helen, thy beauty is to me
>   Like those Nicaean barks of yore,
> That gently, o'er a perfumed sea,
>   The weary, wayworn wanderer bore
>   To his own native shore.
>
> On desperate seas long wont to roam,
>   Thy hyacinth hair, thy classic face,
> Thy Naiad airs have brought me home
>   To the glory that was Greece
>   And the grandeur that was Rome.
>
> Lo! in yon brilliant window-niche
>   How statue-like I see thee stand,
> The agate lamp within thy hand!
>   Ah, Psyche, from the regions which
>   Are Holy Land!

Coleridge

(1945)

WE CAN usually say of any man that he is very like himself, or, in a more English idiom, that he is very much
of a piece: that when you meet him tomorrow he will be
much the same as he was yesterday. That is so, also, of most of
our poets—Chaucer or Spenser, Milton or Wordsworth, Keats
or Byron or Blake, each of these is the poet you know in almost every poem he writes, and each continues to be his recognizable self from his literary cradle to his critic-haunted
grave. Each has his own grammar and prosody, his own vo-
cabulary, and his own way of conducting his own poetic business. The style *is* the man, and, among the major poets, the
style is unmistakeable. Milton could no more write like Wordsworth than Keats could write like Shelley, or Byron write like
Blake or whoever else.

It is different with the minor poets. They tend to write
exactly like each other: they are the clubmen of literature:
they pronounce all their words alike: they are all equally

ashamed of a false quantity or a split infinitive or a faulty rhyme; they have all the same accent, the same sense of humour, and they infest each other's wigwams.

My opening remarks about a poet or a man being the same person per week, per year, and per poem, is true of nearly everybody, but it is not true of Coleridge. He was half a dozen people, all different, all remarkable, all eating at each other's vitals, all getting drunk and dizzy on laudanum and transcendental philosophy, and all, somehow, failing to attain the first rank to which he was entitled on every count. He is the oddest personage in English letters, and he is the most astonishing failure in letters anywhere. He dispersed his talents too widely.

He was, for example, a remarkable political journalist, and could have won fame and fortune for himself in that one craft if he could have stuck to it. He was a philosopher, and there too he could have left a more permanent mark than he has done. He was a critic of the most assured knowledge, taste and sensibility, but, somehow again, no one ever bothers to say so with any emphasis. He was a translator, and a dramatist, and a Unitarian clergyman, and he was the most astonishing conversationalist of his time; he was several other things, and thereupon and thereafter, he was also a poet.

Wordsworth said of him that he was "the most wonderful, and, indeed, the only wonderful person he had ever known." There were many other people who would have agreed with this statement, and indeed he was truly one of the most astonishing personages in the whole range of our literature. But it is as a poet that he is finally to be criticized and considered. His place in English literature is very securely insecure, for it will always be a question as to what that place is, and Coleridge himself never knew where he stood in any poem.

In general the bulk of a poet's best work is compressed

into some ten years of his life. Shelley and Keats are exceptions
to this rule, but these two are exceptions to every rule. They
died very young on the one hand, and they were, in a special
sense, geniuses on the other hand. Coleridge, also, is an exception to the rule, but in a peculiar way; he is genius also, the
authentic "Lost Traveller under the Hill," and his great work
is compressed into about three years of his early life: all the
rest of his poetry, and there is an enormous quantity of it, is
of this or that or the other interest, but it cannot be termed
great.

The great poems of Coleridge are the first half of "Christabel," the "Kubla Khan," "The Ancient Mariner," "Dejection," "Love," and "The Nightingale." If all the rest of his
work in verse were lost and these only preserved, his reputation would be that of a very singular poet indeed, but it would
still be a question as to whether he is great or "singular."

It is odd that both Byron and Shelley admired Coleridge's
poetry, but what they admired is odder still. Shelley thought
that his poem to France was the greatest ode in the English
language; no one else has thought so, and that poem is very
rarely mentioned by anyone. Shelley didn't live long enough
to become a real critic. He spoke and wrote and composed in
the heat of his young blood. The oddest part of this matter,
however, is the poem that Byron liked best, and praised, and
urged Coleridge to publish. This is the "Kubla Khan." Had
the question been put to us we should have asserted that Shelley would have admired "Kubla Khan" and that Byron might
have admired the "Ode to France." How either of these two
poets admired what they did I don't know.

Meanwhile, among those who talk of Coleridge there is a
great divergence of opinion as to which poem is to be considered his best piece of work. The general public will, of

course, plump immediately and naturally for "The Ancient Mariner." They should understand that a modern school is growing up which holds that the running prose commentary to this poem is the only part that should certainly be read. Another type of reader and critic will state that the first part of "Christabel" is his greatest work. A third excellent expert is very busy in claiming that "Dejection" is not only Coleridge's best poem but that it is even superior to Wordsworth's great "Ode on the Intimations of Immortality." There are then competent critics who asseverate that "Kubla Khan" is not only Coleridge's greatest poem but that it is the greatest or the divinest or the purest poem in the English language.

If the question were addressed to me personally I might be prepared to insist that the simplest parts of the "Mariner," most of "Kubla Khan" and bits from the others are his best work. He is scattered and discontinuous, and marvellous in spots, and lunatic, or boring, or disappointing in the total.

It is strange that criticism, after so many years have passed, should be in so many minds about the work of this poet, but then Coleridge is one of the strangest men and one of the strangest poets that ever lived. If one tried to elicit Coleridge from his prose writings one would never guess that he could write "The Ancient Mariner" or any other poem. The virtuosity of this poem is extreme, its fantasy is extreme, its knowledge of music and colour and pace is extreme. There is no poem like it in any language, but in my opinion that does not make it the best poem in the language, or even make it the best poem of Coleridge.

The best long poem in the English language is, of course, Milton's "Lycidas"; the second best is, I think, Chaucer's "Prelude"; the third and fourth best are Spenser's "Epithalamium" and his "Colin Clout"; John Donne's "Anniversary" could be thought of as the next greatest; then Wordsworth's "Intimations of Immortality"; and, as against these, the poor "Ancient Mariner" of Coleridge is just wherever you like, or is even nowhere. This poem suffers from the irremediable ill of being a fantasy of being: that is, in terms of life and in terms of poetry, it is non-nourishing and untrue. The very same unaccountable wandering from truth lies at the heart of "Christabel," and even at the heart of the simple poem "Love." No miracle of talent or technique can quite redeem untruth from being initially and persistently inhuman in both life and letters.

Poetry, English poetry anyhow, is a very reserved and severe art. There are a number of things with which it will have nothing to do. Of these fantasy is one. There is no first-class fantastic poem in English. Humour is another matter that poetry will not touch with a pole. Even wit only enters this domain on sufferance, and when it does so enter it is seen, as in the Courtier Poets, as the remarkable work of very superior undergraduates who are busy impressing equally superior undergraduates. These are prose qualities. They achieve their own limited, versified, man-of-the-world success, but they can never be considered as "great," and can only be considered as poetic by courtesy.

When there is critical uncertainty, as in this case, the critic ceases to be a critic and becomes, say, a reviewer, or he becomes merely such and such a person, detailing his own impressions, his own sympathies, his own taste, and the extent of his own reading and thinking upon poetical and artistic matter. The simple way out is, of course, that of eulogy—when in doubt about something, praise it—but this is a simple way indeed, and it never brings one to grips with the subject. All criticism should be at first destructive criticism; what remains after such corrosive analysis is the indestructible goodness and greatness of the subject.

So, in what I have further to say of Coleridge, I cannot speak as a critic. The material which past criticism should have bequeathed me is lacking, and I must talk to you as from my own solitary judgment, and assert that I dare not claim any certitude or any finality in judgment. This, so, is merely what I think of Coleridge.

The god-in-the-car in every one of Coleridge's principal poems is a kind of lunatic. A bewildered and bewildering Albatross sets all that vast machinery to work in his "Ancient Mariner." In "Christabel" a completely unaccounted-for Devil seems to infest, or even to be, the Lady. In his poem called "Love" (which is very highly praised) there is an equally unnecessary and looney Knight buzzing all over the poem like a demented bluebottle. "Kubla Khan" goes nowhere, starts from nowhere, stays nowhere, does nothing whatever that can be given a name. All his poems are haunted by some unnecessary and importunate and unchase-able ghost. His "Dejection" has himself in it as a spook. He mourns in this poem that he has lost his "shaping spirit of Imagination," but he never had Imagination, he had instead Fantasy, and he mistook this prose goblin for the poetic and creative god. What is the good of creating something that is nothing!

Coleridge was a haunted man: his poetry is a haunted poetry. It is not evil, not at all; there is not one spot of evil in Coleridge's nature; he is nigh to being a poet, nigh to being a philosopher, he is the Jack-of-all-splendours, and the master of none. So his verse is not evil, it is just spooky, and a pipe-dream, with opium for its father and Coleridge let in to be its mother, for he is astonishingly feminine. It is astonishing, and inexplicable, and haunting, and teasing, and would be dreadful but that the real goodness of the man shines through it, and, almost persistently strives to redeem this poetry from the laudanum that gave it birth.

And then—how astonishing, how almost wonderful "The Ancient Mariner" is. The works I mentioned a little while ago, by Milton and others, as being the greatest poems in English, are wonderful indeed, but none of them is astonishing, and this is the ill of Coleridge, as it is the ill of some of Shelley, some of Byron and most of Edgar Allan Poe. But how astonishing it is, and how, particularly when one is young, one wishes that one could write like that, or even half as astonishingly as that.

I am inclined to consider that "The Nightingale" could be considered as his top-note, and that this poem is not astonishing, and is wonderful. . . .

I am, as you can see, speaking a whole lot as against Coleridge. It is not my fault. Criticism has not yet made up its mind about this singular poet about whom, after so long a time, there is still doubt. And yet how can one say one harsh word against "The Ancient Mariner"? . . .

"Dejection," too, is a remarkable poem. It is spoiled for me by being autobiographical. The poet is talking about himself, and that is a bad subject for any poet. To be dejected about somebody else or something else might be something, but to cherish and coddle one's own dejection is anyhow a weakness, and is poetically a crime. The matter has not been transformed, and we are tempted to be sorry for the poet instead of being sorry for sorrow wherever it may be.

William Blake

(1945)

ONE day, a long time ago, a young sculptor asked Socrates for advice about his work, and the great man advised him in three short great words. He said to the aspiring young man: "Chisel your statue."

A poet does chisel his poem. He goes over it and over it. He repeats it to himself almost in his sleep as well as in his waking, and at last, when he must let it go, he does so knowing that nothing more can be done to that poem, and be it good or bad, that he has diligently chiselled his statue and just can't do another tap to it.

Blake never chiselled his statue. He was always too busy about the next poem, the next drawing, to bother excessively about the one that was on the table or on the drawing board. In fact he always preferred the next one to the present one. His are, I think, the least worked-over poems in the language. The consequence is, that a great amount of his work exists in the shape of draft poems, and are the only poems that come to us in this seven-month condition. He didn't have to work like a horse to produce poetry; he left it, unfortunately, to produce itself.

We don't know everything, in fact we don't know much; but we do know our poets. If we have studied their works, we become exceedingly intimate with, say, Coleridge and Words-worth and Shelley and Keats, Browning and Herrick and Donne. We know these personages as well as we know the members of our own families, better certainly than we know the people with whom we habitually wine and dine, or who are members of our own clubs, for it is of the essence of poetry that nothing whatever is withheld from the reader, and that a personal lie in verse is almost unthinkable.

As to the poets I have mentioned, no personal question arises about them. They have told us—if we are good readers —who they are, what they think, how they feel, and indeed how they react to every emotional, intellectual or imaginative situation that is possible to them and to us.

This is not quite true of Blake. Every other poet is given in the piece and in the lump, but Blake is curiously a half-hid-den man. He has secreted himself, first, within Elizabethan lyric; and then he has so gone-to-ground within the mazes of a mythology, his so-called Prophetic Books, that the man, Blake, is not easy to discover in the windings and labyrinths of these strange and challenging poems, and of other poems that are only half written.

How much of what he gives us here belongs truly to him-self, and how much of it belongs to Swedenborg or to Jacob Boehme we do not quite know. One cannot doubt that Blake is indicating a somewhat that he has actually adventured in, but what truth is it when he claims divine collaboration for his verse, for he strictly makes this claim?

When Milton asserts that Urania is the genius of his song we are not bothered, we know where we are. We know that there is no Urania, that there is Milton's own self, and his own muse which is his own heart and mind and being. But Blake's claim is not this classical or poetic pleasantry. He states outright and downright that God's own self, the Unutterable Transcendency, is with him in the day and in the night, and does not merely inspire his song, but actually and audibly and verbally dictates it to him in South Molton Street, London, W.C.

Speaking as a versifier myself, I prefer the poetic "form" of Spenser or Donne or Keats to the poetic "form" of the Prophetic dictation. In his preface to the long poem "Jerusalem" Blake says of its form:

I have produced a variety in every line both of cadences and number of syllables; every word and every letter is studied and put into its fit place.

Every poet, of course, does this in every line that he writes. But it seems to me that Blake did this less, and did it less expertly, than any other poet whatever. He is the most careless poet that ever lived. His ear could pass any dissonance. His eye could overlook any error. His mind could at times be satisfied with any stuff that got or crept or wriggled into it. He was not only reluctant to chisel his statue, he was incapable of it; he was actually terrified of re-reading, or correcting or polishing his poems.

The reader of a poem may not realize the more-than-Yogi-attention which his poet has given to that admired verse. The draft of it may have taken only some minutes to put on the paper, but he may thereafter have lived with it, and on it, and in it, for months before he will say, "I can do no more; this poem is finished."

Three quarters of Blake's poems are merely drafts for poems, for Blake would not live with them, and live them, and be almost ready to die for the bettering of them. His poem, for example, "Tiger, tiger, burning bright," is very famous, very arresting, and is almost shamefully ill-groomed, ill-made. Two verses of it are good and three and a half are very bad. The bad verses are:

> In what distant deeps or skies
> Burnt the fire of thine eyes?
> On what wings dare he aspire?
> What the hand dare seize the fire?
>
> And what shoulder and what art
> Could twist the sinews of thy heart?
> And, when thy heart began to beat,
> What dread hand and what dread feet?
>
> What the hammer? What the chain?
> In what furnace was thy brain?
> What the anvil? What dread grasp
> Dare its deadly terrors clasp?

How could anything be worse than that! What is wrong with these verses is, of course, that there is no sense in them. They are just stuff and nonsense.

The two good verses everyone knows:

> Tiger, tiger, burning bright
> In the forests of the night,
> What immortal hand or eye
> Dare frame thy fearful symmetry?

and:

> Did He smile His work to see?
> Did He who made the lamb make thee?

Another, to me, ridiculous poem is the famous

> A robin redbreast in a cage
> Puts all Heaven in a rage.

It is the poorest jog-trot and doggerel of a poem that any first-class man has written. There is no music in it, and a poem without its music is rubbish. There is nothing to quarrel with in its thought, but it is just rhymed prose.

I don't think I know any poem of Blake's that is perfect. There are perfect verses. But also I do not know any poem of his that I would agree to be without. Criticism hasn't really got at him yet, although he promises indeed to be the most criticized poet that ever lived.

Indeed, Blake-criticism hasn't truly got anywhere yet. There are two schools of it. One, a very impatient one, says simply and downrightly that Blake was a madman. Even as late as only a few yester-years ago G. K. Chesterton said that Blake was mad. Lots of critics had said it before him.

The other school of Blake-criticism is a sentimental one, and holds that this poet is a gifted infant, and is to be forgiven everything and anything, and is to be just loved and praised and petted and marvelled at as the best baby ever.

Through the whole of his work, I have not come across one incident to support the idea of his madness; nor is there much to justify a sentimental evaluation of him or his work. The man who wrote the best epigrams in our language was no

simpleton, and no man's fool. Quite a quantity of his verse was
written between his twelfth year and his twentieth. This is the
greatest poetry ever written by a young person; and this, and
much more, is the best and largest collection of what we call
"pure poetry" in the language. Blake is the master of that
lovely, almost unearthly metric, and of that simple, unreasonable elation which we call "pure."

Critically, there truly is a trouble about Blake. He was not
a serious poet; he was not a serious painter; he was not a
serious philosopher; he was not quite a serious religious—he
got religion and philosophy mixed up, and those two don't
mix well. But he was a poet, he was an artist, he was a philosopher, he was a lover of God, and he was all these as most
of us are not. Artistically and otherwise he never quite grew
up; he just wouldn't; there is a childishness of the Saint which
the philosopher doesn't know much about.

Blake died at seventy years of age—not one day, and not
one disaster older than he had been when he was twelve or
twenty. He had much to contend with, and had he been a
complainer, much to complain of. All through his life he had
been over-worked and under-paid, and under-praised. If any
poetic genius was ever cheated, Blake could have felt cheated.
Year in and year out he gave prodigally and got little in return; so little that if he had stated that he got nothing from
life except what he brought to it that statement could be considered as correct and just.

He lived on about ten shillings a week all his life, and he
said nothing about it. He was overlooked by the great and the
good, and he said nothing about it. He took refuge in God in
a way that Milton didn't need to take refuge in some Urania;
and at the end of his life he was still in love with poetry, still

in love with painting, still in love with philosophy, and still in love with God.

He lived and died in love with Love, whatever that is, and he died singing, like a lark or like a crow, but singing he died. His life and his living of it, his death and his dying of it, were marvellous. His work doesn't bother much about being "great"; it is wonderful instead. He is the genius and there is no one like him, and he is The Beloved, and there is no one better worth loving, and he was given little enough of love either.

John Donne

(1946)

THE art of poetry, every art in fact, needs within the artist a certain tranquillity of being. John Donne had none of this. His desires, his loyalties, his ambitions were at odds with each other.

He had many desires, much ambition, and a certain special loyalty which has nothing to do with either of these, for he was at odds with the world, the flesh and the spirit. He was not only a man racked with conflicting qualities, he was a poet similarly on that rack, and his poetry is too often an immediate, *personal* utterance, and has too often missed that transcending song which evades mere personal experience, and attains and utters the truth and the soul of every man.

Donne was at once a sensualist, a philosopher and a deeply religious man. We may take it that a poet must be these three anyhow, for if one of these is absent the heart of poetry is missing also. But there is yet a quality which gathers these together and makes of their diversity that unity which alone is lovely, and which adds the poetry to the poem.

Milton, defining poetry, stated that it must be "simple, sensuous and passionate," and his definition stands to this day as the most comprehensive that any poet has given us.

John Donne was sensuous and passionate, and he was these in a degree that no other poet can challenge—but he was not "simple," and, indeed, he scarcely knew what that word can signify, for the term "simple" has a significance rather than a meaning. He and his poetry exist together in a complication which was purely personal to him, and which he did not know how to resolve, and, indeed, which he did not know needed any resolution.

He is the wit in verse, and the wit is not at home in simplicity, and scarcely dares attempt it.

Donne should have been the Prince of Poets; instead he is the Prince of Wits. A prose statement continually threatens him because of this, for wit and poetry are enemies, but so powerful is Donne that he stands against this almost as a fortress would, and by sheer power almost he smashes it back. Had he succeeded in this he would be one with, the equal of, Chaucer and Spenser and Shakespeare, and would be the glory that he should be instead of the enigma that he is.

When John Donne was born, Shakespeare was nine years of age, Spenser was twenty-one. Donne was born, that is, into the strangest age of English history. The Great Age begins in 1560 and ends in 1660. This literature begins with Shakespeare and ends with Herrick, and among the names that make up this splendid tale John Donne, strictly upon his talent, should have been the second greatest of them all.

We don't know what the future will decide in this matter —he may yet be given that station, for it is harder to kill John

Donne than it is to slay the Phoenix. He keeps coming up again. When the critic has slated John Donne almost to death there he is the next day, upright and challenging and irrepressible. He is the solitary man: the "strayed traveller under the hill."

The majority of critics hate him—but they pass, and he remains, Poetry's enigma! Ben Jonson said of him that in certain respects Donne was the greatest poet living, and we following Ben Jonson, if we cannot agree with that criticism, as certainly we dare not disagree with it.

Donne's father was a wealthy merchant, his mother was a lady. He was educated at Oxford and Cambridge and Lincoln's Inn, and he was specially trained for the Catholic priesthood. When he was coming to responsible years he had to relinquish this vocation, and this same relinquishment was what his soul and his art had to contend with. Something essential was wiped out of life for him. It was not only poetry that he could not simplify: he had somehow to simplify the religious revolution into which he was born, and simplify his acceptance of a future into which the new Protestant State and his own worldly ambitions both forced and enticed him.

He travelled in Italy, Spain and Germany. He met the full force of the Renaissance, and he lived in these travellings as splendidly as his purse allowed. His father was dead, and by the time he was twenty years of age Donne had dissipated his inheritance.

When he came home he had to get a patron and a job. There was no possible work for such a man except in the Church, and, although he had been trained in the Catholic System, he had to remove bag and baggage into the Protestant State. He was deeply religious, but he was also profoundly ambitious. Everything that was about him thwarted everything that was within him, and the note that is urgent in his work is passion and melancholy, sensuality and pessimism. These are not absent from Elizabethan literature; they are, indeed, main strands in that astounding and declining splendour; but Donne was mastered by them all in a degree that no one else can show, for being at once religious and ambitious, he had to compromise with his conscience, and like it.

He was, by his patron and by the King, ordered into the Church, and he quickly obtained preferment. He was a great wit, a learned and magnificent orator, and he quickly made his way in the Church: he finally became Dean of St. Paul's, and in his preachings there he became the Bossuet of England. There are critics who prefer Donne's prose to his verse: I think they are mad, but Donne himself in his old age agreed with them, and stated that he wished all his verse could be destroyed —here is the most horrid recantation ever made by a genius; his deanery had got him down, and he was recanting, not only Catholicism, but also, and even, "whining poetry" as he called it.

His poetry falls into three degrees and periods. The early amorous verse, the Epistles and Satires, and his later religious and philosophical poetry. I can here only speak of one of these.

Sometimes his amatory poems are referred to as Lovepoems. There is, however, a distinction to be made here. The great love-poems in English are not passionate outpourings, for a love-poem is conceived in tenderness, and is uttered as tenderness. A love-poem is as simple as a poem can possibly be, and it is satisfying as no other poem can be; a love-poem comes as effortlessly and irresistibly as a Spring flower; and a lovepoem belongs to every lover that lives. Passion and wit, and even splendour, what have these to do with love! These, that know nothing of tenderness, and are the qualities of impending anger and antagonism! Too much of Donne's love-poetry is conceived in wit, and conducted in a passion that is akin to rage. But he did fall in love, with his wife, and tenderness did come to his verse when he speaks to her or of her.

The poetic love-statement also is *lyrical,* but Donne's love-statement is too often dramatic, and every dramatic utterance on love is a lie, or does somewhat falsify that, and every other emotional value, that is submitted to it. We lose shamefacedness, and gain cheek. For love is private, and is unheard and unseen of others, while dramatic love is public, and is posturing and bawling. The thing passion belongs to drama, and has nothing to do with love. Donne was shameless—he was a dramatic wit.

And then, when one has said so, there remain Donne's love-poems, each a witty, dramatic, outrageous publicity and posturing, but the critic who would elect to be without these love-poems of Donne has never been born, and will never live. We may mourn, perhaps, that this poet loved a job a little more than he loved his conscience, that he praised patrons a little more than he praised life, and that he wooed prose a little more than he wooed poetry, but Ben Jonson's statement, whether we like it or don't like it, cannot be got away from. "In certain things," said he, "Donne is the greatest poet that lives"; and these "certain things" are not few. For reasons which I have tried hastily to indicate he is not with Shakespeare and Spenser, and then I would also say that his poetic work is the most "remarkable" collection of poetic material in the English language.

JAMES, SEUMAS & JACQUES

On His Poems: I

(1940)

EVERYTHING a man says about his work is a piece of his autobiography. I will try to bring you into the workshop of a
writer of verse, and show you what such a writer is at.

All writing is an odd occupation indeed, but writing verse
is odder still. In prose the worker knows to a large and a
guiding degree what the job is about. In verse he doesn't know
anything of the kind, he doesn't know anything about it at all;
but you put your trust in something, you put your trust in
verse itself, and you feel, on the whole, pretty sure that if you
don't interfere too much she will do the job much better than
you could.

I don't know whether poetry is a man's servant or his
mistress. She certainly takes days off, and she seems certainly to
prefer younger men to wiser men, and she certainly only comes
back when she wants to. It is, as I said, a very odd occupation,
or an even more odd enslavement. But if she *is* the mistress

her wages are good. She pays in delight, although she does warn you that you will make nothing out of it.

When I was a younger man I used to try to do all kinds of things in verse. I should add that I never really knew what I was trying to do until the job was finished, and then the good little poem itself showed me just what it had been at. I think I have never written a poem that didn't astonish me when I got to the end. On the route it had seemed to be about this and that, but at the end it had switched and was about the other.

You will understand, of course, that This and That and the Other are the only things you can write about, and that the What's-its-name called This is about the only thing that most people write about. In other words the popular author writes about This, the good writer writes about That, the poet writes about the Other. No one at all in our history has been able to write about all three except Chaucer and Shakespeare, and these two did it with no trouble whatever.

But to return to my own workshop: when I was ready to write a poem there was never more than one idea in my head. A very simple idea too, for it can be expressed in four words. The four words are: "I have a poem." That is all there was to it. My conscious mind never had any idea, never cared a rap, as to what the poem would be about, but we, my conscious mind and I, were perfectly certain that we had a poem, and that very shortly the poem itself would tell us what was in the bag, and we would then tell it whether it was a good poem or a dud. Duds happen only now and again between one's twenty-fives and forty-fives, but they tend to happen every day after fifty-five, and after sixty nothing else happens but duds—Bless them! there's lots of brains in duds but no blood.

In those days I never wrote just one poem and called it a day: I almost always wrote three of them—one of these was the actual poem that had dared me try a fall with it, the other two were just excess of energy, and I expect the real poem hated them both as illegitimate, and conceived me as a partner she dared scarcely let out of her sight. Nor was I completely satisfied either, for I noticed that she was giving other fellows pretty good poems that she might have given to me.

The plain fact, so far as I can isolate it, is that you think about a poem after you have written it, and that you don't think about it at all while you are writing it. There is a kind of spring-board out and away somewhere, and a poem does a cannon or a somersault off this and pops into your head with a splash that leaves you dizzy and drenched and drunken, and you only know that you have been the busiest man in the world after she's gone, and by the inordinate swelling of your head.

The poems I will give to you are only given as examples from the workshop. This quite small one tantalized me a bit because I could not make out where it was going nor whom it was about, and it wasn't until the last two lines were finished that I spotted it was about a cat, our good, black cat, Mr. Wow. Other people's cats, ordinary cats that is, say "Mieeou" when they want to be let out or let in, but our magnificent, coal-black, golden-eyed, chinchilla-ruffed hero said "Wow" and stuck to it. You will notice that the poem does not let its cat out of the bag until the very last line, and, thereupon, you may notice that the whole poem is pure cat, and a black cat at that —it is called "The Fur Coat":

> I walked out in my coat of pride;
> I looked about on every side;
>
> And said the mountains should not be
> Just where they were, and that the sea

Was out of place, and that the beech
Should be an oak! And then from each

I turned in dignity, as if
They were not there! I sniffed a sniff;

And climbed upon my sunny shelf;
And sneezed a while; and scratched myself.

Now there is another creature, not so much cat, perhaps,
as cattish, and as my poem about this lady went its sinuous way
I wondered why it was making me work so hard at just stuff-
and-nonsense, and if it knew where it had taken the bus for;
and suddenly, again, the last two lines turned up the lights,
and I gave a giggle and a sigh at the trick the verse had played
me. This is called, "Nora Criona":

I have looked him round and looked him through,
Know everything that he will do

In such a case, and such a case;
And, when a frown comes on his face,

I dream of it, and when a smile
I trace its sources in a while.

He cannot do a thing but I
Peep and find the reason why;

For I love him, and I seek,
Every evening in the week,

To peep behind his frowning eye
With little query, little pry,

And make him, if a woman can,
Happier than any man.

—Yesterday he gripped her tight,
And cut her throat. And serve her right!

All along in verse I have found the same thing happening.
The poem leads me down the garden path, chirping all about
roses and radishes and pansies and peas, and then in the last
verse it spills its real beans, and it and I are perfectly satisfied
that, however we got there, there we are.

Every now and again I have found myself wishing that I
could stand a poem a drink. I should love to present a bucket
of carrots to my poem, "The Goat Paths," but I should have to
give a restorative—brandy perhaps—to its last stanza.

On His Poems: II

(1946)

DURING my time I expect that some two thousand men and women have written verse, and published it, and died; and not an hundred people had read their works, and not one soul will ever speak of their poems again. Their work lived with them, and died with them. It was poorish poetry perhaps, but they had their own fun out of the game, they did put every ounce of will and skill that they possessed into their hobby, they never made a penny out of it, and they felt like the top of the world. It was well worth doing, even though it was no good.

Meanwhile, among the few that I knew personally only the very bad writers ever referred to themselves as "poets"; the others said they "wrote verse" and left it at that. The term "poet" is a title that is conferred on you when you've been dead between thirty and fifty years. You get it, or you don't, when criticism has made up its mind about your stuff. It takes about thirty years for reviewing to transform into criticism. There is no such thing as a present critic on present work.

I remember being scandalized—horrified, really—when I was a youngster by a conversation between W. B. Yeats and George Russell. These—as I then thought—old men were talking to me: and as I now see, were warning me not to be too bumptious, and not to expect a dish of fame or a bag of kudos from the verse that I was then writing in a very frenzy of writing. I used to stop people in the street and bawl my new poem at them; so did every other poet in Dublin. "Twinkle, twinkle, little star," said I, proudly, and they all said as much to me.

The two great men held that in the forty-odd millions of our population there is an audience for the well-known poet of about one thousand readers, and that all the rest about fame and fortune is moonshine. Well, about this possible thousand of readers, we had better remember that not quite fifteen people had read Keats when he died, and they all hated him; not fifty had read Shelley when he popped out of this dome of many-coloured glass, and forty of them loathed him. Wordsworth was quite an old man before people stopped calling him words and no worth; and Milton got the most famous ten pounds in history for *Paradise Lost* and nothing at all for the miraculous rest and remainder of his great work.

A poet, a painter—the artist in general—is a person with a hobby, and your hobby is the only thing to which you give the whole of your brain, and the total square inch of your soul, and every bit of the rest of your time that you can spare from making a living. I knew a fellow that gave up a steady fifteen bob a week to be a poet; he made nearly half a crown a month at it, and died hungry but happy.

The Dublin that I was born into was, as I now see, a very odd city. It was just large enough to be big, and small enough to be completely knowable. In one direction, if you cycled for a quarter of an hour, you came on the sea; in another direction a quarter of an hour brought you to the lovely little mountains that were designed by heaven and sculptured by Praxiteles, and a third hike planted you in what seemed an illimitable plain, where lies the ghost of Tara of the Kings, the Secret City of the Heart.

Dublin is a city packed with herrings and apples and public-houses, and that, believe me, is a well-packed city. There was very little show of life in the comely streets, but behind the doors of its houses life was riotous. I think I grew up among the wittiest conversationalists of the world, and every man-jack and woman-jill of them seemed to be writing verse, and reciting it at each other, and at you. There were dreadful moments in which you thought that you would never get your own poem in, but, if you were as determined as they were, you got it in all right, even though nobody listened to it. How can a poet listen to another fellow's verse! 'Tis a kind of incest.

Even the people whom you didn't know, and who were obviously trotting into a tea-shop in Grafton Street, looked as though they had just come out of a poem, or were just going into one. You go into a poem rather soberly; if you don't come out of it drunk 'tis no poem. I made a note about those lovely likeable unknowns with feathers in their hats and plumes in their souls:

> At four o'clock in dainty talk
> Lords and lovely ladies walk,
> With a gentle dignity,
> From the Green to Trinity.
>
> And at five o'clock they take
> In a café, tea and cake;

Then they call a carriage, and
Drive back into Fairy Land.

Every Dublin person can recognize himself and herself in
those two verses. 'Tis a speaking likeness. I think that if you
lived in the Dublin of that day you had to write verse, or
pretend to be a foreigner. As to how *I* came to write it—that
is almost impossible to say, for I had neither the background
nor the training that would warrant a literary way of life.

On His Poems: III

(Undated)

Now this chap that I'm talking about, his name was James, Seumas and Jacques. He answered to all these names like a well trained pup, and he also came if you whistled. He told me how it was that he took to writing verse—"I didn't do it intentionally," said he, "I was told to do it."

Before I turned over a new leaf and became a poet (he went on) I was a gymnast. I was short and light and strong and seventeen years of age, and there's nothing better than that except to be tall and heavy and stronger and twenty years of age (between seventeen and twenty there are fifteen missing years). I wasn't bad at the game and in my second year our team won the championship of Ireland, and I was on it.

I remember that match especially because I had right then the first and only gumboil of my life. It was a marvel, and everyone complimented me on it. It was twice as big as a tennis ball and it felt twice as big as a football, so that I looked like the most lop-sided creature that ever crawled down a tree or up a drain. Every time I had to do something the audience cheered my jaw to the echo, and strong women wept at me about it.

I remember that match also because there was a horrid disappointment in it. There had always been gold medals given for this event, but they gave us silver medals, and my team were so angry about it that we marched into a tobacconist shop, planted our medals on the counter and asked for a packet of Woodbines in exchange.

But what I'm getting at is another thing altogether. There is a thing called tact, and its operation is very strange. You can learn some of the *forms* of it, but if it isn't born in you you never get it really. There is a bodily tact, a mental tact, a social tact, and this is in every event what we prefer to call style.

There used to be a continuous order from our gym instructor which applied to everything whatever that one was doing. The order was "point your toes." That, in a certain way, was a meaningless order. The "pointing" had to be done at a certain split second of a certain very rapid swing, and no one could tell what was the spot of the flying movement at which one pointed one's toes in a split second. This is the mysterious part; we nearly all did know, and we went up and up like a squirrel hopping the twigs or a lark splitting the air.

This is the tact of the body. It is knowledge itself. And the more so because it is completely unconscious, and completely reliable. There were some few men who hadn't got this knowledge. We had a saying in those days about a certain unwieldy lover that he won his girl through main strength and ignorance. That is how these tactless chaps went up. If you can imagine a very highly energized half-ton of coal doing a hop, skip and a jump you will see that the hop might come off, the jump could come off, but the skip never, and without that skip the job is done through main strength and ignorance.

It is odd that the knowledge I am speaking of and which I call "tact" never lets you down, and it never lets anyone else down either.

Some of us men would go to a music-hall to see a gymnastic turn, and as I looked at the feat that was in progress my mind would say to me, "I can do that," and next evening at the gym I would do that particular trick or feat. I think that my mind never once fooled me in this matter. Then, a few years afterwards, the very same thing happened to me in another medium.

I loved reading, and I loved eating, and to do these two things at the same time seemed to me to be the height of bliss. I loved reading so much that when I couldn't get a real book to read I would even read poetry. That happened to me one time. I had nothing to read, and so I was reading the *Songs of Innocence* of William Blake, when, quite suddenly, quite out of the blue, my mind whispered to me, "I can do that."

I was delighted, as I always was when my mind condescended to notice that I was present. So I went to bed with a note-book and a pencil, and during that night of the nights I wrote twenty-five poems, and I could have written fifty but that morning had come, and I had to get up and go to work.

As there is a tact of the body so there is a tact of the mind, and if you are as well bred towards the matter you are handling with your pen as you are to the people you meet, so your stuff becomes effortless, and that "effortlessness" is style, or the tact of the game, in sport and in art and in living.

Here is the very first piece of verse that I wrote that night, "The Rivals":

I heard a bird at dawn
  Singing sweetly on a tree,
That the dew was on the lawn,
  And the wind was on the lea;
But I didn't listen to him,
  For he didn't sing to me.

I didn't listen to him,
  For he didn't sing to me
That the dew was on the lawn
  And the wind was on the lea;
I was singing at the time
  Just as prettily as he.

I was singing all the time,
  Just as prettily as he,
About the dew upon the lawn
  And the wind upon the lea;
So I didn't listen to him
  As he sang upon a tree.

On His Poems: IV

(1947)

O F COURSE I have to pretend that I know how I came to write my poems, but I'll also have to admit, as between us, that I only know in a sort of a way. I've never sat down, and said to myself, "Go to, I'll now write a poem." It really happened the other way about, and I had very little say in the matter.

What actually happened was that a poem grabbed me by the back of the neck, and said, "Sit down and write me." So down I sat, wondering a bit what it would be about, and there I was being dictated to by this utter stranger, who, also, always said to me, "You do me well, or I'll knock your block off." And, believe me, I've always worked harder for that poem-thing than I've ever worked to get that famous old piece of meat and two veg.

When the poem is finished that's another matter. I know now what it was about, and, up to a point, I know how it was done. There's a process, or a ghost, or something or other

222

in the mind, which we call the unconscious but don't let that name worry you. It's called that because it seems to be able to do most of its work without having to bother thinking about it, and it goes along so easily that you, who are conscious, don't seem to have much, or even anything, to do with it. That, generally, is the way a poem is born. That's the way by which art and music and humour, and a whole lot of other things, come into life. . . . First, there they are not, and then, pretty suddenly, there they are.

Now, as to how a poem is written, or as to how a poem writes itself: when I was very young I used to meet a number of quite old people. They looked old, too. They had white hair, and cracked voices, and shivery hands, and their legs used to have a habit of folding up under them if somebody wasn't around to prop 'em up.

People don't get as old as that nowadays. They used to start getting old and fat about fifty, and then they got thin and stiff about sixty and then they got all wobbly and odd; but nowadays we people are as lively as a pet lamb when we're ninety. We live in a different world, I think, and I think too that we are quite different people from what great-grand-papa and great-grand-mama used to be.

When I started to write verse some of these people came into my mind now and again, and I wrote about them as well as I could. I remember that one time I asked an old lady what it felt like to be old, and she answered me very simply, very honestly—"It feels shtiff-like," said she. Well, I'd never felt stiff, so I wasn't able to make much out of that knowledge.

Then, another time, I remembered an old gentleman. I used to sit on his knee now and again, and he used to make faces at me now and again. He had white whiskers under his chin, and his ears used to wiggle a bit. So one time, later on,

I made a little poem about him, and this is the queer thing and the point about this old-age stuff, the little poem revealed to me what it was that I really thought about that old gentleman. His name was "Danny Murphy" and so far as I could get him, here he is:

He was as old as old can be,
His little eye could scarcely see,
His mouth was sunken in between
His nose and chin, and he was lean
And twisted up and withered quite
So that he couldn't walk aright.

His pipe was always going out,
And then he'd have to search about
In all his pockets, and he'd mow
—O, deary me! and, musha now!—
And then he'd light his pipe, and then
He'd let it go clean out again.

He couldn't dance or jump or run,
Or ever have a bit of fun
Like me and Susan, when we shout
And jump and throw ourselves about:
—But when he laughed, then you could see
He was as young as young could be!

And I've got another old gentleman up my sleeve, and I don't know how he got there, but perhaps you won't like him so much. In this poem he's in a very bad temper, for one thing: but then after all he's old, and he's cold, and he's got a cough, and he's rheumatic, and he has a pain in his stomach, and he has an earache, and if there are any more of those

things he has them too, so there's nothing to do about it, and
here he is being as bad-tempered as he can manage. I can't
remember that I ever met him, and yet—it's strange—I know
all about him, and he did get into my mind somehow. I just
thought of him as "Ould Snarley-Gob"—the word "gob," by
the by, in Irish means "the beak of a bird"—and this is how he
goes:

> There was a little fire in the grate;
> A fistful of red coal,
> Might warm a soul,
> But scarce could heat a body that had weight—
> Not mine, at any rate.
>
> A glum old man was sitting by the fire
> With wrinkled brow,
> Warming himself, somehow;
> And mumbling low, this melancholy sire,
> A singular desire.
>
> If I were young again, said he, if I
> Were only young again,
> I'd laugh at pain!
> I'd jeer at people groaning, and I'd try
> To pinch them ere they'd die!
>
> The young folk laugh and jump about and play
> And I am old,
> And grey, and cold!
> If I were only young again, and they
> Were old, and cold, and grey,
>
> I'd pull them from the fire, I'd jeer and shout
> I'd say, for fun,

Get up and run
And warm yourself, you lazy, doddering lout!
Get up and run about!

One time I used to love trotting about in the Dublin Hills. It was very wonderful, for although the hills are close to a fairly big city they are yet almost as solitary as a desert. Personally, I think that everybody needs to be alone now and again, but you've got to choose your place to be alone in. When you go to the country, or when you go to the sea, you should go in your crowd, for you don't take the country or the sea with you—they aren't in your heart.

But when you go up the mountain you should go by yourself, and when you're up there, you might, as it were, open your ears and listen, and open your eyes and look. You will be listening to the strangest thing that is in our world: you'll be listening to solitude, and you will be looking at solitude too, and you may get a sense of it, and of yourself, that you will never get anywhere else.

I'll break off there for a moment, for I remember that I was in a bad temper one day, and what did I do? I insulted a mountain. Maybe there was somebody with me, or maybe it was raining and I couldn't go up the hill. Anyway, the point is that in this little verse—it's very little—there are five or six lines which you must say in one breath; and then you should be as out of breath as if you had climbed the hill. Here are the lines; "The Paps of Dana":

The mountains stand, and stare around,
They are far too proud to speak;

Altho' they are rooted in the ground,
Up they go—peak after peak,

Beyond the tallest house; and still
Climbing over tree and hill,

Until you'd think they'd never stop
Going up, top over top

Into the clouds—Still I mark
That a linnet, thrush or lark

Flying just as high, can sing
As if he'd not done anything!

I think the mountains ought to be
Taught a little modesty!

Every now and then I used to meet something or other up on the hills, and at times I used to meet an odd goat or two away up there in the hills, and one day I followed a goat-path in order to have another look at a certain he-goat who had lovely, hard, clear grey eyes, and also he had beautiful whiskers.

I am inclined to think that the three most beautiful things in the world are: a goat, a donkey and a mountain. I mean by that, any goat, any ass and any mountain.

Now the path that is made by a goat on a hill is very curious. It doesn't go in a straight line through the heather; it twists away from itself every three feet or so, and this little path is only about six inches wide, if that much. It goes round and about, and it doesn't care where it goes. So I tried to write these lonely little paths, and the lonely, lovely little feet that had stamped them out, the daintiest little feet in the world. For there are two sets of dainty feet: there are the feet of the goats, and the hind legs of the donkey. You watch the hind

legs of the donkey some time and you will see the prettiest
movement of feet that you will ever see.

I call this little poem "The Goat-Paths." And here's how
it goes:

> The crooked paths
> Go every way
> Upon the hill
> —They wind about
> Through the heather,
> In and out
> Of a quiet
> Sunniness.
>
> And the goats,
> Day after day,
> Stray
> In sunny
> Quietness;
> Cropping here,
> And cropping there
> —As they pause,
> And turn,
> And pass—
> Now a bit
> Of heather spray,
> Now a mouthful
> Of the grass.
>
> In the deeper
> Sunniness;
> In the place
> Where nothing stirs;
> Quietly

In quietness;
In the quiet
Of the furze
They stand a while;
They dream;
They lie;
They stare
Upon the roving sky.

If you approach
They run away!
They will stare,
And stamp,
And bound
With a sudden angry sound,
To the sunny
Quietude;
To crouch again,
Where nothing stirs,
In the quiet
Of the furze:
To crouch them down again,
And brood,
In the sunny
Solitude.

Were I but
As free
As they,
I would stray
Away
And brood;
I would beat
A hidden way,

Through the quiet
Heather spray,
To a sunny
Solitude.

And should you come
I'd run away!
I would make an angry sound,
I would stare,
And stamp,
And bound
To the deeper
Quietude;
To the place
Where nothing stirs
In the quiet
Of the furze.

In that airy
Quietness
I would dream
As long as they:
Through the quiet
Sunniness
I would stray
Away
And brood,
All among
The heather spray
In a sunny
Solitude.

—I would think
Until I found

Something
I can never find;
—Something
Lying
On the ground,
In the bottom
Of my mind.

I remember the night—it was at night—that I wrote my first piece of verse. I sat up in bed that night from eleven o'clock until five o'clock in the morning, and by that time I had written down twenty-five poems. They were all different and they were all so easy that it was a perfect pleasure to write them. As against that is the fact that I once had to wait three years in order to get the last line of another poem of four verses—I got it.

You see, there are no rules about making poems. You all know from your studies in grammar that there are a few things in English which you cannot do. For example, you cannot make a sentence which hasn't got a verb in it, for a sentence walks about on its verbs the way you and I walk about on our feet. All the same, I once wrote a poem and it is composed of one noun, fourteen adjectives, and no verb.

The reason I wrote it is this: I was reading a long poem by Spenser, the Elizabethan poet. At a certain point in his work Spenser says something like, "And there we were, out in the main-sea deep." I turned the book upside down, grabbed a pencil and said, "Spenser hadn't time to write it—I'll write it for him." And in one minute my little poem was written for Spenser, and it hasn't got a verb in it, but I tried to fill it full with the noise and the roll and the swaying of great waters. I called it "The Main-Deep" and this is how it goes:

The long-rólling,
Steady-póuring,
Deep-trenchéd
Green billów:

The wide-toppéd,
Unbróken
Green-glacid,
Slow-sliding,

Cold-flushing,
—On—on—on—
Chill-rushing,
Hush-hushing,

. . . Hush-hushing . . .

Sometime or other you have all put a big shell to your ear, and listened to the curious sound that seems to come out of it into your ear. Sometimes when you are by the sea, alone, and at night, you can hear something of that sound. I think of it as rather a grey kind of a whisper, not so much a sound as perhaps the ghost of a sound. When I was a very small boy a woman put a shell against my ear, and said to me, "Listen, son, and you'll hear the sea." And then, later on, I remembered that grey and gloomy and astonishing whispering that came to me out of "The Shell" and I tried to put that into words:

I

And then I pressed the shell
Close to my ear,
And listened well.

And straightway, like a bell,
Came low and clear
The slow, sad, murmur of far distant seas

Whipped by an icy breeze
Upon a shore
Wind-swept and desolate.

It was a sunless strand that never bore
The footprint of a man,
Nor felt the weight

Since time began
Of any human quality or stir,
Save what the dreary winds and waves incur.

II

And in the hush of waters was the sound
Of pebbles, rolling round;
For ever rolling, with a hollow sound:

And bubbling sea-weeds, as the waters go,
Swish to and fro
Their long cold tentacles of slimy grey:

There was no day;
Nor ever came a night
Setting the stars alight

To wonder at the moon:
Was twilight only, and the frightened croon,
Smitten to whimpers, of the dreary wind

And waves that journeyed blind . . .
And then I loosed my ear—Oh, it was sweet
To hear a cart go jolting down the street.

And now here's another piece of verse about a man. He lived a couple of hundred years ago. His name was David O' Bruadair, and one day he got into a bad temper, and he wrote a poem about it.

He was out, as we've just been, on the hills, and he got very thirsty walking. He came to a tavern, walked in and asked the girl behind the counter for a drink. She had a good look at him, and she asked him a horrible question. She said to him, "Have you any money?" She was a suspicious soul.

Well, O' Bruadair was a poet. He hadn't got any money, he never had any money, he never would have any money. Of course, he told her the truth that he hadn't got any, and that he wasn't asking her for money, he was only asking her for a drink.

So the girl—she must have been a big girl—got over the counter, and she grabbed O' Bruadair, and she pitched him out of the door. Right there and then David composed a poem at her, and we may be certain that he said it at her, and we may be certain, too, that she didn't like one word of it. This is what O' Bruadair said about her, and *to* her ("A Glass of Beer"):

The lanky hank of a she in the inn over there
Nearly killed me for asking the loan of a glass of beer;
May the devil grip the whey-faced slut by the hair,
And beat bad manners out of her skin for a year.

That parboiled ape, with the toughest jaw you will see
On virtue's path, and a voice that would rasp the dead,

Came roaring and raging the minute she looked at me,
And threw me out of the house on the back of my head!

If I asked her master he'd give me a cask a day;
But she, with the beer at hand, not a gill would arrange!
May she marry a ghost and bear him a kitten, and may
The High King of Glory permit her to get the mange.

Here's a different thing altogether. There are some matters
we all understand. We all feel for whatever is in trouble, or in
pain. So here's a poem which I call "The Snare." And there's
a little creature caught in the snare:

I hear a sudden cry of pain!
There is a rabbit in a snare:
Now I hear the cry again,
But I cannot tell from where.

But I cannot tell from where
He is calling out for aid!
Crying on the frightened air,
Making everything afraid!

Making everything afraid!
Wrinkling up his little face!
As he cries again for aid;
—And I cannot find the place!

And I cannot find the place
Where his paw is in the snare!
Little One! Oh, little One!
I am searching everywhere!

As far as that goes, nearly all creatures get into trouble, nearly all the little things of the world are in danger. So here I'm talking to those same "Little Things":

> Little things, that run, and quail,
> And die, in silence and despair!
>
> Little things, that fight, and fail,
> And fall, on sea, and earth, and air!
>
> All trapped and frightened little things,
> The mouse, the coney, hear our prayer!
>
> As we forgive those done to us,
> —The lamb, the linnet, and the hare—
>
> Forgive us all our trespasses,
> Little creatures, everywhere!

To end with, here's a scrap ["Cadence"] that gives me a very curious pleasure. It's very simple to read, but it wasn't simple to write. It isn't about anything special, or is it?

> See the lightning
> Leaping in the sky
> How fleet he goes:
>
> See the rose
> Leaping to the eye
> How neat she blows:
>
> See the mother
> Running to her child!
> How sweet she goes!

Living in a Chapel

(*ca.* 1942)

THERE are a lot of ways in which we are exactly alike. I have no sense of direction, for example, and that makes me second cousin to nearly everyone I meet. Then, again, I have a great sense of my own importance—that makes me first cousin of everyone I meet. And now, in addition to these other humanities, I'm an evacuee—that makes me the brother, and the best-beloved of everyone I meet.

People say to me, "Were you bombed out, or did you just run for it?" And I reply according to the day's weather. If it's sweet and sunny I say, "I always wanted to see these parts." If it's raining I say, "You are just as badly off one place as another." And if it's stormy I claim that I just blew in.

In these parts, westwardly away, where I now am, there are three things that can be done, one immediately after the other and without, apparently, any interval or any kind of warning. You can be rained to death, and then sunned to life, and thereon be blown to bits.

237

And the odd of it is, that whether it's raining or sunning or blowing, it is always lovely; and that no part of this countryside is ever the same, no matter how often you see it. Of course, all wet things look unhappy. A wet cat, or a wet blanket, look like misery itself: there they are, the wet things, and there isn't any thought of a joke in either; they look nothing at all like the same things dried. And so, when this landscape dries up it is delicious, and even when it's wet, 'tis astonishing.

Meanwhile, as an evac, I'm living on what I am slowly gathering is a mountain. Someone, anyone, might say here, "Hold your horses, you must know whether you are living on a mountain or not, for mountains are visible to the naked eye." My answer is that some mountains are flattish on the top, and this one is so corrugatedly topped, and has such extensive tops, you could imagine that whole counties could be stacked on these tops.

Also, if I may say so, it is a very different thing going up a mountain in a taxi, and going up one in knickerbockers, as most of us sporting people do. Personally I would hold that if you haven't barked all the gristle off your knees and rubbed all the skin off your elbows, you haven't been up a mountain at all. A real mountaineer should also have an imperfectly-broken neck, so that when ordinary people see him looking at them from half-way round they know that he has been up a mountain. But if you come up mountains from a railway station that is among them, and blimp up the rest of the way in a taxi that seems to be going down just as often as it goes up, you can't at last tell whether you're going up or down, you just say, "This is a bumpy land," and leave it at that.

I was, so, very pleased when I was told on the third day after my arrival that I was not only living in the Cotswolds, but that I was dwelling on the very highest lump of them.

During the last twenty odd years wars have completely ruined my sense of geography. In the war before this one we all learned more geography than we knew what to do with, and in this one we are learning a whole lot more. In my case, I can't hold places any more in mind. I get them so mixed up that they are all just simply a marmalade of places in my head, and I get them all wrong when I try to talk about them.

So a few days ago, talking to a man on the road, I praised his countryside, saying to him, enthusiastically, "I do love your Grampians."

He was properly worried when I loosed that one on him; but pulling himself together, he asserted with pride that there wasn't one single Gramp in a cartload of his native parts. And then, noticing that I was abashed, he told me that I was not only standing on the Cotswolds, but was actually living on the highest lump of them.

Then, in order to help him forget the insult of being Grampianized against his will, and against all geography, I asked him what was the meaning of the word "Cotswolds." He told me with the greatest good-will that he hadn't the ghost of an idea. So I tried to work it out for myself—

"Cots," I assured him, "are things that babies sleep in, and 'wold' is the second person, singular, of 'wild.' Thus, 'I am wild,' 'you are wold,' 'they are weald,' would be a correct form of speech."

"But," he interrupted earnestly, "what are you wild, and what am I wold about?"

"We are wild and wold about Cots," I answered, "about babies' prams sticking about all over the place, and they truly not there at all, and each of them with no baby in it that is just bawling nowhere about nothing, and getting the place a bad name."

"It's enough to make any man wold," said he earnestly.

"It's spooky stuff," I agreed, "and the less we say about it the better."

"But them babies that aren't there?" he inquired.

"Let them stay where they aren't," I answered.

I remembered then, and imparted to him, that when I was in Chicago I asked everyone I met what the word "Chicago" meant, but nobody knew. And then in San Francisco, a wise professor told me: " 'Chicago' means 'Wild Onion,' " said he; and I thought back on Chicago, the flattest city in the world, crouching beside a very flat lake, and knew that everyone that lived there was wild as a coot, from merely having to live flatly, and widely, and windily; and that very probably the onions that lived there were the wildest and most unprincipled onions on earth.

Still, I'm not living all over the Cotswolds. I am gathering three meals and a sleep in the oddest dwelling that anyone ever evacuated to. I am living in a Chapel.

I fancy that I must be the only person in the noblest islands of the world who lives in a Chapel without being a saint by profession, or by certificate, or even by saintly permission. And now I'm so used to living in a Chapel that I smoke my pipe in it, and trot in and out of it with buckets of water and bits of coal and yesterday's debris, and think nothing of it.

Still and all, in the watches of the night, when I awaken because of a driving rain or a howling wind or the two that mix and drive and howl into the kind of yowl that might be uttered by a completely desperate cat—then my mind wanders a little away, dwelling on those who came here, years ago, to worship, if their imaginations were vast enough for that vast act; or to pray, if life was pressing on them, or if unhoped-for hopes were dawning in them like the first faint stirrings of dayspring and a promise of the sun. So it is, at moments, a quieting and a disquieting domicile.

I came into occupation of it by the kindness of a famous musician. He gave a cottage nigh-by to a poor woman and her daughter who had been bombed right out of their twenty feet of London life. I think that he gives away whatever he has got, and I hope that he will henceforth get everything he wants from whoever has it, and that he always gets it for the same nothing that he gives his things away for.

If the reader has ever lived in a Chapel, he will know that, when the worshippers are gone home, there is nothing whatever in the Chapel except grace, plus a certain amount of dampness. He will know also that a little country Chapel is composed of four walls, and of precisely nothing else. But my Chapel, in addition to exactly nothing else, has a fireplace, and with that there we are, for where there's a fireplace there's a home.

Still it's a little odd, to a cityish person with London and Paris and New York well in his memory, to trot out every morning to the well for water, and wander away in the wood for twigs, and get away, the almighty remoteness of a few miles, to the town for the innumerable odds and ends that you won't live without until you have to. And then there is the black-out!

They used to say, in the distant ages of a year ago, "Sunrise and sunset": now we say, "Sunrise and black-out." Whatever else man does, whether as labour or for fun, the most unlovable job of work he ever did is the black-out. Everywhere 'tis a difficulty, and unwelcomed, and a drudge. But if you haven't had to black-out a piece of Church architecture, you haven't had to black-out at all.

The windows, seven of them, are a mile up, maybe a

couple of miles up, and they have that curious, inward, sloping-away from themselves which gives plenty of light inside but makes their blacking-out a job for engineers with a European reputation. So every night we go round the seven windows with a fifteen-foot pole, and we poke our black-outs the way they should go, even if it takes a month each night to do it.

But as we grow more expert, so does the Chapel grow more comely. A fireplace and a typewriting machine! What can man want more? And especially so when the neighbours come up the winding ways with presents of cabb-ages, cab-ines, and carr-ots, all won hardly from their rocky soil, and with their scuttles of coal, treasured surely enough, but given to the new-come neighbour with no more than a gesture and a smile of welcome. These are good things indeed, and we all need them, even if we don't want them. Even the rains and the winds are good—they wash and blow the petrol off one, and they make you feel new and clean as a fox or a ferret.

But there is yet something one can miss. I miss the dull thuddings that began at half past seven o'clock at night, in London, and that did not stop until half past six in the morning. One misses the boom-boom that droned round and round your house during all these hours; that was so near, and so far, and so intimidating, and so lived up to, and lived beyond. And one can miss a bit being with those who are still listening to those dull boomings and thuddings; who go asleep to them, and awaken among them, and go out about their businesses, and are not shaken into ill-humour nor shocked into private panic, but have been shaken into the utmost of helpfulness they can give to others.—London, thou art the flower of cities all. And if you could only manage to cart these Cotswolds with their wide and corrugated tops into Hyde Park, how aery, and gay, and lovely life would be; what excellent neighbours you would have, and how life would be even more worth living.

Villages

(1943)

I AM living in a part of the world which might be described as a pretty complete solitude lightly surrounded by villages. If I go, say, three miles in any direction I come to a village; and if I keep on going on, I am out of it again in from five to eight rather twisty minutes.

As to what a village looks like: in my parts it is a rather flattish kind of place surrounded by every kind of slope, grade, steep and contour that hills can dream of. There are also pits and declivities, and among these, two-foot streamlets are meandering and moaning like lost waters.

Of course, villages are not what they once were: for the village, as history knew it, went out with the crinoline and the clouded cane. First, the railway hit them hard, and then the bicycle about finished them off. Now comes the radio and the flivver, and 'tis good-night, village, and good-bye to it for ever.

In the not-so-very-long-ago every village on earth was exactly the same kind of place, and all these were inhabited by precisely the same kind of people. Timidish, ingrowing people they were, living among their cousins to the twentieth degree, and they knew that in the night darkness surrounded them, and that nothing stirred beyond their homes except sly little dangers that can nip and tuck better in the darkness than in the light, and that have their ways and means which are better left just as they are.

It was not the village people who kept the homes fairly secure in the two dark weeks of the moon. It was the cats and the dogs. So in every village there used to be a cat and a dog population almost as large as the human. These it was who kept the badgers and bogles, the red-eyed slavering ones at bay, and the village in security.

Now, here in my Cotswolds, all among the thick hills, in this tumbled land of blind corners and obedient black-outs, the winter nights are beginning to recall ancient days, and an almost lapsed life is creeping back, or slinking back. The "wolf with privy paw"—the fox, that is—is growing hopeful again, and is nosing the wind that he scarcely dared sniff on. He is taking another look round, and everything is no longer as secure as it used to be: for with the black-out there is no protecting window gleam, and with the meat ration there are no more dogs in the houses and few enough cats for that matter.

The privy paw pads where it will. The mouse is getting bold, the rat washes himself in any man's view, and the fox and badger are becoming different creatures. They take the air and promenade their fangs and tushes wherever they please, and the morning snow shows that they have been sitting on the doorstep, or squatting on the windowsill. After three years of no hunting and no dogs the young foxes have lost all fear, and are beginning to think they own the earth. They eat the cats and the hens, and they'll take a snack off the village elder when they weigh him up against the unfair distribution of the world's eatables.

Cats are taking to sleeping in of nights, and the badgers are rearing large hungry and fearless families in the dens and dumps of their native hummocks. Here, not a yard from the doorstep, the best cat the world has ever known, the wittiest angel that ever wore a lap out, has been deeply digested these three weeks past; and sixty hens, that clucked and cackled year by year, lay big brown eggs in heaven, or nowhere.

Not very long ago every village was the same. England or Ireland, China or mid-Africa, they all had their villages, and they were all held together by the local well, the local religion, the courtship of cousins and the horse. One could fancy that the village people talked mainly of these matters, and of each other's washing, and that they never talked about anything else. When there were—and it was only a half a lifetime ago—no newspapers and no bicycles the village was itself, but these things are here and the village is disappearing, or is so transforming that its own cow and pump can scarcely recognize it.

My earliest village was in Ireland, outside of Dublin, and to the mountains away. Mountains or hills in Ireland differ slightly from the same things elsewhere. In this, principally: they are beautifully drawn. The line of those hills, and the spacing of them, is exquisite. The hills elsewhere tend to be lumps; shaped rather by dynamite than by the pencil of Angels.

At the time I inhabited my first village I was about four years of age. I remember four years of age as if I never had got to more than five. I wore a bib and skirt like a girl. I think that a boy in Ireland used to be a girl until he was about ten years of age; he then grew rapidly in wickedness and had to be dressed accordingly. I had no shoes, nor had I ever, consciously, seen anyone who did wear them. The soles of one's little feet were as tough as the hoofs of a deer, and one could tramp on nettles, or jump on jagged rocks, without the slightest bother.

Of course, horses wore shoes. There was a man, indeed, who put shoes on his donkey, but he was thought eccentric. All the donkeys that I knew had their own very odd, flat, long, spinsterish kind of feet, and when they weren't working they wandered everywhere in the village and poked their furry noses into anywhere that smelled good. Only a woman with a broomstick can keep a donkey out of a house where bread is baking.

The nicest donkey I ever knew was named Jeremiah after a Prophet. His bray was loud and long, and was like a profoundly considered malediction among the hills. He was a famous athlete. He would climb on a heap of stones, then jump on to the wall, then he would climb on to the roof, and then he would eat the thatch off the roof. He took no notice whatever of bricks that were thrown at him while he was eating a roof: bricks falling on him might have been raindrops, and he ate with great rapidity.

He had the oddest taste in food. One day he came over to pet me. Then he got a second thought. He pulled off my petticoat and ate it. Then he pulled off my hat and he ate it, and only then did he caress me, which was what he really came to do. As he was telling, very loudly, how much he loved me, the next greatest friend of mine came over to see what was happening. She was the chief cow of the village, and she was called Mogue, after a Saint. She ate my bib. Then Jeremiah got angry at losing the bib, and he kicked Mogue. Then Mogue pucked him in the stomach. Then the three of us began to tell the world, and then the wives of the policeman, the publican, the blacksmith and the cobbler came running with broomsticks and flat-irons and lumps of coal, and they all asked me where I was bit, and where I was poked. And then one said joyfully that I was as right as ninepence, and the next said I was as right as rain. Then their husbands came out of the pub, and wanted to know what they were doing to the child. That nice donkey, Jeremiah, was killed the next year because he took to eating hens.

Among the most remarkable inhabitants of my village there were three or four completely unforgettable dogs whom I have completely forgotten. I expect that there is a small pack of dogs, and as many cats, buried in the childishness of every man; and the fact that he cannot remember a single thing about them doesn't interfere in the least with the fact that he loves them dearly, and can surmise a gentle eye and a wagging tail somewhere beyond bounds and well within grasp.

There is a word which we all use daily, although now it hasn't much sense. 'Tis a village word, and language preserves it from disappearing. That word is "the Neighbour." Once there was no more powerful and meaningful word than that, but now it only refers to the perfect stranger who goes to bed next door to you, and whom you sometimes hear and never see.

In the village of so few years ago the neighbour was the realest thing in your world. There were between fifty and a hundred of them—all cousins and droppers-in on each other—and they knew you from the cradle to the grave. The village knew, as your mother did, when you cut your first tooth; and it knew, as well as your father did, when you told your first lie. They knew when you robbed your first orchard, and when you first mitched from school. They knew when you first looked at a girl, and exactly how much you got for your first job of work. They knew every bit of good or ill fortune that had ever come to you, and they knew, without the slightest possibility of doubt, whether you were a good boy or a bad one.

And you knew as much about them. Every rheumatism that was in the village lodged in your mind and yelped there. You knew everybody's horse and goat and dog and cat; nor merely by sight, you knew them by name and by nature. And all of these creatures knew, just as well as the neighbour did, whether you were a good boy or a bad one; and they came to you, walking on their hind legs and wriggling, or they swerved and slunk and ran, just as the well-known facts warranted.

We are, of course, getting a deal of knowledge about matters in another way now. Literature and art, science and psychology are bringing us masses of information, but I doubt that the intimate human knowledge which was once the common culture of the village will ever visit the human mind again. The animals are gone, the old tales are going, the neighbour has almost disappeared, and no mass psychology will compensate for the fact that man increasingly must become more and more a stranger to man, and more and more an enigma.

That was the village I knew when I was a baby. The people belonging to it are all as unforgettable and all as forgotten as were the dogs and cats that I once knew so well. They are forgotten into the being itself of one's self; not petrified there, but living and lively, as the heart is, as the mind is.

Nothing Much

(1944)

I HAVE a little cottage away among the hills, and we had been gone for a fortnight from it. When we got back everything was as it had been before we left, except, of course, and very naturally, that everything that could turn green—anything made of leather, for example—had gone a thick, rich green.

They keep, you know, a kind of thing in the country which they call mildew, and I can never stop being astonished at what that stuff can do to one's only other pair of shoes to say nothing of a strap, a belt, and a pair of braces. My shoes were of a really remarkable green colour; and they felt green, if you know what I mean—clammy a bit, and a bit cabbagey.

I was standing by the window, upstairs, marvelling at mildew and mourning about shoes, and wondering what in the dickens and the deuce that green stuff could be, when my eye was caught by something else—a different colour altogether, a bright red colour all mixed in on a bright black. That cocktail of colour was a butterfly, and it was sitting just inside the window, on the ledge, looking, as I thought, eagerly and longingly at the outside world. Its airiness and loveliness of red and black was nearly as astonishing as the greenness of my shoes.

I was thinking, "You must be pretty tired of sitting in here, and you must be pretty hungry and thirsty as well." So I set about rescuing my little visitor; but as my hand hovered carefully, the butterfly did not move, and my next spot of noticing was that it was dead. Whatever that stuff "life" is—and I've got a pint or so of it myself, as you have—either the butterfly had lost its drop or two, or a droplet of life had mislaid one perfectly good butterfly.

I was thinking of the poor little creature dying there all alone, and mourning a bit for it, when I noticed that it was *not* alone. Just outside the window, a trifle lower on the ledge, two inches from the glass, there was another butterfly, equally sumptuous in red and black, equally poised and light and lovely. Also, as I soon saw, equally dead.

Two butterflies, one inside the glass and one outside, and both dead! I was a little horrified, as we all are when we see that the life which was here has gone from here, and we grasp the fact that if the coming of life is astonishing, so is its departure unreasonable and incredible. I don't think I bother much about death and myself, but I hate to see it creep or swoop or tumble or stumble on the bright little things of our world and our nature. We are all much of a muchness. A bird singing at you, or a tiger chewing your leg are not foreigners. We know what they are at: they are doing what we do, as we do, and there's the rub . . . and the mystery.

But there was something happening here which was unusual, and so—for after all, I'm not quite a man, I'm a writer— I began to wonder how it came that there were two of them, one a prisoner certainly, but the other free as the air itself, and yet the free one was as dead as the captive; and I began to marvel how such a thing could be.

There is only one way of getting at matters that puzzle you. The philosopher explains things away; the doctor cuts them away; the scientist analyses them away. The writer's way is different. Consciously or unconsciously the story-teller and the poet agree that everything whatever is part and parcel of himself, and that the actions of all creatures are precisely the actions which he would take were he placed in the same circumstances and undergoing the same experience. So I became two butterflies at once in order to understand what had happened.

Of course, I was only really curious about the creature that was outside the window. It could so easily have escaped, and yet it hadn't even tried to. The butterfly inside couldn't get out. It had died of imposed hunger and thirst and despair. That was its story. But here is the beautiful and terrible story of the outside free creature. It, too, had died of hunger and thirst and despair, but it had imposed these wretchednesses upon itself.

No, it had accepted, fully and freely, these final miseries as being all that life had to offer, since these were all that life was offering to its imprisoned comrade. As long as the creature inside had any life left in it, it could see that the comrade outside was still there, and could know that it was not alone; and to be alone is for all creatures much worse than terror and, perhaps, is more desolating than death. It was not deserted: life was standing by, and if necessary, would die with it. Whatever truth there must be in despair and misery and destruction, there was exactly as much truth in faithfulness right unto death, in love right unto death. Something surely was cancelled out of horror for the butterfly within, and a strange, a lovely gravity must have greatly comforted her as she died.

I have just used the word "she" about the captive butterfly

and I think I am justified in claiming that the prisoner was a female. You remember the old joke about how to find out whether your canary is a male or a female: you offer the bird a piece of sugar, and if he takes it it's a he, but if she takes it it's a she. Well, we can't get at the insect world quite so easily and sweetly, so we must do it in another way. Let's be butterflies for a moment. So!

Now we're butterflies. We have lovely red and black wings; we are lighter than the air itself; and we are happier than happiness. Also, we happen—and I am a little proud of this piece of magic—we happen to be female butterflies; but we can't go further into that just now, because, just now, we have caught sight of a friend of our species stuck inside a window-pane. He is doing all he can to get out, flying, fluttering and falling, and tiring and tiring and tiring. We are distressed surely, we are tormented, but we must fly away from that window, for it is not the business of a female to die for love: it is our business to live for love; and, no matter at what price, to reproduce our life and all life in our little ones. She may not die with love, or for love. She has to give birth to love and to all love: the unborn is her love.

So the dead butterfly outside the window must be the male. He is free to live or to die. Is he free? If there is any splendour in him, if he has vivacity and talent and pride he is free to die; not so much to die for her, but, at least, to die with her, seeing merely to it that she is not alone.

An Irishman's Days

(1945)

ONE day, away in a place, I saw a spider. You know the
creature. It isn't an animal because it doesn't bark, and it
isn't an insect because it has eight legs—two legs too many—
and that disqualifies it.

Talk about being in a jam! This spider was in a jam all
right. When you are unhappy and have, at the same time, to be
very careful, you are in a jam. In fact, any time you have to
think (which is the same thing as being very careful) you are
in sight of a jam, even if you aren't right in it.

I'm not very good about the maleness and femaleness of
things, but I knew that this creature was a lady, for the simple
reason that she had all her babies with her, festoons of them,
bunches and clusters and cart-loads of them. They were packed
up on her back so that she looked as though she was carrying
a small mountain. There must have been a couple of hundred
of them: tiny things, each about as big as a pin's head, and she
just didn't dare to move. I think she didn't dare to breathe, if a

spider does breathe. I think it a bit odd too that, while you and
I would just hate two hundred babies, a spider is able to love
every man-jack-and-jill of them. She isn't an animal, and she
isn't an insect—my guess is that she is an angel.

There was a lily-pond in the place I was staying—away in
Kentucky, U.S.A., it was—and one day, as I looked into the
lovely water, I saw her. There she was in the water, crouched
up, humped up, and she was as motionless as a stone. Apparently she had semaphored out, or thrilled out somehow, a
warning to the babies, and they too, all, were as motionless as
stones, and they were all, she must have thought, as good as
gold. She was doing all their thinking for them, and they were
doing that difficult obedience which is first cousin to thinking.

Goodness knows how long she and they had been in this
jam. Hours perhaps. But I haven't told you the whole tale
yet! There's worse to come. There was a blob hanging out of
her by two toes. That blob was a hefty cockroach. You know
the chap. He hasn't got a lovable nature, and he can run like a
jeep. He was bigger than she was, and he was hanging on to
her by the two front toes of one foot. He knew, for he was an
intelligent chap, that if he put any more weight than that on
her she'd capsize and he'd drown. He was hanging on for dear
life truly. Like the babies, she was all he had; and he, too, was
as motionless as a stone.

She couldn't get rid of him, she didn't even dare to try.
He, and she, and they, were waiting patiently—no, were
waiting motionlessly—for the drowning that could be delayed,
but could not be evaded.

Well, I think I've planted you there about as tough a jam
as can be got into, or be nightmared about. A nightmare when
you are asleep is bad enough, but a nightmare when you are
wide awake is another thing, and she, and they, were in the

long nightmare that cannot be awakened from: life itself! That nightmare!

I wonder what they thought about as now and again, every now and again, at long quarter-hours, she looked at the cockroach hanging on to her by two toes; and what, now and again, the cockroach thought of as he looked up at her from between his two toes. When people tell me—and they do—that anatomies with more legs than two don't think, or that they think differently from you and me, I just know that these are uneducated people, and that they are incapable of understanding the Miltonic line: "Is you is, or is you ain't ma baby?"

I got them out of the water with great precaution and a large leaf. Placed on the ground, the cockroach went into top gear and scooted out of sight in one scoot. The lady spider tried to do the same, but as she moved, the slight jolt bumped half a dozen babies off her back. She stopped dead on the instant, and the little things raced to her, climbed up her legs, packed themselves into the pack, and then she went off, with a job of work still before her that I didn't envy her any part of—she had to find food for that couple of hundred very hungry babies, and I fancy that they were all semaphoring to her about it.

I'd like to give that spider a medal, and a pension, and a keg of rum.

After all, there wasn't very much water in that story: only about two feet of it, but if you stay with me for a few more minutes I'll so souse you in water that you'll either swim or drown.

Do you remember the first time you heard the sound of the sea? I remember it to this day.

One time, a while ago—about sixteen years before we started to shave—I was standing with my favourite finger in

my mouth, looking at nothing, when I noticed that I was looking at a woman, and that she was waggling a muffin at me. I
forgot the lovely taste of my finger in one second, and after
falling over myself twice, I got there first; that is, I got there before she could eat the muffin herself.

In another instant I was in her house, in her lap, and I was
eating the muffin. Whatever fun her lap got out of me was its
own business. I and a muffin were in love; the lady was whispering:—

"You stay there for a minute; you go to sleep, little boy."

Then she picked a large shell off the table and held it
against my ear. I tried to sit up at it so as to listen better, but the
lady with the lonely lap wouldn't let me; and then, in the half
of no time of really diligent hearkening to the grey and ghostly
glubberings of the sea, I fell asleep.

Some years afterwards I became very interested in words.
I just adored a certain dictionary that said, "Wine, weal and
winegar are werry good wittles I wow," but I began to notice
that there are certain things, quite a number of them, and we
have no words to really describe them at all. 'Tis so with water.
We have a lot of dry words, for we are dry creatures, but at the
best our wet words are only damp, and so we don't ever get intellectually or imaginatively at that element at all.

All that is just a prelude to the fact that I want to tell you
about the happiest male creature that I have ever known or
heard of.

One day, when I was right bothered about the fact that
there are no wet words in the language, and that consequently
one can't even talk about water, I decided to look into these matters for myself. So I took a header into the sea, off a headland in
Donegal. The water up there that day was astonishingly good-
looking. It seemed to be made of sliding and surging rainbows,

and the whole seascape had gathered together all the opals and rubies and emeralds, all the pearl-whites and jet-blacks of the world. So right off that headland, in I plopped with a wriggle and a swish, and away I skimmed with a hum like the big bass string of a guitar. You've *got* to keep up with me now.

Soon enough I was far out, and deep down, and wide away, and in less than no time I knew more about water than any chemist has ever dreamt of:—Some chemists dream about turpentine, others dream about hydrochloric acid. Thereon, soon enough and very shortly, I began to meet a lot of fish.

Well, the things I talked about to those fish would astonish you nearly as much as it astonished them, and just like you, they didn't agree with one word I said on anything. There was one flat, pink fish that said "Sez you!" to every second word I uttered. I just hated that blighter.

Perhaps I ought to say at once that no fish I ever met with could understand the meaning of the word "wet" as applied to the element they lived in. I had denigrated them about it. "You're all wet," said I. One and all they asserted, and asseverated, that they had never felt wet in their lives, and that water is whatever it is, but it is not wet.

"Wet," said that flattish, three-cornered, pink fish to me, "Wet be blowed."

I didn't like any part of that pink fish. He was too flat and cornery for eating, and too pink for appetite. A pink slab in emerald water is a blot; and anything that is flat is a blot also. He was a blot! Shakespeare said, "Give me fat chaps."

Anyhow, right there, far out and deep down in greeny-yellowy sweeps and deeps and steeps of the main I met the only perfectly happy male creature in our poor old world. He lived in heaven.

His wife told me about him. She didn't really introduce us, but she didn't object to my having a look round.

As I bobbed about—I travelled rather in here-and-there bobs, for I didn't care where I went—so, as I bobbed around, there she was, cleaving majestically through the billows and surges, the chains and ranges and sierras of the great sea.

She was about twenty-five feet long. She was three shadings of silver in colour; namely, pure silver, all shining; light-grey, all flickering; and pearly-trimmings, all half hiding and coy. She was very elegantly, though massively, stream-lined, and she had a ten-foot-wide tail, very delicate, very yielding, and stronger than steel. One swish of that tail could drive her forward at about ten miles a minute. She looked like lightning, and she moved like light!

I intimated to her that she was the darling of the world, and she intimated back that she knew she was. She would have been very vain but that she was very well-bred; and a certain careless vanity is very proper, very attracting, in high breeding.

You will notice that we are now in deep water; three miles deep, in fact. You can't sink, but you had better swim; tread water if you get frightened. We are lapsing and lingering with only a half-inch trembling of the tail. We are bowered and embowered in a translucent emerald, shot with golden spots and laced with silver-sliding shadows. Here there is nothing but the emerald, and the dull gold, and the silver, and if you shut an eye there is the solitude, otherwhere undreamt-of, the almost nothing, the almost nowhere, the all alone.

I got into her undertow, and we went along effortlessly. That was the very poetry of motion, for water carries you along, and holds you up, and it never lets you fall.

No fish can even guess at the meaning of the word "fall"

any more than it can know the significance of the word "wet." It may seem a bit odd, but they don't know the meaning of the word "salty" either. They translate our word "salty" by their own favourite word "lively." They can't fall, and they can't get wet, and they can't taste salt. Fresh water comes dull to them and makes them sick; they think of it the way we think of a bad smell.

My new friend seemed at first to be all alone, but that wasn't so. The next time I came across her she was in the middle of a crowd. Twenty to fifty smaller editions of herself were bouncing and walloping around her. They were an unruly clutter of kids, and she was always threatening their father on them. They were all whistling and snortling and burbling so outrageously that you couldn't even hear yourself getting hungry within a league of them.

On land you get hungry per three hours, but away in the lively salt you get hungry every five minutes. Also, a fish never gets tired, it gets sleepy instead. And also, again, fish don't understand the meaning of the word "thirsty," and I couldn't get it across to them. That flat, pink, three-cornered Insolence, with a bulby nose, chipped in on me here:—

"Trying to pull a fast one on us, are you?" he snortled.

I'd gladly have gutted that Pink Un, but he hadn't any guts. He was too flat.

Another thing, a noise in water is a lot of times louder than a noise in air. And down there, in the green-grey, yellow-smelling mid-deeps, when a periwinkle sneezes off the Irish coast you can hear that sneeze bumping back off the Statue of Liberty in New York Harbour.

You can imagine, then, something of the row these babies were making when they were really making a row. Half the Atlantic Ocean was bawling at them to stop bawling. But when she threatened to call their father they all went as silent as clams. Clams aren't really silent, they cough a bit and they gargle a lot. But you can't blame them, for they spend most of their lives making cement. That clutters them up.

"Where do you get all the babies from?" said I to the big gal.

"I get them from my dear husband," she answered proudly.

I looked around—

"Where's himself?" said I.

"In my ear," she replied.

And she smiled with the wide, sweet smile that you can only get from a fish.

I remarked—cuttingly I hoped—that a witty fish and a crowing hen are always dodged by the gentlemen.

We had a spot of bother about the strange word "hen." The Pink Blot interjected, "He means a Dame."

But my swift lovely lady insisted that her husband lived in her ear—

"Where else *would* he live?" said she.

I didn't know, of course, but that is exactly how it turned out. He was a tiny fish, about an inch long, and he lived in his wife's ear. She carried him about with her everywhere, and she would rather lose her tail, or a couple of fins, than lose sight of him for even a second. The way that good gal used to manoeuvre her ear and her tail would astonish everybody except a perfect lady.

She had arranged everything for him of the best.

Inside her ear, on the lower slope, she grew a kind of fluff that he ate. It tasted, he told me, exactly like liver and bacon, except that it was twice as good. Up in the top corner of her ear she grew a special juice for him; and, according to him, that was the best brew ever. It tasted exactly like fifteen-year-old

Irish whisky, only better, and the old boy used to take a bit of that and sup of this, and 'twas plain that he was as happy as the day is long.

It was the prettiest sight to see him take a swim. He would slip out of his wife's ear, and—unaided, mind you—he would cavort down and around a full twenty feet of her, and then he'd start on the long scram back. 'Twas worth watching. She used to lie as quiet as a mouse while he was having his constitutional, stirring nothing but the tip of her tail, and with that she raised little bubbles that helped him on the tough tack home. Then he came to her ear, scooped himself into it, had a good tuck in of the liver and bacon, and a drop or two of the good juice I was telling you about, and then he'd communicate down to her that she was a good gal, and that he'd be seeing her again when he sobered up.

In so far as living the life of Reilly is concerned he lived the life of Reilly and the life of O'Rourke, and he is the only male creature within the globe whom I could ever be jealous of. You will remember that she looked like lightning, and she moved like light. What a gal she was! What a wife she was! What a tail she had!

When the children—they were ten or twelve feet long already and putting on an inch an hour—when they were naughty she used to proclaim in her lovely mezzo-fishprano that if they didn't stop it and be good she'd tell their father on them, and the mere threat of that made them quit all evil ways, and swim like good little fish, and whistle with their tails in their mouths like little angels.

Of course, they were all she-fish, and they all hoped to get a great and good husband like their father. Their favourite poem ran like this:

Where do husbands come from, come from?
Where do husbands come from?
They live in our ear
And they swim in beer,
And that's where husbands come from.

The way those kids were particular about their ears would astonish you. They had all decided that they would put in a radio-set and a deck-chair for their husbands, as well as the groceries. But there you are, and there's nothing half so good in life as a good husband, as every poor fish of a husband knows.

Well, I tumbled through the surges and the chains and ranges and billows of the deep until I got home again; and I made up my mind that if ever I met a gal who grew liver and bacon in the bottom of her ear and maybe champagne in the top I'd marry her and live happy ever after. Of course, I was a bit scared that she might go to sleep one night on her ear and smother me, so I gave that up. However, when the moon is blue and I take a bath I always sing "A life on the ocean wave, and a home on the rolling deep." And I'm always bothered because the water seems wet although I know it isn't. And anyhow, I hate a bath now that hasn't clams in it.

Living—Whatever That Is

(1948)

I N CHOOSING for my title "Living—Whatever That Is" I tried
to indicate that I'm not giving anyone tips about making a
living.

All creatures have to live, and, to do that, they have to
make a living. That means that they have to get food somehow,
and a shelter somewhere. So have we, but, in addition, we have
acquired a very great deal of leisure, and many people would
hold that the art of living, even the enjoyment of living, consists in finding out what we can do with or pack into our un-
occupied time.

As to living—that strange, extravagant something or other
—I haven't done much of it that I know about. I've written a
lot of prose and a lot of verse, and perhaps I got most of my fun
out of that. I've got into bed and out of bed once every twenty-
four hours for a good while now, and I suppose that I've eaten
enough to load a ship and drunk enough to float her in. Have
I lived at all? Or have you? And, if we have, what is it that we

did? I know only as much, or as little, about living as the next man, and when I try to think about it I'm stuck.

It has often been suggested that we should live danger-ously. This is the advice that is given by courage and boredom, for those two can be very near neighbours of each other. The man who wants to live that way is already half sick of his life, and merely wants to die killing. Nor is there anything original in danger. Every mouse lives in the utmost danger from the moment it opens its baby eyes until the moment when it closes them for ever. Every lamb and rabbit and little grey goat lives all its life within instant reach of violent and agonizing death. And, after all, is there anything in our world braver than a flea? He'll bite anything, except, I suppose, the missus; his mis-sus, I mean.

There is nothing we know better than the thing we call living. It isn't only that we are in it—we are it; and we and it are one unapproachable mystery. Imagine not knowing what life is, and we it!

When I was a youngster I used to do an odd trick: maybe we all do it. I used to squat beside the dog or the cat, or beside a cow or a bird, and try to "be" myself into the being of that creature. I used to moo at the cow and whistle at the bird and they always answered back. You could see them listening to the sounds you made, and you could see them being highly pleased at being taken notice of. The way all things love to be loved, and also love to kill each other is very strange.

I discovered that I didn't have to become cows or cats, for they were me already. There wasn't a scrap of difference be-tween any of these creatures and myself. There was nothing whatever they did that I didn't do, and there was not one emo-tion open to them that wasn't part and parcel of the truck and stuff that I was filled with. They were all capable of being very happy, and they were all capable of being very frightened. So was I; and they were all living the life I was living.

I still think it curious that there should be conflicting capabilities anywhere, and that we should be capable of a joy or of a horror within merely a matter of seconds.

Then, one day I thought that I had come upon an happiness that had no contrary whatever in its nature. I sat beside a small bush that day, and tried to "bush" myself into it. I vegetated at it.

The bush was about four feet high, and it had got itself up regardless. It had covered itself all over with new green; then it had covered its greenness all over with an outbursting of the very gum and glue of health; thereupon it had rioted itself into an exuberance of blossom, and added to that an excess and splendour of scent. It was full of life, it was full of power, it was full of joy. It was a very extravagance and lust of living. It was all the daintiness that dared be, and it was all the life that anything could stand without dropping dead of it. I thought that not God in his heaven could be happier or as happy as this plant was that was living like lightning and that hadn't got a care or a doubt or a shade in all its being, and I conceived that nothing whatever could surpass the ease and beauty and lavishness of life that was in that thing.

There are people who will say that a plant knows nothing about these things. They say! Let them say! But the plant knows, all right, and it couldn't bother to live if it didn't know just these things, and act according.

But they do know the opposite of this too: the contraries can goblin them as certainly as they haunt us. I have seen a half acre of young trees growing too closely together, all growing up longer and skinnier—they were only ten inches round and they were thirty feet high—all trying to reach the sunlight that they couldn't get to; all parched with thirst because they were too many for the available water; all lank with hunger because they were too many for the available food; and I think that sight of hunger and thirst and effort and despair jolted me as badly as anything I have ever seen in the human or animal worlds.

And yet, when it is said that everything in life is difficult, I think that the contrary is just as true. When we look into the complex of things and qualities that make up living we could as easily come to the conclusion that almost everything we can speak of is perfectly easy, and is almost effortless. We do not have to strain or wriggle or twist in order to see anything that is about us: we merely open our eyes, and without the slightest effort an universe of light and form and colour is there. We do more; for just as instantly we can banish all that sight and light by merely closing our eyes again. If we want the light we open our eyes; if we want the dark we shut them. So it is with all the senses. They work for us, and we don't have to do anything whatever about it except just to bid them get on with the job.

The mechanics of the body also shows the same thing. The heart and the lungs and the rest of the lumps and bumps get on with their work without ever taking one second of a rest during all the days and the nights and the years of a long life; and, barring accidents, we don't have to control these, or even remember that they are there. We only know they are there when they have gone out of kilter; but, given that they are all right, we don't have to think about them until we die.

So far as I can see it, there is only one difficulty in living. The one solitary thing that is troublesome is just movement. We do not move with that facility with which we see and hear and smell and taste and touch. We even think without any trouble at all, except when we don't know what we are thinking about. Thought is becoming just an extra sense, and even when a person is old, he may do all these effortlessly and perfectly, and only get hot and bothered when he has to trot about.

So far as I can see it, there is no reason why we should ever move about, except that we've got to get our food; and there's the snag, and there's the rub. The few general laws that underlie life seem to me to be so curious as to be almost totally irrational. There are four things, and we do them or we quit. We breathe or we die, we eat or die, we drink or die, we sleep or die. Is not this an extraordinary penalty to have to pay for a spot of aberration now and again—and what is dying anyhow? The whole of life is merely a preparation for it, for birth is the cause of death, and if death is not a great reward for being a good boy in the Looney-Bin what can it be?

Movement and food and drink are truly the difficulties, and why the effortless miracle called Life should have invented these traps for the unwary is completely incomprehensible.

As to the necessity for eating, I don't know what to make of it. When we open our eyes they are instantly filled with sight. When we open our mouths they should as instantly be filled with calories and vitamins and rations. This would not be one scrap more marvellous than is the miracle of sight and sound and touch, each serving and conveying an universe of its own type and each not bothering us a rap about it. If there wasn't any more bother about food there wouldn't be any more bother about anything, and we should live forever, if we wanted to, which nobody but a fool would want.

All this could be taken as a comical kind of reflection. I don't intend it so at all. We've got to eat, and what is it that we do eat? We eat death: life lives on death: merely because it hasn't invented a sense that would grab grub the way the eye grabs sight. When we get fat on a ham the pig is dead, and so is everything dead that goes into our traps. There is the lovely early bird getting the just as lovely early worm. If I ever become more of a worm than I am now I'll take for my device: Better Late than Never. And the lovely early cat gets the lovely early bird, and the good old early dog gets the poor old early cat for keeps. The odd thing called death is what everything lives on. I kick. I call it stupid. I wrote a couple of verses about it ["In Grey Air"]:

> This living is a curious feat,
> Is very odd!
> It is to murder all we eat,
> And, then, thank God
> That we can murder
> More than most,
> Before we, too,
> Give up the ghost.

> It is to sleep,
> And make life be
> As it were not:
> Dismiss to think,
> To feel, to see,
> And know the lot
> As just a burden
> And a bore,
> And best forgot.

> I do not understand,
> Nor see
> What 'tis about:
> Nor why a curious
> You and me
> Should sleep, and eat,

And boast about
Our slaughters,
And our sleepings,
And our passings out.

There is a sense, of course, in which one should not be either a person or a self; one should be one's crowd perhaps, and nothing else, and neither think nor imagine outside the fears and hopes that belong to our order. Still, as long as the early worm is getting it in the neck—and he is all neck, poor chap—just so long will this present person be a disgruntled wight, and a believer that the best of all possible worlds isn't just worth being born into, for 'tis founded in murder and conditioned by stupidity.

Of course, the thing we call Living (which includes the other oddity, dying) is a very easy thing to do. So many creatures do it, all creatures and things do both. There are camels and Chaucers; snails and Shakespeares; Wordsworths and winkles; Miltons and mildews and mice; there is the well-known man-in-the-street, and the good old toad-in-the-hole. They have all managed to do exactly the same thing that I did, and in precisely the same way, and we all play follow-my-leader when the time comes to pop off. When a thing gets old enough to know better it says, "Let's die," and it dies dead—if that's how you die!

I don't at all know how dead you are when you die, or even if you are dead at all. I doubt it. Philosophy has tried to rationalize this irrational, but philosophy has really only answered questions by shelving them; and then there are the mythological and religious surmisings or irradiations on the matter.

Philosophy says that the proper study of mankind is man; and adds, "Know thyself"; and suggests that is all that needs to be known. Do I really need to know that I am a monster of greed and anger and folly? Religion states its own special knowledge in the great sentence: "The Kingdom of Heaven is within you." When that is realized there is nothing more to realize. Every bit of thoughtless and effortless joy that visits us comes from the source, and its opposites of murder and doubt derive from a belief that the Kingdom of Hell is within you. All ideas are operative, and both of these work as you will them to.

But that there is a top to a thing and a bottom to the thing doesn't make it that there are two things; and that there is a top called birth and a bottom called death doesn't make any difference to that which is free, and sufficient, and joyous, and eternal.

No More Peasants

(1949)

I was born into the outskirts of a city that was packed with
horses, packed with birds, packed with donkeys and goats,
and packed with the living noises of all these, and of ten times
more than these. Goodness—there were human beings there
also, who looked exactly like horses and said "Neigh" to everything, and very excellent men—and here and there a woman—
who looked exactly like asses and only didn't bray because
they were too shy. As to the men and women who looked precisely like goats and shook incredible whiskers at you, they
were legion.

The Dublin streets that I first knew thudded and neighed
and whinnied with every kind of horse that can be imagined,
and they also snorted and screamed with kinds of horses that
can't now be imagined at all. For example, there was a horse
then which you can't now meet anywhere. He was perhaps
proudly referred to as a "wicked" horse, and indeed one could
look into the face of such a beauty and peer into eyes as re-
lentlessly fierce as the eyes of a tiger; more so indeed, for the

poor old tiger only looks like a disappointed cat who's been out-manoeuvred by a mouse, but a wicked horse looked like the devil.

Machen was perhaps not right, but he was also not wrong when he portrayed the devil as "a stallion Englishman, and a gentleman at that." I once thought that the mildest eyes that could be looked into were the eyes of a cow, and that the eyes of a grocer's curate were very mild eyes, and that the so battered and so beautiful eyes of a sailorman were sweeter than the buttercup in bloom. I thought also that the wickedest eyes that could be faced by mortal man were the eyes of a stallion horse, or the withdrawn, suspicious, cold glare of a retired colonel looking at his fellow clubmen, and that the accusing, unforgiving, hard orb of another fellow's mother was about as petrifying a thing as one could stare at.

Imagine a world in which there are no more stallion horses and no more tom cats, where men aren't exciting any more and women aren't maddening, where excitement and lunacy and the devil and his dam are flicked at us from a screen. We're in it and play no part in it, and we've quit the idea of being alive as something that doesn't pay.

In those days one's father always gave two pieces of advice to his son as capital matters in the art of living; they were, "My child, you must never walk behind a horse," and "My son, you must never mix your drinks," and mothers cautioned their daughters who were visiting the town: "Darling, keep your mind on your religion, and your hand on your twopence." Well, these bits of advice are now meaningless, for there are no more horses to walk behind, and you must mix your drinks or be known as a very odd kind of hayseed, and your religion and your twopence have switched westwards away.

The Dublin of that day didn't only thud with the feet of

horses; it clanged and clamoured and squawked and flapped
with the wings and the quarrels of tens-of-thousands of birds
who followed the horses and their nose-bags; sea-birds mostly,
very raucous, amazingly opinionated; they would stand on a
horse's neck and screech defiance at Neptune himself. Donkeys
on the whole don't like birds; they endure them. Crows used
to pinch whole nests off a donkey's back, but the horses loved
them. It's perhaps odd that I never once noticed a horse that
tried to scare one of the ten birds that were hopping around
each of its four feet. Even the wicked horses weren't wicked
that way. I've seen horses shake bits of stuff out of the old nose-
bag for sparrows. The horse that doesn't love sparrows and kit-
tens and mice has never been born. The human being that
doesn't love these three should never have been born.

Still there are pardonable oddities. I've noticed rats that
were quite shy and a bit self-effacing before mice; but elephants
and women are terrified of them, and how curiously female all
elephants are, and how strangely elephantine the women you
don't like—screen stars—tend to become. I will say here and
now that the woman who isn't a mouse isn't a woman, and that
the man who isn't an elephant and terrified of them is no man.

I'm dwelling a bit on horses because they are very curiously mixed up with the human being. The greatest names of
the nobler races derive from the good creatures that used to
carry a man wherever he wanted to go, and used to work for
him when he hadn't a wife to do so, and punctually brought
him home when he was drunk. So you get the Cavaliers, and
the Chevaliers, and the Caballeros, and the Ritters, and it was
once known that while everybody had the right to be a thief,
nobody had the right to be a horse-thief. A patrician was really
a man who owned a horse.

It's very odd that in Ireland this wasn't quite the case. Our great names, beginning with Cu and Con, have taken their names from the hound, and it was considered that the Irish wolf-hound and one's eldest son were the noblest works of nature. I'm prepared to believe that everything whatever, including black beetles, is the noblest work of nature.

People talked when I was a kid about horses and liquor and religion and women and money and the neighbour, and they could raise a fight about every one of these. Well, everyone knows that these six have disappeared. There are no more horses, no more liquor, no more religion, no more women, no more money and no more neighbours. There are forgeries of all these, so the poor old human race has to do all its fighting about nothing at all. America is responsible for some of this. There is the Ford car, and the screen star; the Tin Lizzie obliterated the horse, and the canned Lizzie is rubbing the womanhood out of our women. What fools women are to be taken in by screen things. The woman who loves anything whatever except her baby is a traitor to biology, and the woman who admires the man she can't marry is mad.

In the older days, the two things on which the world moved and lived were the horse and the peasant. They've both practically gone, and with them an irreplaceable knowledge has also disappeared. It used to be called living, and that begins to be something that no one does any more. The entire of their knowledge was cast in the form called proverbs. Most of these had to do with the ceaseless thrift and the ceaseless care that thrift imposes. To be endlessly careful, to be ceaselessly thrifty, these two made sleep sweet and made waking up adventurous. A stitch in time, said Grandmama, saves nine. For want of a nail, said the grizzled uncle, the shoe was lost; for want of a shoe, the horse was lost; for want of a horse, the rider was lost, and the loss of that rider bankrupted nothing.

A phrase that I often heard was "You can't go behind the proverb." In the peasant culture, that was true. There never was a peasant art, but there was a peasant culture, for all art is aristocratic, and all culture is of the peasant and his horse.

Living in their tight communities, these people knew each other in a way that human beings do not know each other any more. They rarely moved more than five or ten miles from their parish. When you were born, every fifty-odd of your neighbours knew when you cut your first tooth, they knew when you were weaned and why, and some held that your mother was dam' quick, and others averred that she was a mathematical genius. They knew when the priest and your father were contented or discontented with you, and they didn't take your side either. How wise the Catholics were to call their priests "Father." They knew that you were the ugliest child that ever was born, and they didn't hold that against you. The first time that you looked at a girl, they all knew about it, and one-half of them, female, wondered what you could see in her, and the other half, male, marvelled what she could see in you, two questions that no Trinity College professor has ever been able to work out, and the first time that a girl got the idea that maybe you weren't as bad as you looked, that was known to every soul that was a neighbour, and they all thought that she should be smacked. Girls were mainly smacked; boys were mainly told off.

If you were cantankerous or stingy or sly or a liar or a coward, all these were forgiven to you, for everyone knew these things about you since you were three years of age, and only expected from you what they knew you could provide, and you knew precisely as much about every man-Jack and every woman-Jill of them all.

There was only one human being who was a bit out of focus in these matters. He was the Lord of the Manor. He was more than a bit incalculable. He seemed to be in love, and he wasn't. He seemed to be very careless about money, and he wasn't. He seemed to forgive you all your sins, and he didn't; but he was fearless, which you weren't, and he would take a chance, which you couldn't, and he might invite the priest to dinner, which you daren't. The peasant today listens in every night to Piccadilly Circus; he hearkens diligently to the Rue de la Paix, and there are some even who have a shot at listening-in to Moscows and where-nots and other ships that are all at sea. Poor old peasants—they have forgotten all of their proverbs, and they are completely unable to imagine what a neighbour looks like. That person the peasant whom the whole world stood on is gone. His horse is gone; his neighbours are gone, and barring the church, his Lord of the Manor is the most dilapidated what-not that nature knows of. Poor old peasant and poor old Lord of the Manor. Ten thousand years are sliding away with you, and you are being replaced by some three thousand millions of us who don't know each other and don't want to, and who have got to find something or other that can be known, and perhaps can even be liked.

Modern change is in being when money and sex and speed are seen as removed from what was a norm. A change in money is equivalent to a change in climate; a change in the sex convention is equal to a change in civilization itself; a change in speed is a new thing. These changes are with us, and the thing called living has to be learned all over again painfully and from scratch. It has to be learned by something more than three thousand millions of us, a number shortly to be doubled, each thousand of whom don't give a hoot for any other thousand of us, and every thousand of which don't want to go to bed because they're lonely, and don't want to get up because what's there to get up for? You pull on your breeches in the morning, and you pull them off at night, and that's that.

Mogue, or Cows and Kids

(1949)

THERE used to be all kinds of creatures in the world when I
was a boy. There was a cow that I remember to this day
because I saw her crying. She was called Mogue. I didn't know
then that a cow shouldn't be called Mogue because Mogue
is a man's name. There was a famous Saint Mogue away in the
days and years of yore. The people who owned this cow were
pious people and they were merely wrong in the gender. A matter that we all go wrong about. There is no doubt that a lot of
women should be called He and that many men should be
called It. The inbetweens might be referred to as Them—and
told to come round next week.

The reason that Mogue, the good red and white angel, was
crying was because her most dearly beloved people had taken
away her calf and sold it. She didn't know they had done it; she
couldn't have believed it. I fancy that perhaps she blamed God.
She stood with her head over the fence mourning about this
and tears as big as marbles were running down her long red
nose. "Lord, Mogue!" said I to her. "Moo moo!" said she to

me. And although I was a hard-hearted ten-year-old, I could have wept with her. "Mogue," said I, "I didn't swipe your calf." "I'm certain you didn't," said she.

I had a row with her a couple of weeks after, for I put my mackintosh on the fence so that I might be free to pet her. You pet a cow by putting your cheek up against her nose. You do the same with women. Well, Mogue pulled my mackintosh over the fence and she ate every bit of it except one sleeve. That was serious, for I was on my way to school and my lunch was in the mackintosh, so she got that too. To be without your lunch at twelve o'clock and watch the other kids wolfing theirs is as desolating a thing as can happen. The way everybody except yourself eats like wolves is very distressing.

I wonder what did Mogue's milk taste like that night? You know that good fresh milk, well flavoured with a four-year-old rubber mac, should have made people's tea taste like nothing else altogether. I think they all thought there was po-teen in the milk, for poteen is a miracle, but it can taste like this and that and the other.

That world used to be well peopled with horses too. And there used to be very wicked horses among them. There aren't any left in the world now. Ah me! The lovely wicked horses! The way they arched their necks and looked at you as if you were an inferior being, and then they snorted you away. They would reach out and bite each other whenever they got the chance and they would reach out and nip your arm or shoulder if these were handy. Also they used to keep a good look back-wards and, if the going was good, they'd try to kick your head off. I remember often thinking that the savagest eyes one could ever look into were the eyes of a wicked horse. They swirled and stared and glared.

I only once met a wicked donkey. He was the one who

used to climb on the roof and eat the thatch. I was sorry for
him though, for he had been teased very badly. First, having
been badgered beyond reason, he began to chase hens. But it's
a pretty good donkey that can catch a hen, for a hen can do
flops and hops that a donkey isn't up to. Then he began to kick
cows. Mogue took a hand in *that* game. When she spotted what
he was at she laid for him, and as he'd be getting into position
for his kick she would charge, and toss him a couple of yards
away. He was the only mad ass I ever heard of, but when I
knew him first he was as sweet and kind a creature as ever
lived. At the end of it the people who owned the poor old ass
had to shoot him. And that was a happy day for everybody
around who owned a hen or a cow. And every hen for three
farms round crowed like a cock and whistled, and was di-
vorced by her husband.

Mogue and my lunch reminds me of something else that
had to do with lunch; but this had to do with a bit later when
I was older passing through London. There was a nice woman
I went to see. Her husband was a poet and loved bulldogs, as
every poet does, and she had a champion one with her. He was
the English bulldog; that is, he had a head as big as a pot, and a
mouth so long that it ran right round his head. He was very
affectionate and he loved to kiss everybody. When that chap
kissed you it felt exactly as if you had been jabbed all over the
face with a very wet sponge just taken out of the bath, and with
nearly all the bath in it.

She asked me to take him for a walk and then to come
back in a quarter of an hour because her husband was out. We
went into the park and I noticed that the dog was looking on
every side with great eagerness. Suddenly he went off at a great
pace. If you have never seen an English bulldog going off at

great pace, with every spot of him in a wiggle, you've missed something. So going in bleeps and blounds he came to a small boy, pushed him over, sniffed all his pockets, found the one that the boy's lunch was in, pulled the lunch out and ate it, and then he started off looking for another schoolboy with a lunch.

I cleared off and made my way back to the house. When I reached it, he was there before me. His master was there too. That dog was delighted to see me, although I'd only been absent for ten minutes. He gave me a great kiss, which I had to wipe off with my hat, for I had forgotten to bring my handkerchief with me; his kiss was very sticky and was full of crumbs.

But let's get back to ten years of age and to Mogue, the only lovely lady that ever lived. And to a certain unappeasable wondering at this and that and these and those.

You will remember that in those days every day used to be a new day, and that everything used to be a new thing. Every night you didn't want to go to bed, and your mother chased you into it with an angry adoration that you would never meet with again, and every morning you didn't want to get up, and your mother threw you out of the bed with the statement that breakfast was the loveliest thing in the world, and that your father would wolf every spot of it unless you came down and beat him to it.

Your father was, if one may say so, a different kettle of fish. He got strange and stranger every day of your life. He was the only human or animal being that you didn't know one single thing about. He said, "Boy, if you do that again I'll give you a kick in the pants." And he wouldn't kick you in the pants, not even if you gave him tuppence to do it. You meanwhile would kick anyone in the pants for a ha'penny.

You did what he said, when he was looking, and you

didn't do one tap more of it when he wasn't. He said to your mother, "That chap takes after you. He is the champion idiot of the world." You didn't care very much for the word "idiot" but you did know that you were a "champion."

But let's get back, as it were, to Mogue, who must by now be the loneliest cow that ever was remembered.

There was a river that ran through the field. Here it was only ten feet wide, a little further on it was twenty or even fifty feet wide. Here again it was a bit deep, with boulders sticking out of it round which the waters swished and hissed. Every few hundred paces in fact it was a different river. On this side it rushed and gushed and sloped through meadows. The further side jutted up in a small hill. And we liked to hop across the water by these boulders and climb up the other side to a far-sloping field. We often got wet, but we didn't mind that.

Well, there were three of us, all about ten years of age, and all given to yelling as hard as we could about nothing at all. One day we jumped across the river and up the slope, and there we were suddenly halted. So would you have been; for there was a bull in the field.

He was Mogue's husband, and his name was Nicodemus. And he was reckoned the most bad-tempered bull in these parts. He was on us before we saw him. And then we heard him, for he bellowed at us in the most low-class Irish accent I have ever heard.

Then he took to pawing the ground, and at each plunge of these fierce hooves great wads of grass and soil were lifted six feet into the air. And then he came at us.

If you have never been charged by a savage young bull from about fifty yards away, then you won't quite get that there are three seconds of about as dizzy a spot of terror as you've ever been mixed into. In five seconds the bull was at us. But we weren't there. We were through the fence, and down the juts, and into the water, and well away.

We were a discontented crew, and then we were an angry crew, and then we wanted revenge, and then we wanted that creature to know that we weren't the sort of people that could be chased by a bull. So we made our plans.

We knew that part of the river well. We picked out three nicely-separated, well-bouldered spots that were easy to cross. The plan of campaign was that one of us should go over, attract Nicodemus' attention, hop and scramble back with lots of yells to keep the bull angry, and then the second of us, a hundred yards away, would get over and up, attract his attention, and escape, and so to the third. Whereupon I, away at the top, would be over again in hops and howls and the bull would come charging again.

The way that chap bellowed and snorted and charged and stamped, with his tail stuck up like a walking-stick; and then he'd begin to twist and twirl and try to rush down his ever-disappearing enemies. Well, that was astonishing. And the tired-lessness of him! The powerful beauty, the unbeatable will, and the speed and the courage of the creature were extraordinary also.

After a while he must have thought there was a million of us, and that we were able to disappear in one half of the blinking of one eye. We kept him on the run for two hours and at the end of that long chasing he wasn't tired. He was pouncing a bit slower now and again, but that was because he was growing a trifle thoughtful; and thought is a condition which bulls don't want to have anything to do with. Tigers, and all the cat tribes, are very thoughtful creatures. So are pigs, although you mightn't think so. I knew a fellow one time, and he had a pet pig—a little black and white chap—he was as clean as a whistle and he knew when he could get up on the sofa and when he couldn't. But the only idea in a bull's mind is to get at the enemy in one direct onslaught, and then let the best bull win.

By the next day we had run Mogue's husband to a stand-still. And on the day after that he walked away from us when-ever he saw us. And by the end of the week, he was the mildest-mannered and best-tempered bull on earth. He became greatly beloved and people brought him carrots and lumps of bread and slabs of salt and wives, including Mogue, from all over the country. And when he ran after people they all knew that he only wanted to sit on their laps.

Appendix: James Stephens Broadcasts

The dates given are the earliest known dates of transmission. Sometimes there are also recording or manuscript dates. Not all the scripts survive. James Stephens, a record issued by Spoken Arts in the United States and Argo in England, includes the broadcast of June 3, 1947, "A Poet Speaks." + indicates a script included in this book. Where the title is different, it follows in parentheses.

§ indicates a script printed, in full or in part, in The Listener. *Date, page number and title (if different) follow.*

* indicates a script of which the B.B.C. Library retains a recording.

1928

+ I Remember: Reminiscences of J. M. Synge. ("Reminiscences of J. M. Synge") Ms. Feb. 2; galley for *Radio Times* March 12; transmission March 15.

1930 (?)

It Is Beginning All Over Again. No date; possibly Dec. 31; script mentions "saying farewell to 1930."

1937

+* On Speaking Verse: with Four Difficult Examples. May 18.

+ Some Irish Books I Like. June 16.

The English Poets (Anon). June 25 or 29. Rough draft.

* Reading his poem "Nora Criona." July 29.

* Reading "The Small Green Leaf." Sept. 1.

* Reading from *Songs from the Clay*. Sept. 27.

1938

Court Poetry. Feb. 7. Rough draft.

Great Poetry. May 10. Rough draft.

1939

§ Here's Wishing. Group broadcast New Year's Day with E. M. Forster, Walter de la Mare and John Masefield. Jan. 5, page 18. Rough manuscript dated Dec. 26, 1938.

1940

Musings on High. August 10. Ms.

To Talk of Many Things. Oct. 9.

+ Books and People. ("On His Poems [I]") Nov. 8.

1941

Joyce. Jan. 18 or 23. Rough sketch and notes only.

§ How Should Poetry Be Read? Discussion with Thomas Hunt, C. Day Lewis, Robert Nichols, Robert Speaight, Fay Compton. May 22, page 732. No date of broadcast.

§ Must Poetry Make Sense? Resumption of discussion, without Speaight. June 5, page 810.

§ Is Verse-Speaking a Lost Art? Resumption, with Robert Nichols, Catherine Lacey, Gwynnith Thurburn, John Laurie, C. V. Clinton-Baddeley. June 12, page 840.

Books and People: Love Poems. July 5.

§ Does It Stick in Your Throat? Resumption of discussion, with Robert Nichols, Marjorie Gullen, Philip Phillips. July 24, page 129.

Makers of History: S'Ankara. Aug. 1.

1942

+§ Books and Authors. ("W. B. Yeats") Jan. 5. Ms. dated December, 1941. Excerpt in *Listener* Jan. 22, page 106, "Yeats and the Telephone."

+§ Books and Authors ("A.E. [I]") March 27. *Listener* April 9, page 467, " 'A.E.': A Wonderful Amateur."

Poetry. Recorded Oct. 19. Transmission 21 and 27. Incomplete script; seems part of series "Hello, Children."

Imaginary Interview: William Blake, etc. Recorded Oct. 18. Transmission Oct. 30.

+ The Man Who Was Going to Die. Recorded Dec. 22. Transmission Jan. 8, 1943.

+ Living in a Chapel. Undated. Would seem to precede following broadcast.

1943

+§ Villages. Feb. 25. *Listener* March 18, page 329.

+§ Great Dramatists: W. B. Yeats. ("Yeats as Dramatist") Ms. May 9. *Listener* June 17, page 728, " 'He Died Younger than He Was Born.' "

Poetry. Recorded May 28. Transmission June 2. Another in series "Hello, Children"?

Science Notebook—Chapter 30, with Narrator Anthony Weymouth: A Peep into the Future. July 7.

+§ Bernard Shaw. Undated. Excerpt *Listener* Sept. 16, page 318, "Two Great Talkers."
Hello, Children. Recorded Nov. 17. Incomplete.

1944

+ The Great Man. Ms. Feb. 18. Transmission March 9.
+ Nothing Much. Pre-recorded Feb. 18. Transmission March 4.
+ The Story of the Goat. Recorded March 22.
§* Thomas Moore. May 17. *Listener* June 8, page 639, "Thomas Moore: Champion Minor Poet."
+ The Making of a Poem. (" 'Byzantium' ") Dec. 28.

1945

+§ An Irishman's Days. Feb. 16. *Listener* Feb. 22, page 214.
Good Morning, Renmark. Undated typescript, perhaps earlier.
Good Morning, Launceston. Undated typescript, perhaps earlier.
+§ A Story of a Good Dog. June 1. *Listener* June 28, page 718.
+ Coleridge. Pre-recording June 11. Transmission June 16.
Books and People: Dr. William Blake. Aug. 26. Rough draft.
+§ William Blake. Oct. 8. *Listener* Sept. 6, page 271, " 'The "Purest" Poet of them All.' " (Transcript date obviously a re-broadcast.)

1946

+§ Talking Shop. ("On His Poetry [II]") Jan. 27. Excerpt *Listener* Feb. 7, page 170, "The World Goes By."
+§ St. Patric. Recorded March 15. Transmission March 17. Excerpt *Listener* March 28, page 393.
§ Novels Dead and Alive. With Gerald Bullett and Rose Macaulay. June 4. *Listener* June 13, page 782.
+ Poets on Poetry. With Gerald Bullett and Dylan Thomas. June 18.
+§ Getting the Most Out of Talk. ("Talk") June 24. *Listener* July 4, page 14, "Talk and Talkers."
§ G. K. Chesterton. Oct. 1. *Listener* Oct. 17, page 513, "The 'Period Talent' of G. K. Chesterton."
+§* The James Joyce *I* Knew. Oct. 8. *Listener* Oct. 24, page 565.
Epic. Oct. 22.
Geoffrey Chaucer. Nov. 19.
+§ John Donne. Dec. 17. *Listener* Jan. 23, 1947, page 149, " 'The Prince of Wits.' "

+§* First Meeting with George Moore. Dec. 30. *Listener* Jan. 16, 1947, page 109, "A Conversation with George Moore."

1947

+ *Finnegans Wake.* Jan. 25.

+ St. Patric's Day in the Morning. March 17.

+ Draft Script. ("On His Poems [III]") Undated; no indication whether part of delivered broadcast.

+* A Poet Speaks. ("On His Poems [IV]") June 3. (See note, page 285)

+§* Living—Whatever That Is. June 8. *Listener* June 19, page 963.

+ W. B. Yeats. (Excerpt: "Yeats and Music") Oct. 3.

* Reading His Poem, "The Bee" and P. Kavanagh's poem, "My Soul." Nov. 14.

Books and Authors: The Cult of Violence. With Calder Marshall. Dec. 27.

1948

+ Around and About Yeats. Jan. 2. (First in a series, "I Knew Three Men")

+* Yeats the Poet. Jan. 9. (Second in series)

+ *Ulysses.* Jan. 10.

+§ A.E. ("A.E. [II]") Jan. 13. (Third in series) *Listener* Jan. 22, page 144, "A Memory of 'A.E.' "

+§ Stephen MacKenna ("Stephen MacKenna [I]") Jan. 18. (Fourth in series) *Listener* Jan. 29, page 177, "Stephen MacKenna: Talker and Philosopher."

+ Stephen MacKenna (II). Undated; unclear whether broadcast.

+§ No More Peasants. Aug. 22. *Listener* Aug. 26, page 313.

1949

* On Making a Poem. May 25.

* Introducing and reading his own poems. July 28.

The Old Gentleman on Matrimony. Oct. 24. (From *Here Are Ladies*)

1950

* Reading from *The Crock of Gold.* May 28.

+* Childhood Days: Mogue, or Cows and Kids. ("Mogue, or Cows and Kids") June 11.